T0361402

# Check

Lean is about building and improving stable and predictable systems and processes to deliver to customers high-quality products/services on time by engaging everyone in the organization. Combined with this, organizations need to create an environment of respect for people and continuous learning. It's all about people. People create the product or service, drive innovation, and create systems and processes, and with leadership buy-in and accountability to ensure sustainment with this philosophy, employees will be committed to the organization as they learn and grow personally and professionally.

Lean is a term that describes a way of thinking about and managing companies as an enterprise. Becoming Lean requires the following: the continual pursuit to identify and eliminate waste; the establishment of efficient flow of both information and process; and an unwavering top-level commitment. The concept of continuous improvement applies to any process in any industry.

Based on the contents of ***The Lean Practitioners Field Book***, the purpose of this series is to show, in detail, how any process can be improved utilizing a combination of tasks and people tools and introduces the BASICS Lean® concept. The books are designed for all levels of Lean practitioners and introduces proven tools for analysis and implementation that go beyond the traditional point kaizen event. Each book can be used as a stand-alone volume or used in combination with other titles based on specific needs.

Each book is chock-full of case studies and stories from the authors' own experiences in training organizations that have started or are continuing their Lean journey of continuous improvement. Contents include valuable lessons learned and each chapter concludes with questions pertaining to the focus of the chapter. Numerous photographs enrich and illustrate specific tools used in Lean methodology.

***Check: Identifying Gaps on the Path to Success Transactional Processes*** contains chapters on implementing Lean, Kanban systems, line balancing, Heijunka-leveling, and the +QDIP process plus case studies of machine shop and transactional implementations. The implementation model describes the different approaches to Lean, compares them to Toyota, and explains each implementation model.

## BASICS Lean® Implementation Series

*Baseline: Confronting Reality & Planning the Path for Success*
By Charles Protzman, Fred Whiton & Joyce Kerpchar

*Assess and Analyze: Discovering the Waste Consuming Your Profits*
By Charles Protzman, Fred Whiton & Joyce Kerpchar

*Suggesting Solutions: Brainstorming Creative Ideas to Maximize Productivity*
By Charles Protzman, Fred Whiton & Joyce Kerpchar

*Implementing Lean: Converting Waste to Profit*
By Charles Protzman, Fred Whiton & Joyce Kerpchar

*Check: Identifying Gaps on the Path to Success*
By Charles Protzman, Fred Whiton & Joyce Kerpchar

*Sustaining Lean: Creating a Culture of Continuous Improvement*
By Charles Protzman, Fred Whiton & Joyce Kerpchar

# Check
## Identifying Gaps on the Path to Success

Charles Protzman, Fred Whiton, and Joyce Kerpchar

Routledge
Taylor & Francis Group

A PRODUCTIVITY PRESS BOOK

First published 2023
by Routledge
605 Third Avenue, New York, NY 10158

and by Routledge
4 Park Square, Milton Park, Abingdon, Oxon, OX14 4RN

*Routledge is an imprint of the Taylor & Francis Group, an informa business*

© 2023 Charles Protzman, Fred Whiton and Joyce Kerpchar

The right of Charles Protzman, Fred Whiton and Joyce Kerpchar to be identified as authors of this work has been asserted by them in accordance with sections 77 and 78 of the Copyright, Designs and Patents Act 1988.

All rights reserved. No part of this book may be reprinted or reproduced or utilised in any form or by any electronic, mechanical, or other means, now known or hereafter invented, including photocopying and recording, or in any information storage or retrieval system, without permission in writing from the publishers.

*Trademark notice:* Product or corporate names may be trademarks or registered trademarks, and are used only for identification and explanation without intent to infringe.

ISBN: 978-1-032-02920-7 (hbk)
ISBN: 978-1-032-02919-1 (pbk)
ISBN: 978-1-003-18581-9 (ebk)

DOI: 10.4324/9781003185819

Typeset in Garamond
by KnowledgeWorks Global Ltd.

This book series is dedicated to all the Lean practitioners in the world and to two of the earliest, my friend Kenneth Hopper and my grandfather Charles W. Protzman Sr. Kenneth was a close friend of Charles Sr. and is coauthor with his brother William of a book that describes Charles Sr. and his work for General MacArthur in the Occupation of Japan in some detail: *The Puritan Gift: Reclaiming the American Dream amidst Global Financial Chaos.*

**Charles W. Protzman Sr.**

**Kenneth Hopper**

# Contents

# Acknowledgments

There are many individuals who have contributed to this book, both directly and indirectly, and many others over the years, too many to list here, who have shared their knowledge and experiences with us. We would like to thank all of those who have worked with us on Lean teams in the past and the senior leadership whose support made them successful. This book would not have been possible without your hard work, perseverance, and courage during our Lean journey together. We hope you see this book as the culmination of our respect and appreciation. We apologize if we have overlooked anyone in the following acknowledgments. We would like to thank the following for their contributions to coauthor or contribute to the chapters in this book:

- Special thanks to our Productivity Press editor, Kris Mednansky, who has been terrific at guiding us through our writing project. Kris has been a great source of encouragement and kept us on track as we worked through what became an ever-expanding six-year project.
- Special thanks to all our clients. Without you, this book would not have been possible.
- Russ Scaffede for his insight into the Toyota system and for his valuable contributions through numerous e-mail correspondence and edits with various parts of the book.
- Joel Barker for his permission in referencing the paradigm material so important and integral to Lean implementations and change management.
- Many thanks to the "Hats" team (you know who you are).
- I would like to acknowledge Mark Jamrog of SMC Group. Mark was my first Sensei and introduced me to this Kaikaku-style Lean System Implementation approach based on the Ohno and Shingo teachings.
- Various chapter contributions by Joe and Ed Markiewicz of Ancon Gear.

For the complete list of acknowledgments, testimonials, dedication, etc. please see The Lean Practitioner's Field Book. The purpose of this series was to break down and enhance the original Lean Practitioner's Field Book into six books that are aligned with the BASICS® model.

Authors' Note: Every attempt was made to source materials back to the original authors. In the event we missed someone, please feel free to let us know so we may correct it in any future edition. Many of the spreadsheets depicted were originally hand drawn by Mark Jamrog, SMC Group, put into Excel by Dave O'Koren and Charlie Protzman, and since modified significantly. Most of the base formatting for these spreadsheets can be found in the Shingo, Ohno, Monden, or other industrial engineering handbooks.

# About the Authors

**Charles Protzman**, MBA, CPM, formed Business Improvement Group (B.I.G.), LLC, in November 1997. B.I.G. is in Sarasota Florida. Charlie and his son, Dan along with Mike Meyers, specialize in implementing and training Lean thinking principles and the BASICS® Lean business delivery system (LBDS) in small to fortune 50 companies involved in Manufacturing, Healthcare, Government, and Service Industries.

Charles has written 12 books to date and is the coauthor of Leveraging Lean in Healthcare: Transforming Your Enterprise into a High-Quality Patient Care Delivery System series and is a two-time recipient of the Shingo Research and Professional Publication Award. He has since published *The BASICS® Lean Implementation Model* and *Lean Leadership BASICS®*. Charles has over 38 years of experience in materials and operations management. He spent almost 14 years with AlliedSignal, now Honeywell, where he was an Aerospace Strategic Operations Manager and the first AlliedSignal Lean master. He has received numerous special-recognition and cost-reduction awards. Charles was an external consultant for the Department of Business and Economic Development's (DBED's) Maryland Consortium during and after his tenure with AlliedSignal. With the help of Joyce LaPadula and others, he had input into the resulting DBED world-class criteria document and assisted in the first three initial DBED world-class company assessments. B.I.G. was a Strategic Partner of ValuMetrix Services, a division of Ortho-Clinical Diagnostics, Inc., a Johnson & Johnson company. He is an international Lean consultant and has taught beginner to advanced students' courses in Lean principles and total quality all over the world.

Charlie Protzman states, "My grandfather started me down this path and has influenced my life to this day. My grandfather made four trips to Japan from 1948 to the 1960s. He loved the Japanese people and culture and was passionate and determined to see Japanese manufacturing recover from World War II."

Charles spent the last 24 years with Business Improvement Group, LLC, implementing successful Lean product line conversions, kaizen events, and administrative business system improvements (transactional Lean) worldwide. He is following in the footsteps of his grandfather, who was part of the Civil Communications Section (CCS) of the American Occupation. Prior to recommending Dr. Deming's 1950 visit to Japan, C.W. Protzman Sr. surveyed over 70 Japanese companies in 1948. Starting in late 1948, Homer Sarasohn and C.W. Protzman Sr. taught top executives of prominent Japanese communications companies an eight-week course in American participative management and quality techniques in Osaka and Tokyo. Over 5,100 top Japanese executives had taken the course by 1956. The course continued until 1993. Many of the lessons we taught the Japanese in 1948 are now being taught to Americans as "Lean principles." The Lean principles had their roots in the United States and date back to the early 1700s and later to Taylor, Gilbreth, and Henry Ford. The principles were refined by Taiichi Ohno and expanded by Dr. Shigeo Shingo. Modern-day champions were Norman Bodek (the Grandfather of Lean), Jim Womack, and Dan Jones.

Charles participated in numerous benchmarking and site visits, including a two-week trip to Japan in June 1996 and 2017. He is a master facilitator and trainer in TQM, total quality speed, facilitation, career development, change management, benchmarking, leadership, systems thinking, high-performance work teams, team building, Myers-Briggs® Styles, Lean thinking, and supply chain management. He also participated in Baldrige Examiner and Six Sigma management courses. He was an assistant program manager during "Desert Storm" for the Patriot missile-to-missile fuse development and production program. Charles is a past member of SME, AME, IIE, IEEE, APT, and the International Performance Alliance Group (IPAG), an international team of expert Lean Practitioners (http://www.ipag-consulting.com).

**Fred Whiton**, MBA, PMP, PE, has 30 years of experience in the aerospace and defense industry, which includes engineering, operations, program and portfolio management, and strategy development. He is employed as a Chief Engineer within Raytheon Intelligence & Space at the time of this book's publication.

Fred has both domestic and international expertise within homeland security, communications command and control intelligence surveillance and reconnaissance sensors and services, military and commercial aerospace systems, and defense systems supporting the US Navy, US Air Force, US Army, US Department of Homeland Security, and the US Intelligence Community across a full range of functions from marketing, concept development, engineering, and production into life cycle sustainment and logistics. Fred began his career as a design engineer at General Dynamics, was promoted to a group engineer at Lockheed Martin, and was a director at Northrop Grumman within the Homeland Defense Government Systems team. As vice president of engineering and operations at Smiths Aerospace, he was the Lean champion for a Lean enterprise journey, working closely with Protzman as the Lean consultant, for a very successful Lean implementation within a union plant, including a new plant designed using Lean principles. Prior to joining Raytheon, Fred was a senior vice president within C4ISR business unit at CACI International and prior to joining CACI was the vice president and general manager of the Tactical Communications and Network Solutions Line of Business within DRS Technologies.

Fred has a BS in mechanical engineering from the University of Maryland, an MS in mechanical engineering from Rensselaer Polytechnic Institute, a master's in engineering administration from The George Washington University, and an MBA from The University of Chicago. He is a professional engineer (PE) in Maryland, a certified project management professional (PMP), served as a commissioner on the Maryland Commission for Manufacturing Competitiveness under Governor Ehrlich, as a commissioner on the Maryland Commission on Autism under Governor O'Malley, and as a member of the boards of directors for the Regional Manufacturing Institute headquartered in Maryland and the First Maryland Disability Trust.

**Joyce Kerpchar** has over 35 years of experience in the healthcare industry that includes key leadership roles in healthcare operations, IT, health plan management, and innovative program development and strategy. As a Lean champion, mentor, and Six Sigma black belt, she is experienced in organizational lean strategy and leading large-scale healthcare lean initiatives, change management, and IT implementations. Joyce is a coauthor of Leveraging Lean in Healthcare: Transforming Your Enterprise into a High-Quality Patient Care Delivery System, Recipient of the Shingo Research and Professional Publication Award.

She began her career as a board-certified physician's assistant in cardiovascular and thoracic surgery and primary care medicine and received her master's degree in Management. Joyce is passionate about leveraging Lean in healthcare processes to eliminate waste and reduce errors, improve overall quality, and reduce the cost of providing healthcare.

# Introduction

This book is part of the BASICS Lean® Practitioner Series and was adapted from The Lean Practitioner's Field Book: Proven, Practical, Profitable and Powerful Techniques for Making Lean Really Work. In Book 5, we discuss the CHECK step of the BASICS Lean® Implementation Model. These steps include exploring the House of Continuous Improvement, Heijunka (level loading), Mistake Proofing, +QDIP and Tiered Meetings (Huddles), Visual Management, TPM, and applying Lean to the Accounting and Finance Functions.

The books in this BASICS Lean® Practitioner Series take the reader on a journey beginning with an overview of Lean principles, culminating with employees developing professionally through the BASICS Lean® Leadership Development Path. Each book has something for everyone from the novice to the seasoned Lean practitioner. A refresher for some at times, it provides soul-searching and thought-provoking questions with examples that will stimulate learning opportunities. Many of us take advantage of these learning opportunities daily. We, the authors, as Lean practitioners, are students still thirsting for knowledge and experiences to assist organizations in their transformations.

The BASICS Lean® Practitioner Series discusses the principles and tools in detail as well as the components of the house of Lean. It is a "how to" book that presents an integrated, structured approach identified by the acronym BASICS®, which is combined with an effective business strategy to ensure the successful transformation of an organization. The Lean concepts described in each book are supported by a plethora of examples drawn from the personal experiences of its many well-known and respected contributors, which range from very small machine shops to Fortune 50 companies.

The BASICS Lean® Practitioner Series has both practical applications and applications in academia. It can be used for motivating students to learn many of the Lean concepts and at the end of each chapter there are thought-provoking questions for the reader to help digest the material. The Lean practitioners focus on both manufacturing and transactional process areas.

People are the critical component to the success of every Lean initiative. The investment in people in terms of training, engagement, empowerment, and personal and professional growth is the key to sustaining Lean and an organization's success. For more on this topic, please see our book Lean Leadership BASICS®. Lean practitioners follow a natural flow, building continually on previous information and experiences, which builds a foundation for the Lean practitioner. There is a bit of the Lean practitioner in all of us. Hopefully, as you read these books to pursue additional knowledge, as a refresher or for reference, or for academia, it can help expand your knowledge, skills, and abilities for all of us in our never-ending Lean journey.

For the list of acknowledgments, testimonials, dedication, etc., please see The Lean Practitioner's Field Book. The purpose of this series was to break down and enhance the original Lean Practitioner's Field Book into six books that are aligned with the BASICS® model.

## Chapter 1

# BASICS Lean Implementation Model—Check

Vision without action is merely a dream. Action without vision just passes the time. Vision with action can change the world.

**Joel Barker**[1]

Life's just a matter of farming—of finding fertile soil in a good field—of breaking ground and being patient. The harvesting comes last—the main work must be done while the least results are showing."

**Herbert Kaufmann**[2]

It is as easy to "over-inspect" as "under-inspect." "Over-inspection" results in waste of money and high cost, while "under-inspection" results in unsatisfactory product reaching the customer.

**CCS Manual**

## Check Principles

The Check portion of BASICS® links directly to the check in plan–do–check–act (PDCA) as BASICS® is also a problem-solving model based on PDCA. The underlying principles are the same:

- One must build quality into the system, not inspect the quality into the system
- Checking is required to make sure the suggested solution is working
- Checking is waste—i.e., if one must check then the process is not in control
- You cannot get rid of checking until you get rid of the need for checking
- Always ask yourself; do you know how to check?

DOI: 10.4324/9781003185819-1

## The House of Continuous Improvement

### Brief History of the Toyota House Model

This original (house) model of the Toyota Production System (TPS) was developed by Russ Scaffede as a challenge to show where total productive maintenance (TPM) fits in relationship to TPS (Figure 1.1). It is one of the first models that starts to show the concept of a house built on a strong foundation representing the TPS. Russ was launching the new Powertrain facility and was being coached by Mr. Fujio Cho. Since the new Powertrain facility was largely a machining shop, the need for preventative maintenance was critical. Once Mr. Cho was satisfied that Russ-san understood TPM in relation to TPS, his direction, he was told, was to proceed with TPM. However, Russ was told by Mr. Cho "You Russ-san must represent TPS (by this model), as that is how the entire team must understand the initiative of preventative maintenance." This resulted in total support for sustainable success of the TPS in Kentucky.

### Purpose of a Model

The TPS model is well known and represents a good model of the philosophies of Lean that helped guide Toyota. The elements of a model should represent the philosophies that your organization will pursue in their Lean journey. The philosophies should remain constant and represent the aspects of your organization's Lean concept that acts as guidelines for decision-making and direction setting. The philosophies are supported by the tools of Lean. For example, Kanban is a tool that supports just in time (JIT). The tools of Lean are constantly improving and can be adapted to various situations. There are multiple types of Kanbans that can be used to support different aspects of your JIT approach. JIT, however, does not change; it is a steady principle that provides direction and challenge for the Lean implementation. The philosophies represent goals that are idealistic and may not be physically achieved but are the guideposts for continuous improvement.

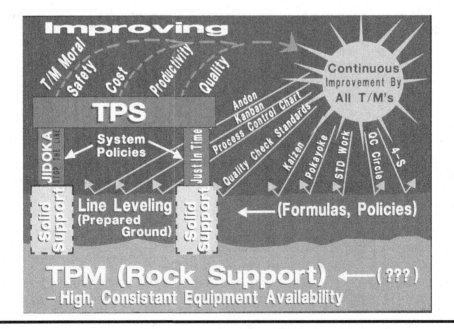

**Figure 1.1    Original Toyota House. (Courtesy of Russ Scaffede—used with permission.)**

The exercise of choosing the philosophies that are important to each individual organization and the dialogue that takes place between the leadership team in determining the organization's model are an important learning and clarifying exercise for the leadership team. It is important that the team develop ownership of the model. Discussing the difference between philosophies and tools can deepen a team's understanding of the concepts of Lean.

The model is used in the organization to clarify the "What" and the "Why" of the Lean initiative. The leadership team must clarify what direction they have chosen and why these principles are important to the Lean initiative. The team members must be engaged to determine the "How."

## Toyota House Model

The purpose of having a model of the company production system was clarified by Russ Scaffede as such: "The model represents the philosophies that the company follows regarding their Lean journey. The philosophies should not change, they are constant, and they provide the vision and direction needed to guide decisions and priorities. The tools that support the philosophies are constantly changing and improving but the philosophies are constant" (see Figure 1.2).

1. The first pillar—JIT
2. The second pillar—jidoka
3. The roof—respect for humanity
4. The base foundational requirements

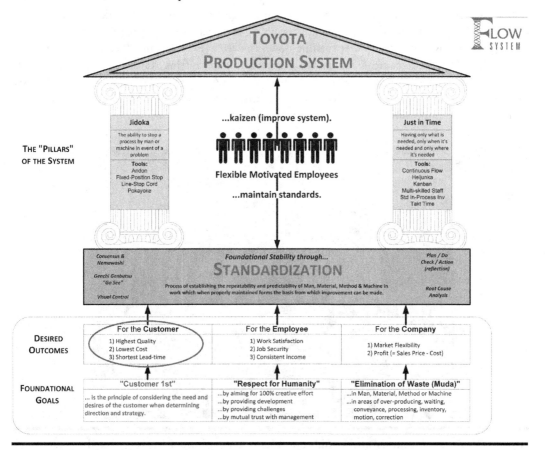

**Figure 1.2   Toyota House. (Courtesy of Nigel Thurlow—CEO, The Flow System.)**

Most of us are familiar with the Toyota House. It has many names as other companies have embraced and developed their versions of the TPS. We will walk through and explain the components of this house of continuous improvement:

## *Just in Time: The First Pillar*

The left side pillar is JIT, which means using the minimum amount of inventory, equipment, time, labor, and space necessary to deliver our products JIT to the customer by creating flow using a pull system. As companies journey down the Lean maturity path and decrease work in process (WIP) inventory levels, they will, if they fix the problems they expose, become more responsive to customers and continue to identify and eliminate the waste in their processes. In his book, Toyota Production System, Taiichi Ohno states:

> In 1956, I toured U.S. production plants at GM and Ford, and other machinery companies. But my strongest impression was the extent of the supermarket's prevalence in America …. Combining automobiles and supermarkets may seem odd. But for a long time, since learning about the setup of super-markets in America, we made a connection between super-markets and the just-in-time system …. Our biggest problem was how to avoid throwing the earlier process into confusion when a later process picked up large quantities at a time. Eventually, after trial and error, we came up with heijunka (production leveling).[3]

The true purpose behind JIT is to reduce the inventory in the systems to make problems more visible.[4] Excess inventory and idle time are always signs of waste and hide problems. The typical analogy for this is to think of water rushing down the river (Figure 1.3). When the water level is high, the rocks in the river create rapids. If you are white water rafting, kayaking, or canoeing, you look for the open space versus to traverse the rocks, but mostly, you move swiftly over the rocks. As you lower the water level of the river, the rapids disappear, and the rocks rise to the surface. At some point, it is impossible to get over the rocks and they must be removed.

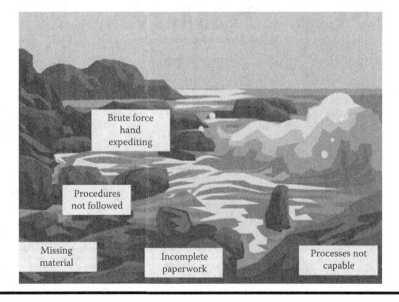

**Figure 1.3  Excess inventory always hides problems just like water rushing over the rocks.**

The problems you
don't see will cost you.

**Figure 1.4   Hidden wastes are always out to get you. You never know when they are going to strike!**

This is the same with inventory. When we have lots of excess inventory (high water), we never see all the waste (rocks) because we are too busy rushing around and over it. It is important to realize that waste hides other waste. The rocks represent waste hidden by inventory, rework, or workarounds created within a process. These are otherwise known as hidden wastes because we don't track them (see Figure 1.4). This will be discussed in more depth later in the book. As one lowers the water (inventory), one not only starts to expose the problems but is also forced to deal with the problems immediately. One must make sure that they are prepared to handle the removal of the waste and there is a continual pursuit to drive this waste down and out, or productivity improvement will be low or even negative and on-time deliveries (OTDs) will be jeopardized.

A common misperception is JIT means zero inventories. This is not the case as all systems need inventory to function. JIT means there is a small amount of inventory available at point of use (POU) before it is needed. It means operators have what they need on the line or at their desk so they don't have to go hunt for their own materials; the material should be right where and when it is needed. We call this POU inventory.

Our goal is to create a more efficient, productive, and effective system with the same or better quality and safety than exists today. It is not acceptable to create the most efficient delivery system if someone gets injured in the process, now or in the future (e.g., carpal tunnel or tendonitis that shows up later in life).

## Going Direct to Retailers: P&G Goes JIT in the 1920S[5]

Much of P&G's success has come from getting close to its customers. It took a leadership role in the US industry toward the end of 1920, when it decided to deliver directly to local grocers across the United States, cutting out the wholesale jobbers and middlemen. It was the first large US company to do so. The number of P&G's accounts jumped from 20,000 to 350,000 to 400,000! As Richard Dupree, chairman when Kenneth Hopper joined P&G in 1948, would remember, "we had to be in a position to deliver 5 boxes of soap to any retail grocer in the country." There was intense opposition from the independent warehouse jobbers. P&G's sales for 1921 dropped to only

*An editorial cartoon that appeared in the* Interstate
Grocer *in 1920, suggested what a bold and dangerous move*
*P&G was undertaking when it decided to sell*
*its products directly to retailer*s.

**Figure 1.5   P&G cartoon. (From Kenneth Hopper.)**

58% of what they were a year earlier and did not recover until 1925 (see Figure 1.5). The company, however, never lost confidence in its decision. Deliveries were still by horse-drawn wagons, but looking back, it can be seen as a beginning of the modern and efficient JIT supply chain to the customer.

Taiichi Ohno, the Toyota executive given the most credit for creating Toyota's JIT, records that he found a model for JIT in the American supermarket, Piggly Wiggly. P&G and supermarkets became almost synonymous in terms of organization. Where P&G's manufacturing employees had suffered unsteady employment at the beck and call of the warehouses, they were suddenly blessed by the steady washing habits of everyone. The company felt able to award its manufacturing employees with what became known as the guarantee of regular employment that resulted, as Kenneth Hopper can confirm, to the freest acceptance he met anywhere of improved methods.[6]

## *Jidoka: The Second Pillar of the Toyota Production System*

The Japanese term ji-do-ka consists of three Japanese characters. The first character, ji, means the worker himself or herself, do means movement, and ka means to change. In the TPS system, the second character was replaced, which translates to work or to labor. Toyoda Sakichi added a character (radical) to the original in the front representing humans. In the words of Taiichi Ohno, "At Toyota, the 'auto-activated machine' means 'a machine which is attached to an automatic stopping device'" (see Figure 1.6). In all of Toyota's plants, most of the machines, whether they are new machines or old machines, are equipped with an automatic stopping device. For example, "fixed position stopping system," "full work system," or "prevention of defective products." (Baka Yoke and various safety devices are additionally installed. Thus, human intelligence is given to the machines.)

Such auto-activated machines change the meaning of management greatly as well. Thus, an operator is not needed while the machine is working normally. Only when the machine stops

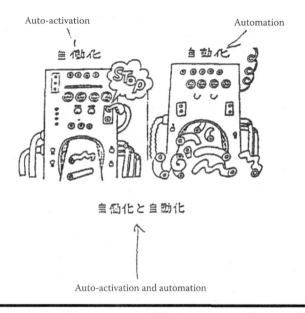

**Figure 1.6 Auto-activation vs. autonomation. (From Ohno's Book, The Bible of the Toyota Production System.)**

because of an abnormal situation does it get attention. As a result, one person can tend to several machines, making it possible to decrease the number of operators and increase production efficiency drastically. Another way of looking at this is that if one attends to a machine and replaces the machine when something abnormal happens, this means the abnormal situation would never disappear. An old Japanese proverb says, "If something stinks, put a cover on it." If the material or machine gets repaired without the managing supervisor being made aware of the fact, improvement is never achieved, and the cost never goes down. Stopping the machine when there is trouble forces awareness on everyone if the problem is clearly understood.

Expanding this way of thinking, we set a rule that even in a production line, which is operated manually, the workers themselves should push the stop button and halt the production line if there is any abnormality. In the United States, the word auto-activation has been changed to autonomation or, when loosely translated into English, automating with a human touch. This idea of jidoka is credited by Toyoda Sakichi,[7] who developed a spinning loom that would automatically shut off if a thread snapped (Figure 1.7). He accomplished this by placing a bunch of pins (floaters) that rode on the threads. If a thread broke, the pin would fall and stop the machine.[8]

The first principle at work is separating man from machine. Once a job is standardized, it becomes repetitive and should be semi or fully automated (Table 1.1). Machines should do

**Figure 1.7 Poka yoke—spinning loom would automatically stop if it broke a thread allowing 1 worker to manage 30 machines.**

**Table 1.1   Separation of Worker from Machine**

| | | Hand Functions | | | | Mental Functions | | | |
|---|---|---|---|---|---|---|---|---|---|
| | | Principal Operations | | | | Main Operations | | Marginal Allowances | |
| | | Main Operations | | Incidental Operations | | | | Incidental Operations | |
| *Stage* | *Type* | *Cutting* | *Feeding* | *Installation/ Removal* | *Switch Operation* | *Detecting Abnormalities* | *Disposition of Abnormalities* | *Detecting Abnormalities* | *Disposition of Abnormalities* |
| 1 | **Manual operation** | Worker | Worker | Worker | Worker | Worker | Worker | Worker | Worker |
| 2 | **Manual feed, automatic cutting** | Machine | Worker | Worker | Worker | Worker | Worker | Worker | Worker |
| 3 | **Automatic feed, automatic cutting** | Machine | | Worker | Worker | Worker | Worker | Machine that stops automatically (worker oversees more than one machine) | Worker |
| 4 | **Semiautomation** | Machine | | Machine | Machine | Worker | Worker | Machine (worker oversees more than one machine) | Worker |
| 5 | **Pre-automation (automation with a human touch)** | Machine | | Machine | Machine | Machine | Worker | Machine (automation with a human touch) | Worker |
| 6 | **True automation** | Machine | | Machine | Machine | Machine | Machine | | Machine |

*Source:*  Non-Stock Production (Shingo, Productivity Press), p. 255.

**Figure 1.8    Gas shutoff. Automated mistake proofing example. (From BIG Archives.)**

repetitive and dangerous work. The next step is to create smart machines or machines which can automatically stop when a mistake is made, or a problem occurs in the machine. This is a central principle of the TPS system, which is why jidoka is the right pillar of the Lean house. The true goal of jidoka that integrates mistake proofing is to prevent the error at the source to ensure a defect does not result. This ensures that quality is built in at each process and triggers an automatic response to an abnormality. It also assures that no additional value is added to the product after a defect occurs. Another benefit of jidoka is that it frees the person up from having to watch the machine (just in case it was to break down). As a result, one operator could run 49 spinning looms!

- Example—the gas pump hose will automatically shut off when the tank is full (see Figure 1.8). This prevents the defect of the gas overflowing from the tank.
- Example—gas tank fueling location will only fit one type of fuel nozzle.
- Example—electrical receptacles with a ground plug and large slotted prong.

Lesson Learned: One can now begin to see how all the Lean tools eventually integrate and work together. One cannot implement just part of the system and expect the system to work as a whole. This theme will be discussed throughout the book.

Author's Note: Ritsuo Shingo in his Master Class in 2021 stated that he felt it was a mistake to have Built in Quality, as it was formerly known, replaced by Jidoka. We consider jidoka synonymous within Built in Quality within the context of this series. The bottom line is you must have quality at the source, and it must be designed in versus inspected in.

## Difference between an Error and a Defect

In Figure 1.9, there is a railing at the exit which is often found in many fast-food establishments with a drive thru. The railing is an unconscious reminder or warning to the customer not to walk directly out into the path of the drive thru. The error is walking in front of the car. The defect occurs when the customer is run over.[9] Toyota's goal is to arrange a production line to ensure that when something

**Figure 1.9 Mistake proofing example—the railing doesn't prevent the defect but is a subtle reminder to the person exiting with the intention to prevent the error leading to the defect.**

goes wrong, the equipment itself detects the error or mistake and stops automatically. From the people's side, the line is set up so that it can be stopped by the team members whenever a quality problem is discovered. Jidoka is part of the fabric and the very foundation on which the TPS is built.

## Jidoka at Toyota

When there is a problem on the line at Toyota, the andon light goes from green to yellow but the line continues to move until it gets to the takt time (TT) stopping point. The andon (visual control) notifies the team leader that there is a problem and on what line and at what station the problem occurred. If the team leaders cannot solve the problem within a TT, the light goes from yellow to red and the line can stop without injuring anyone working on the line. During tours of Toyota, we witnessed the andon lights going from green to yellow quite often, but we did not see any going to red. As soon as it turns yellow, the team leaders can be seen literally running to the source of the problem. Toyota has material buffers at strategic points to enable operators to stop the line while not interrupting the overall production line.

### Toyota Tools to Obtain Jidoka

Consistent with Built in Quality, Toyota integrates the following tools to obtain jidoka:

- Constantly improving machines to automatically stop when a mistake is found or prior to the dies crashing or other breakdowns
- Poka yoke—mistake proofing
- Andon—visual controls for each line such as flags, lights, or escalations
- Fixed position line stops for conveyors

The purpose of jidoka is to prevent defects and equipment breakdowns by arranging the equipment so that either the equipment itself or the operator can detect the occurrence of an abnormality and stop the equipment immediately. It is particularly important to discover the cause of the abnormality and take prompt action to prevent a recurrence.

## Labor-Saving (Monitoring of Equipment Is Unnecessary) Machine Jidoka

The goal is to always strive for 100% quality in products by producing zero defects; thus, systems must be designed to catch the error prior to it becoming a defect. The first goal of Lean is to never produce a bad part. In the worst-case scenario, if a defect is created, we must be able to detect the defective part before passing it to the next process. Machines should check parts before they work on them, while they are working on them, and after they work on them. By incorporating jidoka, we design, modify, or customize machines to detect errors prior to producing a defect. The other goal of jidoka is to make sure that the machines don't break down, but if they do, make sure they stop before making a bad part or crashing.

Examples of jidoka are as follows:

- A probe in a machine that detects when a tool breaks and shuts down the machine.
- A machine uses visual detection to find a defect and stops.
- A machine stops when the bar feeder is empty.
- The machine doesn't start or stops and alerts the user when it is programed improperly or has a fault.
- The machine is designed to stop before crashing the dies.
- The credit card company system knows you are calling from your home phone to activate the credit card.[10]
- The car signals when it is too close to another vehicle during parking maneuvers.
- The car can sense when it is too close to the next car and slows down automatically.
- Many copiers and printers now have jidoka built in. Most copiers stop the machine after a mistake (paper jam) occurs and provide specific instructions with pictures on how to fix it. The goal would be to fix it, so it detects the error (poor alignment, wrong type of paper, etc.) prior to creating the defect (i.e., the crumpled-up document in the roller) and fix itself!

## People Jidoka and the Use of Safety Glasses

The second jidoka principle is to protect the human and to eliminate human mistakes. Machines and equipment should be designed so humans do not need safety glasses or protective gear. The mere presence of safety glasses implies the environment is basically unsafe for the human. Safety glasses, after careful thought and analysis, should be the last line of defense but instead they have become an accepted practice and many times are issued even when not needed for liability reasons. The use of safety glasses is an example of the boiled frog syndrome at work in most companies worldwide. Wouldn't it be better to create safe environments where people can't get hurt? The use of safety glasses is a work-around to creating an environment where people can't get hurt and is a disincentive to modifying the equipment. By installing safety devices such as protected cages and light curtains, one can prevent injuries to workers and create an environment where safety glasses are no longer needed.

The third idea of jidoka is that humans should be able to stop the line if opportunity for an error is discovered or a mistake is made. This is a difficult concept to embrace worldwide in manufacturing and can also be difficult in government and other service industries. In the United States, our short-term make the quarterly numbers and shoot from the hip mentality fundamentally and strategically conflicts with this concept. For example, most US government numbers (i.e., unemployment rate) are revised several times after they are initially released.

## The Safety Bonus System Story

At a company in Europe, their safety program was tied to a bonus system. Each month, when there were no recordable injuries, the employees received a bonus. While the intention was to promote safety, it did the opposite. When someone was injured, they were made to feel extremely bad because now the rest of the company would suffer due to their carelessness. As a result, many safety problems went unrecorded, and "You owe me one's" were created in the organization. Everyone received their bonus, and the perception of a safe work environment was created. However, none of the real problems were addressed and eventually someone had to be taken out by ambulance. Bonus programs are always well intended but may end up masking the problem and driving the wrong behavior. If the problems are not encouraged to surface, they cannot be addressed. The bonus program should be based on the number of safety problems exposed and corrected or mitigated.

## What Sigma Level Are Humans?

Errors and mistakes cost all of us money and, more important, the reputation of our companies. We must take caution if humans are doing any job, since humans are at best two or three sigma. Three sigma (with the 1 1/2 sigma shift) quality is approximately 66,000 mistakes per million opportunities. If the process depends on a human, the system will probably never get better than two or three sigma because humans make mistakes. Therefore, the capability of most manufacturing processes worldwide is in the two to three sigma ranges. To mistake proof or foolproof processes, we need a way to take the humans out of the equation. Mistakes and errors not only cause human tragedy but also add expensive hidden costs to our manufacturing systems.

**Five Phases or Steps to Jidoka—Encompasses People and Machines[11]**
We have always referred to this process as "earning your way to stopping the line …"[12]

1. Implement systematic problem-solving skills:
   a. Use to stabilize the process (must be done before going further)
   b. PDCA/A3 techniques to get to the root cause of problems
   Note: If you cannot get this step right, it does not make sense to move forward as you will only be applying bandages!
2. Develop methods to detect problems as they occur:
   a. Day by hour chart
   b. Encouraging workers to point out problems
3. Implement quality gates—creating inspection points in the process (mistake proofing parts of the process):
   a. Judgment inspection
      i. People inspection—product is compared to a standard and accepted or scrapped
      ii. Successive checks inspection—second person reviews it
   b. Informative inspection
      i. Statistical process control (SPC), control plans, etc.
   Note: Both types have both warning and control devices
   c. Implement in-source inspection
      i. The poka yoke, developed by Shigeo Shingo—implementing both warning and control devices
      ii. Poka yoke means preventing inspection at the source, most used by Toyota
      iii. Modifying equipment to stop after it makes a mistake, or to prevent tools from crashing (i.e., presses) or to stop before it makes a mistake

4. Inducing process quality—never pass on a bad part to the next step—mistake proofing the overall process:
   a. Applying 5S, poka yoke, standardization techniques, and the built-in-quality process
   b. Ensured by preventing defective products/service from reaching the customer
   c. The process should be designed to identify problems immediately after they occur and induce workers to always follow the correct procedures
5. Decouple quality and process flow from direct supervision:
   a. Andon boards, escalation charts, and the ultimate interruption cords (andon cords) in place.
   b. Built in quality without direct supervision

## The Jidoka Process

Figure 1.10 shows an example of a jidoka process:

■ Step 1: The process begins with an abnormality being detected. The andon light goes yellow! It is interesting to note that if there are no visual controls or triggers for the abnormality, the process will continue to go unchecked and produce bad parts until someone discovers them and stops the process. (The objective is to detect the abnormality as near as possible to its occurrence, so it doesn't progress forward and never reaches the customer.)
■ Step 2: The team leader responds immediately to the andon and checks with the team member to understand the abnormality that has occurred. A standard work process must exist documenting this system for it to work and sustain. Many companies put in andon lights but with no standard work or system behind it. The team member turns on the andon light

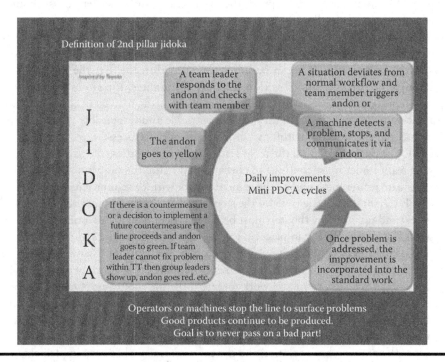

**Figure 1.10 Jidoka Process—BIG® training materials.**

and no one shows up. The system is now dead. In addition, for this system to work, the team leader must be on or near the line and be able to see the andon.

If the team leader is in meetings all day or constantly pulled off the floor, what are the chances for this system to work? The team leader must also be familiar with the process and have done the process himself or herself to understand the problems and gain the respect of their team members. Many companies bring in team leaders that have never worked the line and don't have a clue what the operators go through each day to build their products. A similar situation occurs with many engineers.

Lesson Learned: Most operators will do the best job they can do with the process, tools, and training provided by the management. If they don't have the right tools to safely do the job, they will find other typically non-safe tools to do the job. As Deming said, 94% of employees want to do a good job![13]

The team leader must ask the team member to explain their problem in detail and ask the team member what they would do to fix the problem.

Note: If the team leader just solves the problem, they have missed a wonderful coaching opportunity (Kata) for the team member to learn and develop their problem-solving skills. Together, the team leader (coach) and team member (student) discuss the problem (plan) and see if they can determine the root cause. If so, they discuss possible solutions. If they can come up with a countermeasure, they implement the solution. If the root cause cannot be discovered, they brainstorm a temporary fix (containment measure) and again implement only one at a time until the problem is solved (andon return to green) so they can continue to meet the TT or cycle time at which the line is running.

- Step 3: If a containment action cannot be determined within the TT, the line is stopped and the andon goes to red.
- Step 4: As soon as the line is stopped, the group leader (team leader's boss) should immediately show up at the line. Once again, an opportunity for Kata exists and the group leader will discuss the problem with the team leader and entire team (generally five to six employees) and ask for ideas. If a countermeasure is determined, it is implemented and the andon returns to green. If it can be implemented within the TT, the light stays red. If a solution cannot be determined within the next 15 minutes, the group leader's boss shows up and repeats the process. This continues until the plant manager shows up, because the assumption is that at this point, they are the ones able and responsible to solve the problem. Therefore, promotion from within is a crucial part of the process.
- Step 5: Once the line restarts, the team leader has several duties:
  - The team leader must continue to check to make sure the problem has been solved.
  - The team leader must update the standard work with the countermeasure (this is the act in PDCA) and the cycle time for the step as well as any key points on how to do the step safely and reasons why the step must be done. Of course, this assumes there is a standard work document already in place and that everyone follows the standard work.
  - If a containment action was put in place, then, we have not discovered the root cause. The next step would be to work with the team members at lunch or off shift to continue the PDCA process (plan) and work to determine the root cause. Once the root cause is determined (this process could take from hours to months), a countermeasure can be implemented. The solution must be checked short term and long term (6 months later) to make sure the problem does not return.
  - Once the problem has a solution and the countermeasure has been implemented successfully, the team leader must once again update the standard work with the countermeasure

and the cycle time for the step as well as any key points on how to do the step safely and why the step must be done.

– They must also put a check card into the tickler file (file organized by date) to remind them when to come back to check to make sure the problem has still not returned and validate that the root cause was indeed fixed. Part of the standard work for this process must dictate the conditions for when to stop the line and how the andon light system is supposed to work.

■ Step 6: Reflect and Yokoten—what could we have done to improve the overall problem-solving process just encountered and can we spread the improvements to other areas?

Lesson Learned: In reality, this is a PDCA process with potentially several smaller PDCA cycles generated until the line is back up and running.

## Why Is Jidoka So Difficult to Implement?

One of the reasons we struggle with jidoka is that many of the Lean principles, thinking, and tools must be in place for it to work. Jidoka combines the principles listed below for it to work with machines:

■ One-piece flow, visual controls
■ Poka yoke
■ Creativity before capital
■ Flexibility
■ TPM
■ Standard work
■ Culture
■ Problem-solving

Because most companies do not really understand Jidoka, it makes it very difficult to implement. Most engineers prefer to purchase equipment out of a catalog versus designing right-sized equipment tailored to suit the specific operation. Companies do not understand the competitive advantage which can be gained by jidoka and see it as an unnecessary cost. As Dr. Shingo said, "We must become the machine."[14] We must have the resources to dedicate to modify the machines, so they stop prior to crashing or making a mistake.

One certain indicator, we see internationally, for jidoka being required is when you hear a team member on the line or in the office say, "I cannot leave the machine." When we ask why, the operator says that it might crash, produce a bad part, or have some type of problem, and they also say that when it does, it's a mess. When we ask how often it has a problem, the operator usually doesn't know, or they must think back to 10 years ago. Imagine putting a clock right in front of the machine operator and see how long their day becomes.

In most companies worldwide, we find operators spend most of their time monitoring the machines; where the company pays the operator to stand idly by just in case the machine breaks down or has a problem. Once we tell operators they no longer need to watch the machine, they think we do not care about quality when we are doing exactly the opposite, which is building the quality into the system. When you think about it, having the operator inspect the machine or parts does not guarantee six sigma or even three sigma quality levels.

In most cases, the idle time is not captured in any accounting metrics. In the non-jidoka world, this makes sense because machines and tooling are expensive. When the machines crash, it costs

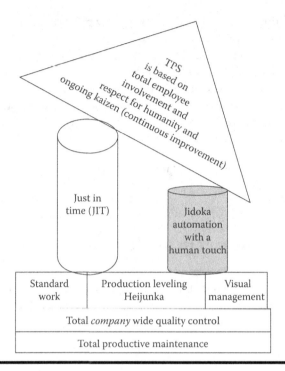

**Figure 1.11  Jidoka—the forgotten second pillar—if an operator has to babysit a machine, you need jidoka. (From BIG Archives.)**

money and downtime to repair them. Yet we continue to reactively fix our machines but never take the time to outfit them so they won't crash or so they stop before, or worst case after, making a defective part or document (in the office world). We believe the failure to apply or even recognize the term jidoka as one of the major hindrances of implementing Lean worldwide today. It is interesting to note that there are two pillars to the Toyota house. One is JIT and one is jidoka. In the house analogy, these pillars support the overall house once built on a good foundation. Yet from a big picture-systems view, we find most companies working on Lean focus 80%–95% or more of their effort on JIT and virtually none on jidoka. A Google search on JIT yielded 630 million results.[15] The search on jidoka yielded 219 thousand.[16] A search on YouTube netted 2.4 million JIT results versus 130 for jidoka of which only 7 dealt directly with jidoka.[17] During our seminars all over the world, when we ask the class "who can tell us about JIT?" everyone's hand goes up. When we ask about jidoka, we get blank stares. This creates a lopsided house as shown in Figure 1.11.

## Man-to-Machine Ratios[18]

What is your man-to-machine ratio? Do you measure it? Is it a key process indicator (KPI)? Most companies around the world think they are world class if they have one operator for two or even three machines. However, these pale in comparison to the Toyota's statistics below:

- In 1896, Toyoda Loom Works averaged 30–40 machines per operator.
- In the 1940s, Toyota Motors averaged five machines per operator.
- In 1993, Toyota Motors averaged 16 machines per operator.

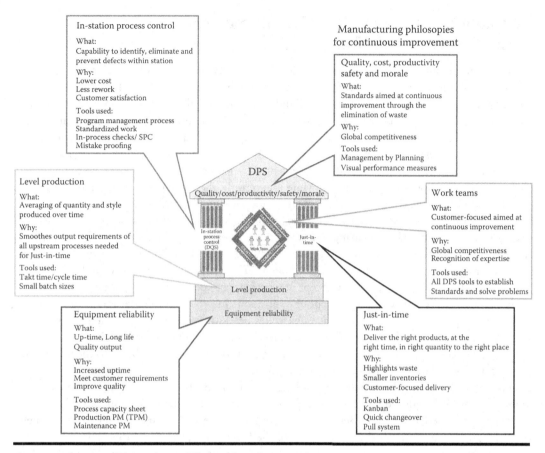

**Figure 1.12 Manufacturing philosophies for continuous improvement for the Donnelly Production System House of Quality. They have since been bought out by Magna International.**

Jidoka is the tool that makes these types of ratios possible.

In 2001 Toyota engaged in a yearlong study to address the issue of difficulties they were having in rolling out the TPS in plants around the world. The basic realization from some of the startup facilities was a failure to realize the importance of the people tools versus the task tools. It was at this time that Toyota released their Toyota Way 2001 house that outlined the philosophical guidelines important to understand the culture or people tools of Toyota. Donnelly corporation, after the arrival of Russ Scaffede, used the house pictured in Figure 1.12 based on the Toyota House. The philosophical pillars were respect for people and continuous improvement. Respect for people had a deep meaning for Toyota that included the idea of providing people with all the support they need to be successful and fulfill their potential. They expect great things from their employees and put them in a system that allows them to achieve at high levels. Continuous improvement encompasses an attitude that is never satisfied and always striving to find a better way. The expectation is that people will challenge themselves and their peers to reach higher and higher levels of performance.

It was an important realization for Toyota that there was more to their success than just the tools of the TPS. They had also developed a culture that developed people skills that were the engine behind the application of tools and methods. The development of lifelong learners, teachers, coaches, and mentors that created a positive spiral of a classic learning organization was a large part of the Toyota success story. There had always been a focus on people selection and development but now the formal philosophies of the company reflected this approach.

## Containment Action versus Countermeasures versus Solutions Solution

It is important to differentiate containment action from countermeasures and solutions. Containment actions temporarily fix or work around the problem but don't solve the problem. In the United States, we call them Band-Aids®.[19] Eventually, the Band-Aids® fail and the problem returns. In the TPS, all the improvement actions, tools, and systems are considered countermeasures. Problems within a manufacturing system can be complicated with multiple root causes and system interactions. The term solution implies that there is a single root cause, when there may be many interacting root causes that will need multiple countermeasures implemented over time. The magic root cause solution that leads to a permanent solution rarely exists. More importantly, the problem solvers need to develop the culture that realizes that there is no permanent solution or single root cause. Every countermeasure can be improved; every root cause could lead to other root causes within the system. The mindset of the team must be focused on realizing that improvements can always be found. Some countermeasures can be very effective, and the goal of every problem solver should be to eliminate the problem from ever returning; however, Thomas Edison stated, "There is always a better way; find it."

Dr. Deming was opposed to the concept of a permanent corrective action because the concept of permanent was contrary to the concept of continuous improvement. Preventive actions should always be supported and devices such as poka yokes need to be implemented. The poka yoke is a good example regarding Yokoten. While the current poka yoke may work well, is there a way to make it cheaper, easier to install, more durable? If so, those ideas should be implemented before sharing the countermeasure across the plant or company.

Problems have a nasty habit of hiding for long periods of time before resurfacing. We have found problems rear their ugly heads years later. Benjamin Franklin[20] summarized his lead discoveries back in 1786 in a letter written to Benjamin Vaughn (see Figure 1.13). Some researchers even believe that lead poisoning contributed to the decline of the Roman Empire. Yet in the 1950s,[21] US paint manufacturers started using lead pigment again in their paints, seemingly unaware of the risk. This created an unbelievable health problem in the United States as billions of dollars have been spent in the repercussions of this one decision. The decision resulted in uncounted lawsuits, deaths, child brain injuries and learning disabilities, hazardous waste cleanup and dumping costs, etc.

On August 2, 2007, Fisher-Price, a subsidiary of Mattel, Inc., recalled 967,000 plastic toys with lead paint made in China. Still, millions of Chinese children suffer from lead poisoning despite a crackdown on contamination.[22] Once again, we have a resurgence of the problem. Why does this keep happening? To this day it is still a problem in the US. We had the knowledge for centuries that lead is very hazardous to humans. Yet throughout history, it seems to be forgotten and then relearned the hard way.

Factory problems follow similar patterns. Even if you find the root cause, we must find ways that will prevent the root cause from ever coming back. This is very difficult to do. Most of us feel it will take too much time to find the root cause. Once we find a work around the pressure is now off finding the root cause or fixing the problem, so it never comes back. Many have asked how Toyota sustains their management system over the years and the answers are many, but it all starts with the "soft" precepts of Toyota discussed earlier, the constant attention to the learning organization, people development, promotion from within, succession planning, and then infrastructure "hard" tools mainly led by standard work.

Remember, if there is no standard work, there can be no sustained improvement. How do we update a process to eliminate the root cause if there is no standard work in place? Standard work must be in place to fully implement jidoka or any process improvement. This does not mean we

Historical Awareness: "If we were to judge of the interest excited by any medical subject by the number of writings to which it has given birth, we could not but regard the poisoning by lead as the most important to be known of all those that have been treated of, up to the present time." Orfilo, 1817

- The oldest piece of lead found in British museum dates from 3800 BC
- 500 BC–300 AD: Roman lead smelting produces dangerous emissions
- 200 BC: Health effects of lead first stated by the Greek physician Dioscerides: "Lead makes the mind give way"
- 100 BC: Epidemic outbreak of saturnine gout and sterility among Roman aristocracy
- 100 BC: Greek physicians give clinical description of lead poisoning
- 15th century: Lead known as poudre de la succession (succession powder)
- 16th century: The introduction of lead containing cosmetics such as Venetian ceruse and spirits of Saturn
- Lead mentioned by Shakespeare (1564-1616) at least 25 times in his published plays
- 1848: Tanquerel des Planches, in his treatise, remarks on children placing lead painted toys in their mouths and developing lead colic
- 1886: Publication of first periodic table (Mendeleyev periodic table), lead is included as one of the 63 known elements
- 1887: US medical authorities diagnose childhood lead poisoning
- 1897: Lead poisoning among Queensland children is documented
- 1904: Child lead poisoning linked to lead-based paints (article in Australian Medical Gazette by J. Gibson)
- 1909: France, Belgium, and Austria ban white-lead interior paint
- 1914: Pediatric lead-paint poisoning death from eating crib paint is described
- 1914: [Many people wrongly believe this to be the year that lead was banned from house paint in Australia. In fact, lead was only limited to 0.1% in house paint in Australia 83 years later, in 1997!]
- 1920: Introduction of tetraethyl lead as a key for improvement of engine performance
- 1921: National Lead Company (United States) admits lead is a poison
- 1922: League of Nations bans white-lead interior paint; United States declines to adopt
- 1922: Tunisia and Greece ban white-lead interior paint
- 1922: The Health Acts Amendment Act of 1922 in the state of Queensland, Australia, says:

114A(1) No paint containing more than five per centum of soluble lead shall be used or put within four feet from the floor or ground on the outside of any residence, hall school, or other building to which children under the age of fourteen years have access, or on any veranda railing, gate or fence.

- 1923: First tetraethyl lead poisoning deaths occur
- 1926: Great Britain and Sweden, ban white-lead interior paint
- 1927: Poland bans white-lead interior paint
- 1931: Spain and Yugoslavia ban white-lead interior paint
- 1943: Report concludes eating lead paint chips causes physical and neurological disorders, behavior, learning, and intelligence problems in children
- 1952: Many cases of children lead poisoning associated with white-lead paint are reported and publicized in popular press in United States
- 1955: CPSC lowered the limit of lead in paint to 1.0%
- 1971: Lead-Based Paint Poisoning Prevention Act passed
- 1971: CDC lowers the limit for a lead poisoned child to 40 micrograms/decilitre (µg/dL)
- 1975: CDC lowers the limit for a lead poisoned child to 30 µg/dL
- 1977: The WHO recommends the tolerable dietary intake of lead as 430 µg/day micrograms/day
- 1978: United States bans white-lead paint (limit of lead in paint below 0.06%)
- 1979: Association of lead exposure and neuropsychological deficits in children described in the New England Journal of Medicine
- 1980 : National Academy of Sciences calls leaded gasoline greatest source of atmospheric lead pollution
- 1985: CDC lowers the limit for a lead poisoned child to 25 µg/dL
- 1990 : Leaded gasoline in cars is banned in Canada
- 1991 : CDC establishes lead concentration safety limit as less than or equal to 10 µg/dL
- 1991: Establishment of Lead Group in Australia

**Figure 1.13    Lead discoveries summarized by Benjamin Franklin.**

can't start fixing machines when they have a problem, but we need to document what we did to fix the machine (standard work) and how to maintain it with total productivity maintenance (TPM), etc. There should be a database tracking ongoing problems and solutions. This way, as we encounter future problems, we can check to see if we have experienced the same or similar problems in the past and what was done to fix it or to know that the last fix did not work. The fact that we have encountered the problem again means one of two things; either we didn't truly fix the root cause the first time or we deviated from the standard process from some reason which allowed the root cause to surface again. In this case, some type of mistake proofing is warranted.

## Long Action Item Lists that Keep Growing for the Wrong Reasons

The best way to keep the action item list from growing is fix the problems so they don't come back. At a plant in China, the welding station and a computer terminal (see Figure 1.14) were attached by a long wire to the machine. The holder that came with the unit to hold the terminal in place was very loose. An operator dropped the terminal on the floor, and it shut the machine down for 2 days. Maintenance fixed it but left it in the same holder. Can we predict what will happen in the future? We must mistake proof our actions or our action item list will keep growing but with the same actions occurring repeatedly. Every maintenance request should have the question: "Was this repaired so the problem can never happen again?"

## Respect for Humanity: What We Call the People Piece[23]

There are many books and videos which explore this topic. In the book Training within Industry,[24] the people piece is referred to as job relations. While learning and implementing Lean tools are not easy, implementing the people piece or what Toyota calls respect for humanity is much more difficult. Anyone who has implemented Lean knows this to be true. The people piece includes getting people not only to buy in and accept Lean but also to embrace continuous improvement,

**Figure 1.14  Computer terminal in a loose holder.**

continually identify problems constantly, provide their ideas, and help sustain the changes. The real goal of Lean is to create a continuous improvement culture where employees are contributing, and supervisors and team leaders are budgeted 50% or more of their time to implement small improvements daily. This is a very difficult culture to create. In discussing this with Jerry Solomon, multiple Shingo Prize winner,[25] Jerry said, "Why would you want to embark on the Lean journey when over 90% of companies fail in their quest to truly become Lean? What will you or your company do differently to be successful?"

Lesson Learned: It is extremely important if you are starting a Lean journey that you answer Mr. Solomon's question above. We ask this of any company considering going down the Lean path. Think through it, plan and map it out, get the right people on board, don't waiver, and never look back. Hopefully, we can flip the outcome to 90% of companies being successful in implementing Lean and Six Sigma.

Exercise: Answer the following question: What are you going to do differently to be part of the 10% of companies in the world to be successful in implementing Lean?

## Top of the Toyota House: Respect for Humanity

At many companies, we have found a major misunderstanding of the respect for humanity term.

### Respect for Humanity Is Not

- Being nice to people all the time
- Moving non-performers to another area
- Annual subjective evaluations
- Letting people do whatever they want in the workplace
- Doing everything people want to be done
- Giving people the answer every time they have a problem
- Hiring any breathing body just to fill a position
- Ignoring your team's input or asking for input
- None of these options are fair to our team members (employees)

### Respect for Humanity Is

- Being respectful to employees
- Employing active listening and empathy
- Coaching employees to think of the answer for themselves
- Making sure the employee can be successful in your environment prior to hiring them
- Making sure we constantly solicit ideas from the employee on how to improve
- Constantly challenge team members with new problems
- Holding employees accountable to promises and deadlines
- Creating development plans and paths for employees
- Disciplining employees as needed
- Allowing employees (team members) to fail and then coaching them on how to learn from the failure
- Empowering employees to the proper level
- Giving back to the community

At Toyota, all employees are taught they own and are accountable for the job and improving the job, which is part of Ji Kotei Kanketsu (JKK) and problem-solving skills called Toyota Business Practices (TBP). They are taught how to use JKK and TBP as part of their on-the-job development where they must go and see (Gemba) to grasp the actual situation and observe carefully, with a TPS eye.[26] They are taught to humbly benchmark and listen carefully to others. They participate in kaizen activities (jishuken). They are also taught presentation skills, how to establish systems and tools, and how to focus management attention using visuals, production analysis boards, process diagnostics, KPIs, and stacked element charts. They create a problem-solving environment utilizing standard work and problem-solving tools, including the 5 Whys, the 5W2H, and breaking problems down into more finite parts to solve them. Team members (workers) are encouraged to surface problems quickly and honestly and create swift solutions and countermeasures followed by updating their standard work. They learn project management skills, problem-solving skills (PDCA), and visual management.

Toyota executives' park in a different spot every week—there are no parking spots reserved for senior management close to the entrance. Executives talk to people on the way in and out and thank them for the truth. Executives are measured by how well they build and encourage supportive culture utilizing consistency of direction, priorities, respect, trust, and involvement of team members. They encourage active listening and feedback, sometimes called two-way communications, where they are open to listening to problems and feedback. They create a culture devoid of threats, intimidation, or fear. Meetings are short and usually stand-up. If problems are not fixed within 2 weeks, the team and group leaders must answer to the general manager (GM).[27] Respect for humanity is embraced by the culture created throughout the organization as described earlier with the focus on true north. It is a culture where 80% of the company's continuous improvement ideas come from the frontline team members, 95% or more are implemented, and 95% or more of the team members participate.

## Respect for Humanity and Ideas

A good Lean system implementation or what some may term a system kaizen (vs. a point or spot kaizen) targets the overall process or the system with improvement. This provides staff with the opportunity to suggest improvements within their work areas, which improves the flow of communication and ideas. Listening to staff and implementing their suggestions always yields an improvement in morale and participation and is part of the respect for humanity concept. Implementing Lean does not only impact each person on the floor but everyone in the office as well. Eliminating waste in administrative processes will free up people and the need for middle management personnel will also be reduced over time. Moving to value stream managers or focus factory managers or service line organizations will provide better line of sight to the customer. Some of this will involve converting staff positions into line positions. Those in administrative positions or middle management positions need to constantly expand their skill set and stay current with training if they are to continue to add value to the company. Imagine if we had a Cpk or process capability measurement in place for knowledge-based processes.

## Make the Employee's Job Easier

Wouldn't it be easier to retain and recruit for an organization that strives to make the employee's job easier? Anyone in a management or staff support role doesn't directly make money for the organization; therefore, what is management's job? One of our favorite quotes is from Mike Walsh

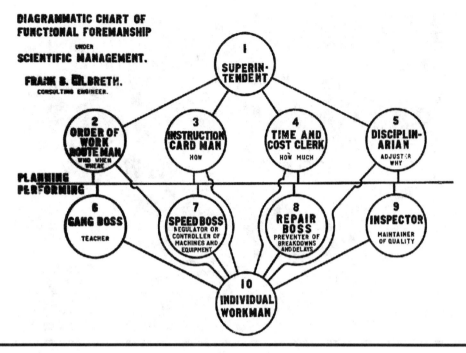

**Figure 1.15   Division of superintendents' job. (Public domain.)**

in the video Speed Is Life, where he said, "Management's responsibility is to be worthy of its people."[28]

Why does management exist? The whole concept of middle management was started by the railroads back in the late nineteenth century (see Figure 1.15).[29] Frederick Taylor benchmarked the railroads and brought the whole concept of middle management and cost accounting practices from the railroads to manufacturing and, eventually, service industries like hotels and health care.[30] Taylor and Gilbreth[31] took the supervisor's job and split it up into eight different positions: planning, production, route, inventory stores, instruction card and time study, order of work, recording and cost accounting, and disciplinarian.[32] This was the beginning of the functional organizations we have today. At the time these jobs were created, they were designed to help the operators get more efficient with a focus on the customer and were co-located in the production area with those performing the work (see Figure 1.16). Yet, where are most overhead indirect staff and managers located today? The answer would be in their offices, normally far, far away from the front line. Some don't even know where the shop floor is located. All one can do in an office is manage history, answer e-mails, go to meetings, and write reports. We have a saying: "You can't fix tomorrow what is happening now!" Does any of this make the operator's job easier? When you think about it, in a truly Lean organization, staff positions should be converted to line positions wherever possible and co-located on the shop floor wherever possible.

Lesson Learned: Management's goal should be to work on making the frontline person's job easier by removing waste and making improvements. They should know, own, and constantly be working to streamline their processes.

In summary, the BASICS Lean® Business Delivery System Lean (BLBDS) has been shown to have application within any organization, such as manufacturing companies, hospitals,

**Figure 1.16  Supervisor is co-located on the shop floor. Next improvement was to raise the desk to stand up height. (From BIG Archives.)**

government agencies, banks, nonprofits, insurance companies, home builders, and service industries such as lawn and garden companies as well as our education systems. Lean will continue to grow as more organizations realize the benefits gained through the BLBDS.

## Make the Employee's Job Safer: The Best Safety Test

The best safety test is to video or watch an operation on the shop floor or in the office and ask yourself the following question: would you let your child, or your spouse do that job, as it is right now?[33] If the answer is no, you need to stop the work immediately and fix the problem. It is amazing how many excuses there are for not making a job safe. Examples include the following:

- We have always done it that way.
- We only do that job two or three times a year.
- We must make the numbers.
- It won't take him long.
- It's not really "that" unsafe.
- We will fix it the next time we do it.
- We can have this done by the time we make it safe.
- Management won't spend the money.

We could list a million of them. The only way to fix a safety issue is to stop work immediately. The operator should refuse to do the job and we should support them. It is amazing when you stop work or stop the production line how fast people will figure out a solution or safe way to do the job. The real question is how we are going to fix it so it will always be safe in the future.

## Scanlon Principles

In the book, The Leadership Roadmap,[34] the authors outline how to roll out Lean in virtually any organization. The book, of course, starts off with the six immutable realities based on the Scanlon principles (see Table 1.2), which are as follows:

1. People
2. Competence
3. Identity
4. Participation
5. Lean enterprise and innovation
6. Equity

The authors spend 88 of the approximately 200 pages defining these, what we would call in MBA school, soft skills, or values. However, when we hand this book out to executives, they typically scan the book and dismiss it out of hand. They generally never finish the book, or they skip to the roadmap templates (hard tools). When I asked them what they thought of the book, I would get responses like "I already knew all that." This is a typical

**Table 1.2   Scanlon Principles**

| |
|---|
| *Identity:* This means that everyone understands his or her relationship to the organization. How do I fit into this team, this company, this industry, this economy? Am I doing the right job? Am I doing it right? The answers to these questions are essential because everyone needs to have relevant, useful knowledge about where they fit into the grand scheme of things. Without understanding where the organization is heading and what is expected of you, you cannot participate in a meaningful way. |
| *Participation:* Employees have the right to the appropriate opportunities to influence decisions and outcomes within their areas of competence. Participation is both an opportunity and a responsibility—the responsibility to be involved and to accept the consequences of the decisions we make. Participation at Donnelly is a search for truth, justice, and excellence—popular or not. Participation is not a game to make people feel good. It is a way to discover truth and better ways of doing things. |
| *Equity:* The principle of equity is probably the most frequently misunderstood. People often think it means equality—doing the exact same thing for everyone—but that's not the case. Equity at Donnelly means that among all the company's stakeholders, there is a fair return for their investment. Equity also means issues of fairness within the company are to be resolved with a spirit of fairness to all: "we" instead of "me." Equity is a question of balance and fairness. The responsibility for managing that balance is shared by all stakeholders. |
| *Competence:* Competence means that everyone in the organization needs to be qualified to do their job, and also needs to continuously increase their skills to meet the demands of tomorrow. No company can survive in a static state. Ever increasing competency includes not only job knowledge, but also the willingness to take the initiative in helping solve problems and improve performance, along with the ability to effectively interact with others. |

*Source:* Public domain also book called the Scanlon Principles.

CEO mentality. Ironically, the book was written by Dwane Baumgardner, former CEO of Donnelly Corporation, and Russ Scaffede, former senior vice president of Global Manufacturing, Donnelly Corporation, past GM/vice president of Toyota Motor Manufacturing Powertrain and consultant. Donnelly Corporation, during their tenure, was probably the closest to Toyota of any US manufacturers and was profiled in many Society for Manufacturing Excellence (SME) videos, and many of their team members are now Lean consultants working with other companies.

What most companies don't understand is that just implementing Lean tools and establishing one-piece flow, standard work, visual controls, etc., does not make a company Lean. What makes a company Lean is the culture that is based on the six immutable realities. Without a vision (the Toyota precepts) and values (the Scanlon principles), there is no real foundation on which to build a Lean culture. Therefore, we would estimate that less than 5% of companies in the United States even come close to approaching Toyota's production system or more accurately called the Toyota thinking system as it is a company-wide system.

We found an example of this at hospital in New Mexico (NM). We were working with the physician director of the emergency department (ED) and had minimal buy in. We discussed the standard work with him, got his input, and then sent the draft out for review. However, based on a nurse's suggestion, we included a facetious line as a joke to see if they really read the document. First, we sent it to the director and surprisingly received his ok during a meeting with us. The nurse and I looked at each other and smiled and I said I guess you all are going to have a good Christmas. The director gave us a puzzling stare but dismissed it. Then we sent it to the rest of the docs. We asked each doc if they read it and they all gave us a resounding yes. We knew none of them did. Look at the "Reassessment" Section and see if you can tell why?

## Reassessment

- Unit clerk will keep you updated on test results and "all back" completed charts.
- If you specified reassess in your plan of care, the acute care nurse will notify you accordingly when it is time to reassess the patient.
- Let the acute care nurse know if there are any new orders, etc., once you have reviewed the reassess chart or provide direction to wait for "all back" and hand the chart back to the acute care nurse or place it in the appropriate unit clerk exam room bin.
- All the docs agree to provide the nurses with a 10% Christmas bonus each year.
- If you need to see the patient to advise next steps and there is no new patient waiting, then proceed to reassess the patient.
- If there is a new patient waiting, please see the next new patient before seeing the reassess patient.

The true power of the TPS is not in the tools but in the philosophy and value systems. How do you create a culture where 80% of the ideas come from the shop floor personnel and are implemented every day? Where does the true power of the TPS lay? Many companies have slogans, such as, "people are our most important asset," but look how they treat their people. Do they lay people off? Do they develop them? It is important to look behind the slogan to the strategies and tactics in place to support their people. Many companies fall short when pressed for the details of how people and culture are being developed. It is not what you see on a tour of any Toyota factory that you should pay attention to; it is what is behind what you see that you need to pay attention to.

## Lean and Layoffs

Most workers at companies we visit fear that Lean is designed to eliminate their jobs. When we ask employees what they think of when they first hear the word Lean, we normally hear cutting costs and eliminating staff. This is certainly not the impression we would like our employees to have as we embark on a cultural revolution. We normally measure productivity as input in terms of direct labor (hours) divided by the number of units (labor hours/unit). In Lean, we like to measure productivity as output in units divided by the input in terms of total labor dollars paid (which includes overtime). Make no mistake, the goal of Lean is to increase productivity, efficiency, and effectiveness at the same time, which could translate into excess capacity if not back filled with additional sales quickly. This means getting the same or more output with less labor, while making it easier for the team member to do the job while at the same time making a product as good as or better than the specification that the consumer desires while continually improving the processes.

As processes are standardized, we can begin to semi-automate or totally automate processes, thus freeing up more labor. The reason Lean is sometimes associated with laying off people is because there are companies that will implement Lean for the specific purpose of laying people off. However, truly Lean companies may lay off temporary employees, but they do not lay off their permanent employees unless the business declines to a point where they have no choice. When starting the Lean journey, normal attrition rates and invoking hiring freezes on new staff or positions can normally mitigate this risk, especially if the company is proactive. Most companies do not go into Lean with the desire to lay off people and it has been our experience and insistence with companies we work with to communicate those layoffs are never related to process improvements.

Lean should never be the driving force behind layoffs. Laying off permanent employees is a sign of poor business management. Kiichiro Toyoda resigned as president in 1950 after he was forced to implement a layoff! He felt this reflected on his abilities and he was no longer worthy to remain as president.[35] How many company presidents today would resign when they have a layoff? In 1995, the year Mr. Okuda became President of Toyota, he stated, "If you're happy your company's share price firmed up thanks to laying people off, you're not qualified to manage a business. First, did the executives drive themselves till they puked to protect their employee's jobs? If your business isn't doing well, don't fire your employees, take responsibility and the axe."

Toyota has been tested repeatedly on their no layoff policy. In 1998, Moody's downgraded Toyota's rating due to the economic problems in Japan. Toyota argued that they transcended the boundaries of the country. Moody's came back and said, "Toyota is fixated on lifetime employment. Maintaining this system poses a risk to future operations of the company."[36] Most recently, during the recession of 2008–2011, no one could believe Toyota didn't lay off its employees in the United States. What companies fail to understand is this is part of the systems thinking behind Toyota's culture and success. They call it Anmokuchi, which means silent or tacit knowledge.[37] It was not until April 2012 that Toyota laid off 350 workers (10% of the workforce) at its Altona Plant in Melbourne, Australia,[38] due to factors including the strong Australian dollar, reduced cost competitiveness, and declining demand.[39] As Russ Scaffede stated in this chapter, Toyota does not guarantee lifetime employment, but layoffs are absolutely a last resort due to extreme business conditions.

Lesson Learned: To truly make Lean successful, there should be a written management commitment not to lay off permanent employees because of continuous improvement; otherwise, people will not work to eliminate their jobs. There was a time when laying people off was a sign of poor management. Now, it has become an acceptable practice spread by MBA teachings. Truly Lean companies do not strategize to lay off their full-time employees due to continuous improvement. Layoffs are normally the result of a significant drop in business conditions.

### Unions and Lean

We have found no real difference implementing Lean in union versus nonunion environments. Union environments can be a bit more challenging, but if you involve the union leadership from the start and make them part of the process, it works. To solicit ideas from their employees, companies are going to have to gain cooperation from the union.

Eiji Toyoda spent ten years working with the union to build trust and secured a joint labor management agreement in 1962 stating, "We, the company and the union, aware of our public nature in the automobile business, vow to work together to take effective and appropriate measures to overcome imminent liberalization, to cooperate towards the general development of Japanese industry and the national economy, and to contribute to the successful transition from Toyota Japan to World Toyota." Eiji's mantra was that a company must not deceive its employees."[40] It was these bonds of trust that allowed Taiichi Ohno to implement jidoka and JIT (starting with Kanban) to establish the TPS. It was during this period that Toyota moved from a seniority-based cost of living pay system to a skill-based pay system.

Back in 2000, at a plant in Buffalo, NY now known as Xylem, we worked on an implementation in a union plant that was very successful, including a new bonus program for the union employees as well as increased pay for enhanced training. In addition, we ended up bringing jobs back from Mexico to Buffalo, NY, one of the highest labor rates in the country.

Union leadership was part of the development and changes and therefore brought into the process. The union was initially skeptical, and there were areas of friction, such as videoing and removal of chairs. In general, most Lean lines work without the use of chairs, which can be a source of concern for the union, particularly as the workforce ages. There were no easy solutions for such issues; however, each such issue was addressed carefully before proceeding to ensure that the issues did not become roadblocks. Once union personnel saw that videoing was there to help them and make their jobs easier, there was no more objection. In many cases, we are asked by the union to introduce bumping and balance the work so that it is fair for all employees.

## Foundation for the Lean House: Total Company-Wide Quality Management

### Quality Circles (Jishuken)

Quality control (QC) existed in Japan before World War II, for instance, in NEC and Toshiba, where control charts were utilized but were kept company confidential[41] (see Table 1.3). The concepts of statistical QC were taught to the Japanese by the Americans starting in 1949 during the Civil Communications Section (CCS) seminars.[42] The American QC experts advocated a do things right the first-time philosophy.

I meet with Izumi Nonaka in 1996 to discuss her article on the History of Quality published in Quality Progress 1993. She told me that "Clearly the CCS Management Seminars, Deming's seminar, and lectures given by J.M. Juran were the basis for creating quality circles." She went on to state the first small group to look at quality was at the Naoetsu Factory, Shin-Etsu Chemical Company Ltd., in 1959 (in Japan). Another example was at Sumitomo Electric (Bunzaemon Inoue who which participated in the original CCS seminar and translated the CCS Manual) in 1960. The term quality circle was not used in Japan until 1962. A quality circle is where the supervisor meets voluntarily with his group of workers to undertake various activities with the aim of solving

**Table 1.3   Statistical QC (SQC) Teachings History**

| | *CCS Management Seminar* | *Deming's Lecture* | *Basic Course (First Time)* |
|---|---|---|---|
| Date | September 26 to November 18, 1949 (Tokyo), November 21, 1949 to January 20, 1950 (Osaka) | July 10–18, 1950 | September 16, 1949 to August 17, 1950 |
| Industry of attending audience and audience size | Vacuum tube, telephone, and radio manufacturers; about 20 people in both places (Tokyo and Osaka) | Various types of manufacturing companies; about 220 people | Chemical, iron, steel, and electric manufacturers; about 40 people |
| Lecturers | Homer M. Sarasohn, Charles W. Protzman | W. Edwards Deming | Japanese statisticians and people in JUSE who learned about statistical quality control |
| Contents | Company policy, organization, control, and coordination. In the chapter regarding control, SQC was taught. Lessons included the use of control charts and sampling inspection. | How to make control charts and how to perform sampling inspections | Translation of the books written by Walter Shewhart and others. Research the QC department engineer's work in foreign countries. |

*Sources: Dr. W.E. Deming's Lectures on Statistical Control of Quality* (Tokyo: JUSE 1950), p. i; "JUSE to Hinshitsu Kanri" *Engineers*, November 1965, pp. 14–15; *Management Seminar*, Daiyamong-sha, 1952, Hinshitsu Kanri Seminar 1BC Getupo, JUSE, 1949–1950; Kenneth Hopper and Izumi Nonaka (during visit to Japan in 1996), Quality Progress September 1993.

quality problems relating to the circle members' work. Efforts are made to link these activities closely with the company's overall company-wide quality control (CWQC) program.

In Professor Yoshio Kondo's book, Company Wide Quality Control, he explains how quality circles began to emerge in Japan. In 1956, there was a 13-week shortwave radio series titled "Dai-Issen Kantokusha No Tame No QC" subsequently taken over by the Japan Broadcasting Corporation (NHK) and shown on television until 1962. Another weekly series on QC was started in 1959, and the book QC Text for Foremen, edited by Ishikawa, sold more than 200,000 copies in the 8 years after it was published. In 1962, the Japanese Union of Scientists and Engineers (JUSE) launched the monthly journal Genba to QC as a sister publication to the monthly Hinshitsu Kanri (SQC). The goals of these shows and publications were to:

1. Inform supervisors and workers about statistical techniques
2. Encourage the formation of QC circles
3. Encourage workers to use their knowledge in their daily work, to achieve objectives, and to keep on improving their own abilities

It was realized that, without the unremitting day-to-day efforts of rank-and-file employees, it would be impossible to secure product quality. May of 1962 saw the first registration of quality circles with JUSE, and as of October 1994, there were almost three million registered QC circles.

The purpose behind quality circles was as follows:

1. To allow people to exercise their full capabilities and develop their unlimited potential
2. To practice respect for the individual and create cheerful, positive, purposeful workplaces
3. To contribute to the improvement and development of the enterprise

The quality circles developed over time into the following:

1. Division of QC circles into sub circles and minicircles
2. Formation of joint QC circles
3. Leading of QC circles by ordinary workers
4. Self-organization
5. Expansion of QC circle topics
6. Development of techniques
7. Introduction of QC off the production floor
8. Extension to suppliers and affiliates

The most notable benefit from QC circles is the empowerment that the front line has in ensuring the quality of the product they deliver. This has benefited the hospitality industry as well as the production floor. It has also given the responsibility of quality to the ones with direct control instead of pushing it back to the manager or engineers. Quality circles were reexported back to the United States in the 1970s and 1980s with the total quality movement; however, they have met a lot of resistance in the US workplace. One of the failure modes in the United States was that the leadership of quality circle teams was delegated to human resource (HR) instead of the supervisor of the group. When layoffs were looming, these quality circle HR personnel became easy targets for the first layer of reductions.

Lesson Learned: While it is certainly effective to use QC circle consultants and facilitators, problems arise when they become the ongoing leaders of the quality circle. Ongoing leadership of the quality circle must be left up to the supervisor of the area or it makes it vulnerable to cancellation.

## Total Company-Wide Quality Control

There is a big difference between how quality was perceived in Japan versus the United States. There was a time, from 1950 to 1970, when Japan was mostly known for very-poor-quality toys, for poor-quality transistor radios, and for the perception that the Japanese were copying everything. However, it was during this time, primarily due to the teachings of the CCS in 1948–1950, where American business and QC techniques were reintroduced to Japan on a large scale after the war. The CCS was led by Frank Polkinghorn, Charles W. Protzman Sr., and Homer Sarasohn, and later in 1950, Dr. Deming and Dr. Juran at the recommendation of Protzman and Sarasohn continued to teach SPC as the CCS courses were being taught by the Japanese in parallel. However, it was stated by those who had attended the CCS classes, "We didn't really learn anything new from Deming the CCS hadn't already taught us."[43]

The CCS taught the Japanese employee participation and quality circles (jishuken[44] self-study or autonomous study groups), both techniques long utilized in the United States by companies like Western Electric, IBM, and P&G. The Japanese rolled out total quality company-wide and called it total CWQC.

What's in a name? Apparently, a lot. The United States rolled out total quality management or TQM in the 1980s and 1990s and it turned into mainly a shop floor program that is virtually nonexistent today. Some of the tools have been repackaged as Six Sigma; however, the quality circles have all but disappeared in the United States and Europe. Maybe the resurgence of huddles now could be considered a precursor to the reestablishment of quality circles.

## Problem-Solving: The 5 Whys

Engaging in a total quality initiative means everyone should understand how to problem solve. You can't really solve a problem without knowing the problem. One of the basic techniques leveraged when problem-solving is the 5 Whys. This familiar tool (see Figure 1.17[45]) involves asking why up to five times to help get to the root cause of a problem. The hardest part of the 5 Whys

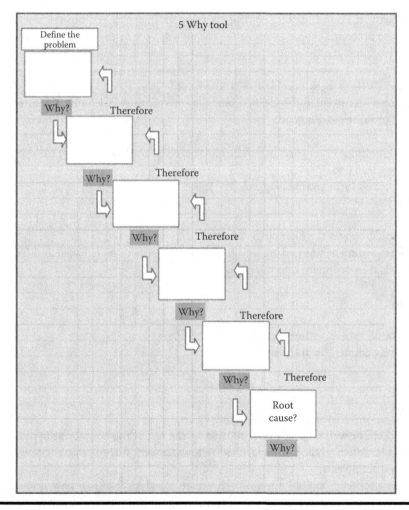

**Figure 1.17   5 Whys. (Courtesy of Ken Skiles.)**

is getting people to use it. Here is a true 5 Why story about a pool that kept growing algae. The problem didn't show up until 3 years after the pool was installed and it took a year and a half to figure out the root cause.

Asking the First Why:

- Question: Why is the pool water green?
- Answer: Not enough chemicals added.

Countermeasure: Add more chemicals—turned out to be a dead end because silt is collecting on the bottom. It provides a great base for algae to grow.

Next Why:

- Question: Why is silt collecting on the bottom?
- Therefore: Because there is a problem with the filter. Countermeasure: Replace filters in pool filter system—turned out to be a dead end.

Countermeasure: Found missing O-ring allowing sediment to get into the pool. Helped but did not solve the problem.

Third Why:

- Question: Why is there a problem with the filter?
- Therefore: Filter needs to be cleaned out. Countermeasure: Cleaning the filter every week still had problems—dead end.

Additional findings: Filter parts had to be replaced. Replaced O-rings and redid piping outside the pool filter—dead end.

And the filter was still getting clogged.

Fourth Why:

- Question: Why was the filter clogged?
- Therefore: Sediment was getting into it and caused parts to be replaced and frequent cleaning that had let sediment into the pool.

Fifth Why:

- Question: Why was sediment getting into the filter?
- Therefore: Sediment is in the water.

Final Why:

- Final question: Why was sediment in the water?
- Root cause: The well filtration system (used by the rest of the house) was bypassed when the pool was installed, so the sediment-filled well water went directly into the pool and clogged the filter after 3 years.
- Corrective action: The pool water output was re-piped for it to first pass through the house filtration system. This was the root cause, and the problem was finally solved although it was very difficult to remove all the sediment from the pool after 5 years.

Author's Note: When I found the root cause for my swimming pool, which was the lack of filtering out the sediment from the pool, I knew I had finally found the permanent corrective action. However, one must be careful as this can lull one into a sense of complacency. The problem could still return if the mesh filter developed a hole and started letting the sediment back into the pool. A way to improve upon the "permanent" fix would be to install a sensor which would shut off the water in the event it detected sediment coming into the pool. But again, the sensor could still go bad.

So, while we are always going after a permanent countermeasure or corrective action, we must always realize that it will still require a check because in fact no corrective action is necessarily permanent.

Lesson Learned: If the questions of why did not continue, the root cause would have never been determined leading to wasted costly efforts without resolution.

## What We Know versus What We Don't Know

Many times, we hear the saying "the operators are the experts." And for the most part, this is true, but not always. See Figure 1.18 that divides knowledge into four quadrants:

1. You know, you know: The meaning behind this one is obvious.
2. You know, you don't know: The meaning behind this one is obvious.
3. You don't know, you know: Many times, we finally realize we knew something, which at first, we did not think we knew. For instance, many times we do Lean things without realizing it, or sometimes just thinking about a problem, we can logically sort it out.
4. You don't know, you don't know: This is the most dangerous quadrant. Many times, we think we know things, which we really don't know. We call this knowing enough to be dangerous. The other interpretation is we don't know what we don't know. It behooves us to find an expert or continue to dig and research a problem, so we get to a point of knowing what there is to know.

Lesson Learned: Those with some Lean knowledge can sometimes be more destructive than those with none. One of the big obstacles with Lean is discovering—or helping others to discover—what they do not know they did not know. "It ain't what you don't know that gets you into trouble. It's what you know for sure that just ain't so."—Mark Twain.

1. Know you know
2. Know you don't know
3. Don't know you know
4. Don't know you don't know

**Figure 1.18   Things you know vs. don't know. Knowledge quadrant. (From BIG Training materials.)**

### Know How versus Know Why

How often have you had a problem, for example, with a computer, then tried several things all at once to fix it, and suddenly, it works? Alternatively, we have a problem with testing equipment on the shop floor, we tap it (or hit it with a hammer), and it works. Sometimes we know how to fix things, but we do not know why. Eventually, the tapping does not work anymore. We must learn the know why in addition to the know how to truly fix the root causes of problems.

Lesson Learned: People usually react to the symptoms of the problem without seeking the facts. The problems are often hidden, and sometimes, we think we are experts only to find out we don't know what we don't know. For example, many times, we only know how to do what we need to do on the machine but do not know why we do it that way and we do not understand the complete machine capabilities. As we reduce the waste, the time it takes to get the product through the process shrinks. If products get through the process faster, it means the velocity and capacity have increased. We look at capacity as equal to work plus waste. We must learn to manage by fact, not by anecdote.

### Poka Yoke

How do you know when you have identified the root cause? The answer is poka yoke—when you have fixed the problems, so it never comes back.[46]

### 5W2Hs[47]: Another Tool to Get Rid of Waste

The 5 Ws are composed of asking (when? where? what? who? and why?). The 2 Hs are (how? and how much?)[48] (see Figure 1.19). The following questions apply:

- When is the best time to do it? Does it have to be done at a certain time?
- Where is it being done? Does it have to be done here?
- What is being done? Can we eliminate this work?

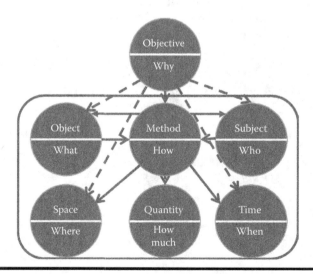

**Figure 1.19  5W2H. (Modified from The Shingo Production Management System p. 36.)**

- Who is doing it? Would it be better to have someone else, do it? Why are we doing it?
- Why is the work necessary? Clarify its purpose.
- How is it being done? Is this the best way to do it? Are there any other ways to do it?
- How much does it cost now?
- How much will it cost to improve?

The goal of asking the 5 Ws and 2 Hs is to get to the root cause and lay the groundwork for creative problem-solving. We can combine this tool and the 5 Ws tool to ask why for each of the 5 Ws and 2 Hs. For example, why is it done when it is done? And why is it done where it is done? The power of continuous improvement of any process, manufacturing or administrative, is directly correlated to the application of these steps in concurrence with the 5 Ws and 2 Hs. Creative thinking is the true foundation of problem-solving and innovation, yet many of us are never trained how to think in this way nor do we take the time necessary to stimulate our thinking processes.

Joel Barker talks about how dangerous paradigm paralysis can be in his video Business of Paradigms.[49] This is where your idea becomes the only idea, and you refuse to see the opportunities for problem-solving. Innovation is the flip side of this. Lean ties directly to the idea of paradigms that are part of an overall problem-solving system. Lean is, in and of itself, a paradigm for creating a new continuous learning culture based on problem-solving utilizing creative thinking. Every company should standardize on a problem-solving model and teach it to every employee. This provides employees with a common model, approach, and terminology when team members work by themselves or get together to work in groups to fix problems. It is like standard work for problem-solving.

Many companies have standardized on the Six Sigma define, measure, analyze, improve, control (DMAIC) model, Shewhart's plan–do–study–act (PDSA), or the PDCA CCS model (see Figure 1.20). The automotive companies standardized on the eight discipline (8D) problem-solving

As engineers and management people, we are convinced that the logical approach to determining what changes are needed and the benefits to be derived from them stems from the use of the Scientific Method. It merely involves careful, common sense, analytical thinking. Simply stated, the scientific method approach consists of five steps. They are:

1. Define the problem precisely.

2. Get the facts — all the facts.

3. Analyze those facts to decide upon a proper plan of action.

4. Put that plan of action into effect with the expected results identified.

5. Monitor the plan in process; make necessary timely adjustments.

The problem that we are dealing with in this course is quite easy to define. Manufacturing productivity and reliability is at an economically unacceptable low level. That calls into question the effectiveness of management organizations. We want to turn the situation around. In order to

**Figure 1.20 PDCA. (CCS Manual, ©1949, p. 23.)**

The Global 8 Disciplines Are:
1. Form The Team
2. Describe The Problem
3. Contain The Problem,
4. I.D. The Root Cause
5. Formulate And Verify Corrective Actions
6. Correct The Problem And Confirm The Effects
7. Prevent The Problem
8. Congratulate The Team.

**Figure 1.21   8D problem solving model. (Rambaud, PHRED solutions, 2007.)**

model (see Figure 1.21[50]), AlliedSignal (now Honeywell) had a nine-step problem-solving model (see Figure 1.22). Toyota has an eight-step problem-solving model that links to 8D as well as to PDCA (see Figure 1.23).

## PCDSA: Dr. Shingo's Model[51]

When researching the origins of this model, we discovered that act did not seem to be part of the original model or Dr. Shingo considered the act implied as part of check. The model Shingo

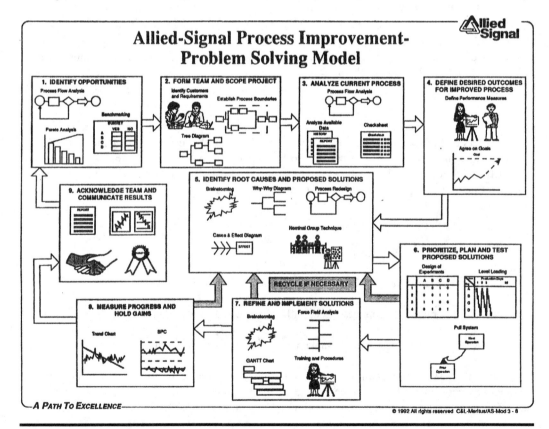

**Figure 1.22   AlliedSignal nine-step problem solving model taught to the entire company.**

(The 8 steps of Toyota business practice [TBP] written in Japanese are below, with translations. There are some slight but interesting differences in nuance, and these always make me wonder how much loss results from translation of Toyota principles, precepts, and philosophies. Step 1, *set a target* seems a bit loose while Japanese contains the word *achieve* that plants the idea that targets are things that must be met. Step 4 is not *analyze* but *think through* or *think until you find* and step 8 in Japanese doesn't talk about *standardize* (this being an implied part of the Toyota ways of working [WOW]) but instead stresses that the results muse to become *established* or *take hold*.

トヨタの仕事の仕方8ステップ(the 8 steps of the Toyota way of working)
  1. 問題を明確にする (clarify the problem)
  2. 問題をブレイクダウンする (breakdown the problem)
  3. 達成目標を決める (set the target to be achieved)
  4. 真因を考え抜く (think through to the true cause)
  5. 対策を立てる (develop countermeasures)
  6. 対策をやりぬく (follow through on the countermeasures)
  7. 結果とプロセスを評価する (evaluate the result and the process)
  8. 成果を定着させる(make sure the results take hold)

As a standard problem-solving process, it is excellent and widely applicable. Inevitably, *PDCA* alone was too vague. The Socratic teaching method and talk of "it takes 40 years to learn" at Toyota has given way to a more deliberate method of teaching this thinking process at Toyota, based on what I have seen. We could say the TBP is the result of clarify, break down, and so forth, applied to the teaching of PDCA. Sometimes I think the genius of the Toyota approach is that this process is so simple, obvious, and offensive to the intelligence and self-worth of most senior executives and go-getters out there that they close the book and say, "That can't be right. There must be more to it." Most people won't understand TBP or try it. You can't really understand it until you try it. So it comes back to a question of packaging and motivation.—From Jon Miller)

**Figure 1.23  Toyota eight-step problem solving model.**

started with was plan–do–check which was a spin-off of Shewhart's plan–do–study. However, Dr. Shingo added control after the plan. We will refer to this model as PCDCA:

1. Plan
2. Control
3. Do
4. Check
5. Act

Dr. Shingo stated:

I believe that acknowledging the existence of the control function and optimizing its effectiveness is the key to achieving a zero-quality control (ZQC) system, one that produces zero defects ....

Especially in the U.S., the setting of standards for contract systems has led to the replacement of time study with time setting. It seems American Management has lost sight of the original goal of doing away with waste. Too many improvements are aimed at superficial phenomena in pursuit of short-term goals .... Moreover, we constantly overlook opportunities for fundamental improvements and current accounting techniques will not expose them. We see this where excessive concentration on the idea of economic lot sizes obscure major reductions in setup times.

Plan-Do-Check demonstrates, the control function of management is missing in Western management philosophies. The management function must encompass plan, control, do, check. The Do function lies beyond the control function, and it is precisely in this process of control and do where many production problems arise.

Based on our experience, the lack of awareness of the control function is a major defect in production management worldwide. We see this same mentality at many companies today because they lose the control function in PDCA. Dr. Shingo continued to say:

> My view differs in two respects, namely (1) the implementation function is an independent function lying beyond management and (2) implementation and management control functions are inseparably linked by the two functions as being intimately related (See Figure 1.24).

In actual practice, managers are primarily responsible for performing management functions and workers are responsible for performing the implementation functions. Implementation functions are continuously affected by the control function. At times, it is also possible for workers themselves, who are responsible for implementation to perform the control function. At any rate, since the control function is always part of management functions, the control function should not be considered as separate from the implementation function.

To pursue this line of thought, control and implementation functions can maintain quality, i.e., guarantees it, but they cannot improve quality. If quality improvement is desired, it is necessary to rotate the management (Deming) circle and to take this into account during the planning stage. Following this line of thought clarifies the purpose of establishing poka yoke measures during the control and implementation stages. The use of statistics is very effective at this stage. However, in advanced industrial nations doesn't the problem of production defects have more to do with quality assurance during the control and implementation stages rather than the planning stage? In this regard, the statement that, "quality is determined during processing," is true. Dr. Shingo believed that traditional production management had overlooked the importance of the control function and careful reconsideration was needed. See Table 1.1.

We asked Russ Scaffede[52] for his opinion of plan–control–do–check and he responded:

> I feel the first issue of Control has several different potential meanings. I fully agree with the analysis of management responsibility to control (or better yet guide implementation allowing the team to control). That is one application. However, I would be more inclined to think of the word control in Dr. Shingo's context or Ohno would be in control meaning stabilize. In that context all my working with Cho and Sato, we

**Figure 1.24   Shingo's plan control do check.**

always discussed before you could even identify waste and eliminate it. You must first stabilize the process. Using the term that way I would say control would be the first element and the cycle would be Control, Plan, Do, Check and Act. Leading to ensuring control first (stabilization) and improving again.

Note: This description by Mr. Scaffede ties in very nicely with the BASICS® model. The idea behind the BASICS® model was to provide a context to utilize the tools to stabilize the process prior to implementing the ongoing PDCA cycles of improvement. We think it is important, however, to consider the alternate use of the control function, which would be during the planning (suggest solutions in the BASICS® model) phase, to determine how one is going to statistically control the output of the process (this would be the Six Sigma/zero defects linkage). Throughout the balance of this text, we will refer to the model as PDCA so as not to confuse people while keeping this discussion in mind.

## Chapter Questions

1. What are three characteristics that display respect for humanity?
2. What benefits are derived from embracing and implementing jidoka in a typical manufacturing factory producing automobiles?
3. Why is jidoka difficult to implement?
4. What are the two networks of operations described by Dr. Shingo?
5. Discuss similarities and differences between Herzberg and Maslow motivational theories.
6. What is the 5 Ws tool? When should we use it?
7. What are the 5 Ws and 2 Hs?
8. What are the two pillars of the Lean (Toyota) house?
9. Explain JIT.
10. Explain jidoka. Give an example.
11. What is the difference between total quality and total company-wide quality?
12. Explain the difference between PDCA and PCDCA?
13. What is the importance of a standard problem-solving model?
14. What is a quality circle?
15. What is poka yoke? Give an example.
16. What did you learn from this chapter?

## *Exercise*

Design a CI house for your company.

## Notes

1. Used with permission from Joel Barker.
2. Principles of Efficiency, Emerson, ©11924, New York, The Engineering Magazine Company, page 58.
3. Taiichi Ohno, Toyota Production System: Beyond Large Scale Production (New York: Productivity Press), 1978.
4. Taiichi Ohno, Toyota Production System (New York: Productivity Press), 1988.
5. Furnished by Kenneth Hopper and reprinted with permission, e-mail personal correspondence.

6. "Hedley and I: Information for Hedley Employees," undated. p. 34. "THE COMPANY FIRMLY BELIEVES ... "Our employees should have security of employment and protection in time of need." This guarantee could be given because of the steady demand for P&G's products just as Japan's companies could offer lifetime employment after the 1960s because its electronics industry was unique in producing goods of such consistently outstanding quality.

7. The Toyota Leaders, Sato, Vertical Inc., ©2008, pp. 70–71.

8. TPS_History YouTube video public domain.

9. This example was first taught by Mark Jamrog, SMC group, as part of the AlliedSignal Lean Training Material.

10. By knowing your home phone, it is making sure it is not activating the wrong card. No human interaction is necessary to activate the card short of calling the activation number. So, it mistake proofs the process over someone manually calling and then the operator having to ask you five to ten security questions.

11. Samuel Obara and Darril Wilburn, Influenced by Toyota by Toyota (CRC Press), New York NY, 2012, pp. 51–53.

12. This example was first taught by Mark Jamrog, SMC group, as part of the AlliedSignal Lean Training Material.

13. Deming, The System of Profound Knowledge® (Cambridge, MA: MIT Press), 2018.

14. Shingo, Non Stock Production (Oregon: Productivity Press), 2006.

15. Google Internet search, February 14, 2012.

16. Google Internet search and many of these were not true jidoka-related items, February 14, 2012.

17. YouTube Internet search, February 14, 2012.

18. Source: TPS—Monden, 3rd edition, Inst of Industrial Engineers, 1998.

19. Band-Aid is a registered trademark of Johnson & Johnson.

20. http://www.ledizolv.com/LearnAbout/LeadHazards/benfranklin.asp, The Famous Benjamin Franklin Letter on Lead Poisoning Phila, July 31, 1786 (to Benjamin Vaughan), http://www.fi.edu/learn/brain/metals.html#historyslead, http://www.wnd.com/?pageId=41959

21. http://www.huffingtonpost.com/2011/06/15/china-lead-poisoning-epidemic-coverup_n_877351.html, http://www.lead.org.au/fs/fst29.html

22. http://www.huffingtonpost.com/2011/06/15/china-lead-poisoning-epidemic-coverup_n_877, Discovery Health "Lead Poisoning in China", http://health.howstuffworks.com/wellness/preventive-care/china-lead-poisoning.htm

23. Leveraging Lean in Healthcare, Protzman, Mayzell and Kerpchar, Productivity Press, ©2011.

24. Donald Dinero, Training within Industry (New York: Productivity Press), 2005.

25. Jerrold Solomon, Accounting for World Class Operation (Fort Wayne, IN: WCM Associates), 2007, Who's Counting (Fort Wayne, IN: WCM Associates), 2003. Both books won the Shingo Prize.

26. Lean Leadership BASICS®, Meyers, Protzman, Protzman, Keen, Owens and Barbon, Productivity Press, ©2022.

27. Gary Convis Speech to WCMC annual meeting 2008.

28. Mike Walsh, at the time CEO of Northern Pacific railroad, Speed Is Life, Tom Peters, a co-production of Video Publishing House and KERA, ©1991.

29. https://www.flickr.com/photos/kheelcenter/5279836252

30. Charles D. Wrege and Frederick W. Taylor (Irwin Publishing), ©1991; Copley, Frederick W. Taylor (Harper and Brothers), ©1923; Kanigel, The One Best Way (Penguin Books), ©1999.

31. Applied Motion Study: A Collection of Papers on the Efficient Method to Industrial Preparedness, Frank and Lillian Gilbreth, Sturgis and Walton Co, ©September 1917, p. 22, Public domain.

32. Charles D. Wrege and Frederick W. Taylor (Irwin Publishing), ©1991; Copley, Frederick W. Taylor (Harper & Brothers), ©1923; Kanigel, The One Best Way (Penguin Books), ©1999.

33. This saying came from Davide Barbon, ITT Industries.

34. Dwane Baumgardner and Russ Scaffede, The Leadership Roadmap (MA: North River Press), 2008.

35. The Toyota Leaders, Sato, Vertical Inc., ©2008.

36. The Toyota Leaders, Sato, Vertical Inc., ©2008, pp. 197–199.

37. The Toyota Leaders, Sato, Vertical Inc., ©2008, p. 198.

38. In e-mail correspondence with James Bond, May 4, 2013. Toyota's history regarding layoffs is quite an accomplishment for any organization! The most innovative organizations including Toyota invest

the time up front during the recruitment process not only to ensure a good fit based on dimensions for the organization but also for the applicant through open two-way communication. This is accomplished through a multiphase/step approach. The successful candidates in these organizations have values very similarly aligned to the vision of the organization. Innovative organizations select and develop people before products. Where are these types of organizations now? They are industry/sector leaders and recognized for their innovative employees and competitive advantage. The layoffs in Australia I believe were due to reduction in economic demand. The Australian plant is small, producing 149,000 units in 2007 declining to 95,000 in 2012 (a 36% reduction). Employment declined to 4,250 from 4,600 in 2012. Compare with Toyota plants in Canada with 7800 team members producing more than 500,000 units per year. You are correct though. I believe some of those laid off were permanent team members.

39. http://www.theaustralian.com.au/news/nation/toyota-to-march-workers-off-altona-plant-as-job-cuts-take-effect/story-e6frg6nf-1226327486781
40. The Toyota Leaders, Sato, Vertical Inc., ©2008, p. 194.
41. The History of the Quality Circle, Izumi Nonaka, Quality Progress, 1993.
42. CCS Training Manual, Charles Protzman Sr., Homer Sarasohn, 1949–1950. An e-book transcription of the version presented at the 1949 Tokyo seminar has been prepared by Nick Fisher and Suzanne Lavery of ValueMetrics, Australia, and is widely available on the Internet. The documents that formed a final English version that was translated by Bunzaemon Inoue and others and published in 1952 in Japanese by Diamond Press are in the Hopper, Hackettstown, New Jersey, Civil Communications Section archive.
43. Personal phone correspondence from Kenneth Hopper.
44. What is jishuken? by Jon Miller postdate August 27, 2006, 9:03 AM. Comments: 3, I was told that the origin of jishuken comes from "Kanban houshiki bukachou jishu kenkyuukai" or かば 方式部課 自主研究会 in the original Japanese. This translates as "Kanban system department and section manager autonomous study groups." This was shortened to jishuken, which is self-study. Jishuken is often called autonomous study groups in English, http://www.gembapantarei.com/2006/08/what_is_jishuken.html.
45. Figure supplied by Ken Skiles, ITT site leader.
46. 1991.Shigeo Shingo and Poka Yoke, Zero Quality Control (New York: Productivity Press); 1986, Yuzo Yasuda, 40 Years, 20 Million Ideas (New York: Productivity Press).
47. Shigeo Shingo, Kaizen, and the Art of Creative Thinking (Hakuto-Shobo), 1959; English translation (Enna Products Corp. and PCS Inc.), 2007.
48. This method is described in detail in Dr. Shingo's book, Kaizen, and the Art of Creative Thinking.
49. Video by Joel Barker, The New Business of Paradigms, ©2001. Joel Barker—Original Business of Paradigms, 1989, Charthouse International Learning, Distributed by Star Thrower.
50. Rambaud, 8D Problem Solving, PHRED Solutions, 2007. With permission.
51. Non-Stock Production, Shingo, Productivity Press, ©1988, pp. 23–28, 226–230.
52. Russ Scaffede, owner, Lean Manufacturing Systems Group, LLC, and Management Consulting Consultant, and vice president of manufacturing at Toyota Boshoku America. Past GM/vice president of Toyota Motor Manufacturing Power Train, past senior vice president of Global Manufacturing at Donnelly Corporation, and coauthor with Dwane Baumgardner.

# Additional Readings

Bodek, N. 2004. Kaikaku. Vancouver, WA: PCS Press.
Collins, J.C. 1997. Built to Last. New York: Harper Business Press.
Dennis, P. 2005. Andy and Me. New York: Productivity Press.
McGuire, K. 1984. Impressions from Our Most Worthy Competitor. Falls Church, VA: APICS.
Miller, W.B. 1997. All I Need to Know about Manufacturing I Learned in Joe's Garage. Fort Collins, CO: Bayrock.
Smalley, A. 2004. Creating Level Pull. Cambridge, MA: Lean Enterprise Institute.
Stalk, G. and Hout, T.M. 1990. Competing against Time. New York: Macmillan.

# Chapter 2

## Heijunka, Planning and Scheduling, Sequencing Activities, Load Balancing

A bad system will beat a good person every time.[1]

W. Edwards Deming

## Procter and Gamble (P&G): Level Loading[2]

A very visible feature of production control (PC) at P&G when Kenneth Hopper joined the company in 1948 was the department managers gathering outside the plant manager's second-floor office on a Friday around midday, waiting to learn how much of their products each of the packing departments would require each day of the following week. A department providing a product to be packed had the freedom, limited only by the nature of its equipment, as to how and exactly when to produce it, but as to delivery, they had no choice. Products to be packed each day had to arrive evenly over the day. What practitioners of just-in-time (JIT) now call "production leveling" or "smoothing" was provided by "the Buggy field," a fleet of large containers each on four wheels with a bottom slide valve …. Fast forward 30 years …. When Japan's postwar JIT specialists arrived in Western factories, their comment was that they were not factories but large dark warehouses full of out-of-date items.

### Takt–Flow–Pull

In Lean circles, there is a saying that is takt–flow–pull. This is short for implementing a Lean system. The idea is to first understand the customer demand and that everything starts with the customer. Once we know the customer demand and our available time, we can calculate our takt time. Next, we work to establish flow within the factory (or service company) from raw materials to finished goods/shipping in accordance with the beat of the takt time. Finally, we create a pull

DOI: 10.4324/9781003185819-2

system where we have a synchronized linkage to our customer and supply chain. As they use our parts, they let us know in real time, which then triggers an order at our workshop. The orders at the workshop then trigger orders throughout our supply chain. This system embodies JIT and jidoka and the respect for humanity-based Lean culture.

## Establishing Takt

To establish our takt time, we need to know our true customer demand and available time. We have gone over these calculations earlier in this book series. We then need to understand our total labor time, throughput time, and plant capacity. We can determine the capacity with the tools we have discussed earlier, that is, the analysis tools, part production capacity sheet, group tech matrix, and plan for every part.

## What We Find: The Evils Created by "Demonstrated Capacity"

As we said earlier, the first step is to establish takt time. However, most companies we see have very little or sometimes even no linkage between the customer order required date and what goes on in their master production schedule (MPS), shop scheduling, and capacity planning systems. Many don't even have MPS! Most departments we see today tend to be scheduled and staffed based on what we call: "Demonstrated Capacity" or "Demonstrated Capability." An example of this is staffing the line, or office, based on what one sees every day on the surface, thus not managing based on facts or data. Don't forget

*Present Capacity = Realized Output + Waste*

Another example is when the line or area experiences unanticipated surges or wide variability in demand. Sometimes the need for the additional staff is only for 3 or 4 hours, but they are scheduled for a full 8-hour shift. Since they are utilized only for the peak demand, they are only trained for one task. Once the demand is met, they may sit around or find busy work to fill the remainder of their shift. You can be sure that if the supervisor is walking around, they will "look busy."

Sudden increased customer demand cycles, not managed properly, result in supervisors going to management and saying they need more staff. There is rarely any data presented with the request and it is not always demanded by the manager unless they are in tough times. If the manager goes out to the area, they will find the staff complaining about a variety of things, such as being too busy or having too much work, co-workers out on sick leave, and even complaining of safety issues. Many times, these complaints are directly tied to the surges in demand or date back to years ago when something extraordinary happened, but more senior employees always refer to it as happening in the present. Most of these things are the result of inherent wastes, which have built up in the process over many years. People are not trained properly, jobs change, people change, and with no standard work in place, over time the recipe for how the job was done gets lost. Sometimes the tools are lost or were thrown out as part of a 5S project. Over time, it becomes difficult to see the situation clearly because the "boiled frog" syndrome takes over, and we forget the way it used to be done and the output we used to get.

Managers go to their boss year after year and ask for more people and space to do the job because it is obvious by looking at the area that more people and space are needed. Over time, equipment is purchased and just stuck wherever it will fit. Engineers are too busy to support the area or the line, or companies have laid off all their manufacturing engineers due to budget cuts. The supervisors must put a case together each year to fight for more people or more space as the waste increases, while they try to convince management to "fix the problem." Over time, there is this migration from the old way of doing the work that "actually used to work fine with less people" to this new way of work now demonstrated on the floor with an ever seemingly increasing need for more people.

Declining productivity + Increased waste = Perceived need to increase people

Over time, the experienced staff members get fed up and leave, and the remaining people forget how the work used to be accomplished. Often, we find that the addition of more people has created more waste. We find managers and staff that understand what they think they need versus what they truly need based on the real customer demand. This results from a variety of reasons: from personnel requests for a particular shift to the manager not tracking or monitoring demand in their line. Shifts in customer demand may occur without a corresponding adjustment to scheduled times for staff. Often managers adhere to traditional set "shift times" without analyzing whether they should be staggering personnel schedules to meet demand cycles. These all can contribute to staff being mismatched to demand and result in excess overtime costs.

If there is no standard work or standardized training program, all these problems are even more exacerbated. Because everyone is trained by someone different and, eventually, the same tasks and the same jobs are done in different ways by each person or shift, it leads to quality and safety concerns. Making decisions regarding space or labor based on "demonstrated capacity" is dangerous and can be extremely costly.

## Lean Should Be Able to Beat Any Existing Standards

We interviewed many employees during a company Lean assessment.

First, we went to a company and interviewed all the supervisors. Each one told us how they were measured to these very tight standards. I then asked each one how the standard was calculated. No one could tell us exactly. We then asked what their results were for the last month. They pulled out a report and showed us their standard versus actual and the variance. They all complained that the standard was wrong, could never possibly be met, and how they must spend a lot of time preparing to explain their variance each month, but the bottom line is that they fight with accounting each month over the standard.

We then met with the "standards" guy who thought he was going to be in for a big fight and then we reviewed the calculations with him. When we agreed his calculations were correct and there was no reason, we shouldn't be able to meet them, he became somewhat animated. We were the first to ever agree his standards were correct. Every month he had fought with production over the argument that his standards were wrong and could not be met, and now he was finally vindicated.

Interestingly, over time, to pacify operations management, the standards guy had been forced to revise the standard downward, believe it or not, to 30% of the original. This means that if the original standard to put together a subassembly was 1 hour, they were setting the production schedule at 200 minutes, approximately 2 per day. So, the company was now scheduling 70% waste into their schedule and increased their quoted lead times by 70% to their customers. When you extrapolate this to the overall business, the effect was huge as this company had five plants. If you think about it, 70% of their plants existed due to this reduction in standards based on demonstrated performance each day.

"Demonstrated capacity" is when companies or departments use their actual daily or weekly demonstrated output totals as a measure of what they can produce versus scientific methods like time and motion study, which would tell them what they should really be producing. Ninety percent of companies we work with initially have metrics based on "demonstrated capacity," including government and health care. A sure sign of this phenomenon is when you ask the supervisor how he knows what can be produced each day and they tell you, "I know from experience." As a footnote to this story, the supervisors were correct when they stated they could not meet the standard. Their work process was so "hosed up" that there was no way they could have come close to the standard at which they should have been producing. When we set up their Lean line, we met the original standard the first week and surpassed it in the weeks to follow. While this company was still doing well from a financial standpoint, can you even begin to imagine how much more money and market share they could have obtained over the years if they were working to the standards guy's original standard!

Lesson Learned: In the past, companies worked to standards set by true time and motion industrial engineers. Today, we work based on totally unscientifically derived standards and on observation. It is shocking to find that many industrial engineering students today who have graduated from top tier business schools have no idea who Frederick Taylor or Frank Gilbreth are, not to mention Dr. Shigeo Shingo, Taiichi Ohno, Charles Sorenson, Ralph Barnes, etc.

## Build to Order versus Push Production versus Pull Systems

These terms get confusing, and we have had more than one good discussion involving them. Let's assume that we are building directly to a customer schedule. This is called a build-to-order system. Build to order is a true "pull" system from the customer. However, what it looks like in our company depends on how we use the customer's order to schedule the factory.

Most companies use some type of enterprise resource planning system. Within that system is a master schedule and a material requirements planning (MRP) or some type of shop floor control system. These systems gather up requirements, order materials, and release scheduled orders based on lead time offsets. Lead time offsets are the lead times plugged into the system for the supplier, receipt, inspection, manufacture, etc. This creates what we call a "push"-type system. In this system, MRP (based on the planner's review and approval) is the "trigger" for the order. The work orders are released and then scheduled in the various work centers in the shop. If the company triggers each order based on the shipment of a previous order where the shipment creates the trigger, this is considered a pull system. If the pull is from finished goods, then it is not a true "build-to-order" system, but it is still considered a "pull" system.

> At Company X, during a State of Maryland Lean Certification review/audit, they claimed that they had a pull system from finished goods to final assembly. However, they scheduled the subassembly operations with MRP based on customer orders. There was no Kanban linkage or triggers to the subassembly area from the final assembly. We got into quite a discussion where the operations director insisted, they had a pull system because it was "build to order." Our point of view was that he had a pull system to final assembly, but it was a "push" system from the customer order to their subassembly area. His point of view was that since it was built to order, it was entirely a "pull" system regardless of how he scheduled the sub-assemblies. However, we argued the fact that if one has finished goods means it is not a true "build-to-order" company.

## Scheduling Issues with Lean

Many companies now have electronic data interchange (EDI) systems where they are inextricably linked to their customer systems. However, many times they are two different systems, requiring the supplier to take their customer's EDI information and manually enter it into their planning system. The goal is to understand your true capacity and then start scheduling to your true customer demand. This sounds easy but can be very difficult to do.

## Pulling in the Schedule

Many times, our need to meet the end-of-the-month goals forces us to pull in shipments from weeks or sometimes months outside our current planning horizon. This creates a lot of chaos in the factory. Once we pull in an order, purchasing and the factory must go into major expediting modes since the material wasn't planned to come in yet. All the suppliers must be rescheduled. Toward the end of the year, we want to decrease inventory so we start pushing out all the supplier deliveries. All these issues come with "batch" production, but generally carry over to Lean production. When this behavior spills over to Lean, it creates real problems in the system.

## Building to Shortages

In the Lean world when orders are released with shortages, the line stops or the line is told to build up to the point where the shortage exists. Now we force the factory to regress back to batching. It is human nature to build up to the point where the shortage exists, but it just kills Lean implementations. Now we need a place for all these partially assembled units (work in processes [WIPs]), but there is no room designed into the layout. This situation can create results worse than the original batch lines. We must learn to discipline ourselves to build to the customer demand and not to make the end-of-the-month-driven results. For this reason, we always create guidelines for running the Lean cell, the first of which is to not release orders that are short parts.

## Triggers: MRP versus Kanban

One of our biggest issues with scheduling comes when we convert our systems over to Kanban. The idea behind Kanban is that the Kanban signal triggers the replenishment. However, when companies insist on using MRP to trigger the orders, the Kanban systems will not work properly and it will not sustain. Unless MRP is a real-time system with 100% accurate information, it will never trigger an order at the correct time. Kanbans always trigger the order when needed (assuming the Kanban calculations are correct and there is not an unexpected surge in demand).

At Company X, we instituted Kanban in all their on-site machine shop buildings. By using Kanban, we cut their lead times by 80% and took their plants from an 8-week backlog to having extra capacity within a month. We increased the final assembly on-time delivery (OTD) by over 40% in just 3 months. The key was to have the Kanbans trigger the machine shop orders versus MRP. We increased the final assembly on-time delivery (OTD) by over 40% in just 3 months. The planners using MRP always pulled in orders to take advantage of their setup times, and the machine shop orders were always scheduled to capacity, yet the final assembly lines always "stocked out" of parts they needed. Once we put Kanbans in place, we were essentially building only what was just previously used and therefore what was truly needed. (Remember, when you are working on what you don't need you can't be working on what you do need.)

We had several training sessions with the planners and taught them to rely on the Kanban triggers and ignore the MRP signals. While we were successful in the first couple of months, it later turned into a constant battle where we finally had to get the leadership involved because the planners were so ingrained with MRP that they could not let it go and continued to release work orders based on MRP instead of Kanban. Despite the training, the original results, and upper management support, middle management did not support the effort so, as soon as we left, the planners went back to the old system using MRP to schedule the machines. On-time delivery (OTD) dropped, and the machining plants are now in Mexico with some parts outsourced to China!

Lesson Learned: It is not enough for upper management to support an effort. They must learn Lean, understand Lean, and lead it! If you make just what you need and reduce your setup times, there is normally plenty of capacity in your shops.

## Establishing Flow: Order Staging Rack in Place

Once the Lean line is implemented, it is important to make sure that you are working on what is really needed. The first step is to set up a work order scheduling rack (see Figure 2.1). Some people loosely refer to this as a heijunka rack. But this is a misnomer; we generally don't object as it gets people thinking about level loading and about the timing of scheduling their production. We are in effect starting to level load the workshop. To implement this rack, you (the Lean Practitioner) generally must take over the line from the planner and or the current supervisor to get the ordering

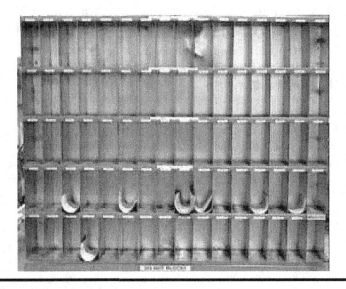

**Figure 2.1   Heijunka level loading scheduling box.**

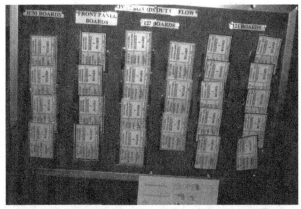

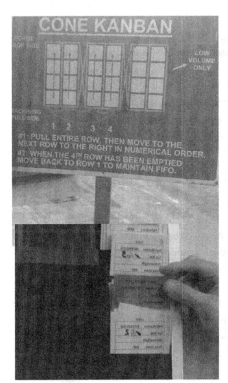

**Figure 2.2 Examples of various Kanban triggering systems. (From BIG Archives.)**

system set up correctly. It should ideally be set up where production is triggered by a Kanban (see Figure 2.2) or work orders.

We should no longer be making what we think the customers are going to want or working to what someone thinks or feels the schedule should be. The schedule should be based on the actual customer demand and sized by customer forecasts. The staging rack can be set up for paper or bins depending on the product with a goal of building to order. Building to order requires the least amount of WIP inventory but may require additional raw material inventory. Many times, our lead times are too long, which forces us to build finished goods and then triggers production orders to replenish it when it is consumed by the customer. This is commonly referred to as a "pull"-type system. In some cases, some staging point Kanbans are required depending on the manufacturing throughput time versus the customer's required delivery time. For example, at one company we had two staging Kanbans, one after the presses (8-part types) and one after heat treat and prior to grinding (32-part types). After grinding, the parts were made to customer order (3,200-part types). The next stage was setting up their parts at their customer sites (vendor-managed inventory [VMI]) where they were able to replace their Kanbans on a daily or biweekly frequency.

Our goal is to directly link our processes together as much as possible. This means having sub-assemblies be part of and synchronized with the final assembly line. Wherever we can't tie in the subassembly processes, we link them with Kanbans with a goal of linking them directly at some point in the future. This is flow production.

> Results: At Company X, we reduced the space in their master layout by over 60% by combining the subassemblies with the final assembly line. The final line was also supplied by welding and machining. We had to batch through welding and machining and link them to the final line with a Kanban before and after the washer. When we finished phase II of our Lean implementation, we were able to receive the tubes from the supplier at 7:00 p.m. the night before, run it through welding, grinding, leak test, wash, and have it to the final line, and ship it out by 3:00 p.m. the next day …. And they only worked one shift! That is JIT flow. We literally had to calculate the batch size required to keep the parts moving through welding and grinding as we were supplying two production lines.

## Scheduling Board Rules

Once the Lean line is implemented, it is important to make sure that you are working on what is needed. An initial step to setting up heijunka is starting with some sort of visual scheduling system. We should be able to walk around the shop and visually know (without asking anyone) the current order in process and the next several orders in line.

This may mean that you must work very closely with planning or PC and the current supervisor to get the ordering system set up correctly. It is important to understand the current work order system and what triggers the release of an order. Here is an example of rules we set up for one planning group:

1. Planning will provide a weekly schedule to the team leaders.
2. Planning will walk the floor with the team leader two times a day to review the progress of the work orders from the shipping area to final assembly, to welding, to machining, and to raw material.
3. Planning will put the work orders in the visual work order boards (see Figure 2.3) on the appropriate day based on the start date.
4. Planning may change the work order schedule only if the work order has not been pulled from the work order scheduling board. Once a work order is started in the cell, it may not be stopped to start another.
5. No work orders are to be put in the scheduling board queue if they have part shortages.
6. The planner and team leader are responsible to make sure that the parts are available when needed for final assembly and the staging areas with no shortages.
7. Planning is responsible to create a visual queue at each machine to show what work order is in process and to determine a way to label the WIP with the appropriate work order number.

It should be set up where production is triggered by Kanban or work order (see Figure 2.4). Work orders can be set up by the number of hours we expect them to take or simply loaded by due date based on what we think a day's worth of orders represent. In the event a work order will take several days, then we would leave the slots for the subsequent days that the work order will run empty (see Figure 2.5).

**Figure 2.3** Visual scheduling board by Value Stream Work Center—Feeding Lean final Assy line. (From BIG Archives.)

**Figure 2.4** Work order scheduling by work center. (Courtesy of Marquip Ward United [now BW Papersystems].)

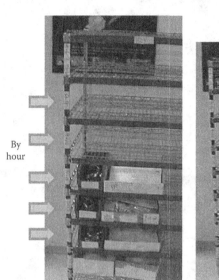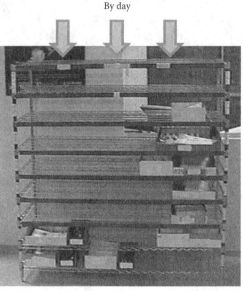

By day

By hour

**Figure 2.5 Visual scheduling rack by day by hour. The picture on the right shows they have not gotten to the bottom two orders. If it was beyond the hour on the rack, we would know those orders were behind. One can tell the second order remaining on the first day will take most of the next day. The last order on the 2nd day will take up the first hour of the next day. (From BIG Archives.)**

## Heijunka: Production Leveling–Level Loading

Production leveling, also known as production smoothing or by its Japanese term—"Heijunka" which means "a plain, flat level," which also means "standard level" and "change." Level loading is a technique for reducing the mura waste and is vital to the development of production efficiency in the Toyota Production System and Lean manufacturing. The general idea is to produce intermediate goods at a constant rate and to allow further processing to be carried out at a constant and predictable rate.

## Level Loading/Kanban Scheduling Rules

- Linking processes together and pulling from the preceding process.
- Never producing more than what is required.
- Machines and materials must be JIT.
- Machine utilization no longer dictates the schedule: some machines may be slowed down or idle.
- Workers, machines and materials, and methods are all organized to facilitate this process.
- Timing and volume are critical: if a later process takes more than it needs from a preceding process, the preceding process must gear up to produce more (time and materials). If the later process, then, doesn't take from the preceding process, it may have idle time (beer game).

## Production Smoothing Example

A key concept for level loading is production smoothing. This involves taking the production schedule and averaging it into daily or even hourly demand. Let's look at an example. Let's say an automotive company uses a press to make parts for multiple vehicles. The press does not have

**Table 2.1   Production Smoothing Example—Calculating Daily Demand**

|        | *Weekly Demand* | *# Working Days per Week* | *Daily Demand* |
|--------|-----------------|--------------------------|----------------|
| Part A | 1,000           | 5                        | 200            |
| Part B | 750             | 5                        | 150            |
| Part C | 250             | 5                        | 50             |

*Source:* BIG training materials.

infinite capacity, and we must figure out how to best utilize that capacity to meet the customer's demands. Traditionally, we would simply build a week's worth of orders for each part and then produce the next weeks' worth of parts in another batch and so on.

But in a Lean world, we look to reduce the amount of parts and inventory we keep on hand. This leads to reductions in inventory, material handling, and required space to store the materials. This concept of leveling the weeks' worth of production into smaller daily lots is called heijunka or production smoothing (see Table 2.1). For instance, if we have a weekly demand for part A of 1,000 pieces, part B of 750 pieces, and part C of 250 pieces, we can perform a mathematical equation of dividing each part quantity by 5 (to obtain the daily demand). For part A, this means we need to produce a quantity of 200 pieces per day (1,000 ÷ 5), part B 150 pieces per day (750 ÷ 5), and part C 50 pieces per day (250 ÷ 5).

In a typical manufacturing setting, we would produce in segmented batch 200 pieces of part A, then 150 of part B, and then 50 pieces of part C. To make this happen, we must first have a better understanding of the time available for the press to produce these parts, the cycle time, the first pass yield (FPY), and the changeover time. Again, using our example, we know that part A takes 60 seconds to produce each part. This means that to produce 200 parts, we need 200 minutes of machine time to make that happen. We also need to account for the FPY. For part A, it is 99%. This means that to produce 200 good parts, we need to plan on producing 202 parts (2 parts are assumed to be scrapped or not good at the first pass). This adds an additional 2 minutes to our cycle time for a total time of 202 minutes. For part B, it takes 67 seconds to produce each part. We need 150 of these, so it should take 10,050 seconds or 167.5 minutes. The FPY on this part is only 90%. So, we need to assume that we will need to produce an additional 17 parts, which means an additional 16.8 minutes for a total of 186.2 minutes for part B. Part C has a cycle time of 46 seconds. The daily demand is 50 pieces. The FPY is 98%. From our data, we now know that it takes 38 minutes for the daily quantity plus we need an additional one part for the yield loss; we add roughly another minute for a total cycle time on part C of 38.9 minutes (see Table 2.2). So, the grand total of machine cycle time is:

$$\text{Part A}\left(202\,\text{minutes}\right) + \text{Part B}\left(186.2\,\text{minutes}\right) + \text{Part C}\left(38.9\,\text{minutes}\right)$$

$$= 427.1\,\text{minutes of machine time}$$

If we work an 8-hour shift on this machine, the time available would be 480 minutes. But people take two 10-minute breaks and a 30-minute lunch for a total available time of 430 minutes. We can see our total cycle time is only 427.1 minutes so we need to run this machine only on one shift, correct? But we still haven't considered the amount of time it takes to change over from one

**Table 2.2  Production Smoothing Example—Calculating Daily Machine Time Based on FPY**

| | Weekly Demand | # Working Days per Week | Daily Demand | Time to Produce per Piece (Seconds) | Minutes Required to Meet Daily Demand | FPY | Extra Parts Required | Number of Parts Needed based on FPY | New Cycle Time (Minutes) |
|---|---|---|---|---|---|---|---|---|---|
| Part A | 1,000.0 | 5.0 | 200.0 | 60.0 | 200.0 | 0.99 | 2.0 | 202.0 | 202.0 |
| Part B | 750.0 | 5.0 | 150.0 | 67.0 | 167.5 | 0.90 | 16.8 | 166.8 | 186.2 |
| Part C | 250.0 | 5.0 | 50.0 | 46.0 | 38.3 | 0.98 | 0.8 | 50.8 | 38.9 |
| Totals | 2,000.0 | | 400.0 | | 405.8 | | 19.5 | 419.5 | 427.1 |

*Source:* BIG training materials.

part to another (see Table 2.3). In our example, let's say part A and part B are significantly different, and it requires 40 minutes to change over. After running part B, it takes only 10 minutes to change over to part C. These changeover times add another 50 minutes to the overall time required of the machine.

We cannot tell you how many times we have worked with people and they have forgotten to calculate yield loss and changeover times in their calculations. They start running the parts and then are often surprised as to why they can't produce everything required in an 8-hour shift due to yield loss and changeover times. Another consideration is the actual machine reliability or machine downtime. Again, countless times we have witnessed significant arguments regarding production's inability to "meet the schedule" due to equipment. Often routine maintenance is scheduled for this machine but isn't considered when calculating the available time. Also, a press often breaks down, especially if they are older or are run to full capacity.

Whenever we encounter production part shortages or missed schedules, we typically look at the assumptions made regarding yield, changeover, and planned equipment downtime. Somewhere in these areas, we typically find a gap between the plan and the actual. When we implement heijunka for a press, line, or a plant, we must routinely review the assumptions and ensure that the actual performance meets the planned assumptions. If not, then we have the choice of either correcting the variance by problem-solving and implementing corrective actions, or as a last resort after we have exhausted our improvement opportunities, we then adjust our assumptions.

> I was working with Company X, which had a plant that hadn't changed any of their calculations in over 5 years, and one of the machines deteriorated to the point where it was down more than it was available during the day. This downtime was factored into their scheduling system based on demonstrated capacity and was therefore never targeted for improvement.

## Production Sequencing

In manufacturing, this concept is utilized to level out production of various or "mixed" models. This concept allows Toyota to run multiple car types down the same line one model after another. This can be accomplished only with flexibility built into the layout, equipment, utilities, and people. The idea behind this concept is to schedule your products evenly so as not to create batches

**Table 2.3 Production Smoothing Example—Calculating Daily Machine Time Based on FPY with Setup and Downtime Figured in**

| #Working Days per Week | Daily Demand | Time to Produce per Piece (Seconds) | Minutes Required to Meet Daily Demand | FPY | Extra Parts Required | Number of Parts Needed Based on FPY | New Cycle Time (Minutes) | Changeover Time (Minutes) | New Cycle Time Minutes w/Setup | No. of 8 Hour Shifts Required on Machine | Unplanned Downtime Minutes | New Cycle Time Minutes w/ Downtime |
|---|---|---|---|---|---|---|---|---|---|---|---|---|
| 5.0 | 200.0 | 60.0 | 200.0 | 0.99 | 2.0 | 202.0 | 202.0 | 25 | 227.0 | 0.53 | 20 | 247.0 |
| 5.0 | 150.0 | 67.0 | 167.5 | 0.90 | 16.8 | 166.8 | 186.2 | 40 | 226.2 | 0.53 | 30 | 256.0 |
| 5.0 | 50.0 | 46.0 | 38.3 | 0.98 | 0.8 | 50.8 | 38.9 | 10 | 48.9 | 0.11 | 40 | 88.9 |
| | 400.0 | | 405.8 | | 19.5 | 419.5 | 427.1 | 75.0 | 502.1 | 1.38 | 90.0 | 592.1 |

*Source:* BIG training materials.

of products coming in at one time. In some areas of companies, this is easy to do, and in some areas, it may be nearly impossible to do.

This mixed model concept could be interpreted as running multiple types of a product family at the same time. To properly sequence activities within an operation, one must understand the order of the activities and, in most cases, the information flow. The process flow analysis gives us this data, and then we combine it with the "amount of demand" and "type of demand" in products or services to determine the sequence. Figure 2.6 shows a sequencing worksheet.

Once the proper sequence is determined, the flow of the models must be balanced and evenly distributed to the extent possible. In Lean, we call this demand smoothing, level loading, or heijunka. We then need to match the process flow analysis (understanding the "critical value-added and non-value-added but necessary activities") to what is "required" by the operator or staff person within the amount of time (cycle time) it takes to perform those activities which come from our workflow analysis. We need to be able to optimize the delivery of products or services within the time frame the customer desires or that which is demanded by the process takt time. When parts are batched, they all arrive at the same time, which creates a domino effect across the system, pulling on all system resources at the same time, disrupting earliest due date (EDD)—formerly first in first out (FIFO) and the ability to concentrate and effectively prioritize the work.

One example in a factory is heat treating or any monument type process, which must be scheduled. If the total cycle time for the area was 300 minutes and we were running on 1-minute cycles, to meet the demand, we would need 300 units in the process. If we batched the area, we would have to staff the area for loading and unloading 300 units at a time, and a bottleneck would occur. If we could continuously process the parts, we would eliminate the bottleneck.

Figure 2.7 walks through an example of how to set up sequencing starting from monthly customer demand calculations. First, we break down the monthly demand to daily demand. We then show how the parts would run segmented batch by model type whether by day or hour depending on the setup times. This means that we would run 240 A parts in a row followed by 60 B parts, etc. We then show the mixed model sequencing. This sequencing is based on the takt times calculated next to the daily demand. We first look at the longest takt time, which is 960 seconds. We can run two C parts at 480 seconds in the same amount of time as one each D or E part at 960 seconds. We can run four each B parts at 240 seconds in the same amount of time as one D or E part, and we can run eight A parts at 120 seconds in the time it takes to run one D or E part at 960 seconds. Our overall takt time is 60 seconds, which means that we need to have one part coming off the line every 60 seconds to meet customer demand. So, one complete cycle of our sequencing matrix equals 16 minutes and includes eight each A parts, four each B parts, two each C parts, one D part, and one E part per cycle.

## Pitch

Pitch is the time required to supply a standard pattern of parts to a line. It is calculated by multiplying the takt time (or cycle time) by the number of pieces in the pattern of parts needed for the line which is normally a shipping box or container size. The sequencing box is typically separated into pitch intervals. Each box is unique to the parts they are running. As an example, it was calculated that a container of part A, which holds 12 parts and has a cycle time of 60 seconds per part, requires 12 minutes to produce a finished container. Since it takes 12 minutes to produce each container and we need to produce several containers to meet the daily demand, we can easily see that each slot in the sequencing box should be separated by 12 minutes. For a daily requirement of 200, we need 16 slots. For parts B and C, we can quickly calculate the time spacing to ensure that we meet their demand also.

**Weekly Robot Scheduling Sheet For Product X**

Available Time Hours/Minutes/Seconds: 26640 / 444 / 7.4  Takt Time Minutes: 246.7

| Model Size | RF | RG | RN | RLF | RLG | RLN | SRS | Total Weekly Demand | Total Daily Demand | Takt Time Sec | Takt Time Minutes | Takt Time Hours | Sequencing Based on TT | Pass 1 | Pass 2 | Total Daily | Total Weekly | Variance from Weekly | Notes |
|---|---|---|---|---|---|---|---|---|---|---|---|---|---|---|---|---|---|---|---|
| 3.0 | 6 | | 6 | 6 | | 6 | 1 | 25 | 5.0 | 5,328 | 88.8 | 1.48 | 2.8 | 3.0 | 2.0 | 5.0 | 25.0 | 0.0 | |
| 4.0 | 13 | 1 | | 6 | | | | 20 | 4.0 | 6,660 | 111.0 | 1.85 | 2.2 | 2.0 | 2.0 | 4.0 | 20.0 | 0.0 | |
| 5.0 | 5 | | | 4 | | | | 9 | 1.8 | 14,800 | 246.7 | 4.11 | 1.0 | 1.0 | 1.0 | 2.0 | 10.0 | −1.0 | Once a week run 0 on second pass |
| 6.0 | 11 | 1 | | 11 | | | | 23 | 4.6 | 5,791 | 96.5 | 1.61 | 2.6 | 3.0 | 2.0 | 5.0 | 25.0 | −2.0 | Once a week run 1 on first pass |
| 8.0 | 2 | 2 | | 7 | | | | 11 | 2.2 | 12,109 | 201.8 | 3.36 | 1.2 | 1.0 | 1.0 | 2.0 | 10.0 | 1.0 | Once a week pass 2 = 2 |
| 10.0 | | | | | 0 | | | 0 | 0 | – | 0.00 | 0.00 | 0.0 | 0.0 | 0.0 | 0.0 | 0.0 | 0.0 | |
| 12.0 | | | | | 0 | | | 0 | 0 | – | 0.00 | 0.00 | 0.0 | 0.0 | 0.0 | 0.0 | 0.0 | 0.0 | |
| Totals | | | | | | | | | 17.6 | 1,514 | 25.2 | 9.8 | 9.8 | 10.0 | 8.0 | 18.0 | 90.0 | −2.0 | |

| Sequencing for Model | 3.0 | 4.0 | 5.0 | 6.0 | 8.0 | 9.0 | 10.0 | Totals |
|---|---|---|---|---|---|---|---|---|
| First Pass | 3 | 2 | 1 | 3 | 1 | | | 10.0 |
| 2nd Pass | 2 | 1 | 1 | 2 | 1 | | | 8.0 |
| Total Daily | 5.0 | 4.0 | 2.0 | 5.0 | 2.0 | | | 18.0 |

| | Total Daily Demand | Takt Sec | Takt Min | Takt Hours | Seq TT | Pass 1 | Pass 2 | Total Daily |
|---|---|---|---|---|---|---|---|---|
| Robot Machine Time | 430 | 840 | 1250 | 1660 | 2070 | 2320 | 2638 | |
| Robot Time Minutes | 7.17 | 14.00 | 20.83 | 27.67 | 34.50 | 38.67 | 43.97 | |
| Robot Time Per Size | 35.8 | 56.0 | 41.7 | 138.3 | 69.0 | 0.0 | 0.0 | 340.8 |
| Percent of capacity based on Avail Time | | | | | | | | 76.8% |
| Cell should be running (hours) | | | | | | | | 5.68 |
| Assembly Time Sec (from time study) | 2847 | 3244 | 3702 | 4012 | 4429 | | | |
| Bottom head, 1st stage, 2nd stage, prep Time Minutes from System | 47.5 | 54.1 | 61.7 | 66.9 | 73.8 | | | |
| # people required | 6.6 | 3.9 | 3.0 | 2.4 | 2.1 | | | |

**Figure 2.6  Weekly Sequencing worksheet. (From BIG Archives.)**

| Products | Monthly Demand | Daily Demand | Takt Time |
|---|---|---|---|
| A | 4,800 | 240 units | 120" |
| B | 2,400 | 120 units | 240" |
| C | 1,200 | 60 units | 480" |
| D | 600 | 30 units | 960" |
| E | 600 | 30 units | 960" |
| | 9,600 units | 480 units | 60" |

Sequence Alternatives: **Segmented Batch**

Monthly  4,800 - As / 2,400 - Bs / 1,200 - Cs / 600 - Ds / 600 - Es
Daily    240 - As/ 120 - Bs / 60 - Cs / 30 - Ds / 30 - Es
Hourly   30 - As / 15 - Bs / 7.5 - Cs / 3.75 - Ds / 3.75 Es per hour

**Mixed Model**

Hourly  1- 2- 3- 4-5- 6-7-8- 9-10-11-12-13-14-15-16-17-18-19-20-21-22-23-24-25-26-27-28-29-30
        A B A C A B A C A B A  D  A B A  E  A B  A C  A B  A  C A B  A D A  B
        A E A B A C A B A C A  B  A D A  B  A E  A B  A C  A B  A C A B  A D

**Figure 2.7   Heijunka mixed model sequencing example. Converting monthly scheduling to sequencing schedule. (From BIG Archives.)**

What other factors must be considered when using sequencing boxes? How about supplies or components needed to make the finished parts? If we are going to consistently produce parts to meet the pitch interval, we must have the parts there when we need them. This typically requires line side storage and a water spider to keep pace with the line. A water spider is said to translate from a Japanese word meaning water beetle which spins in a circle on the water. This concept translates to how we use a shop floor materials person who follows a consistent routine delivering material in a timed pattern. Oftentimes, we use water spiders to deliver to several cells and calculate the time required to perform their task to match the pitch of the sequencing box. This concept goes back to Frank Gilbreth, who used water spiders to keep the concrete at an even consistency and quantity for the bricklayers.

## Milk Runs Timed within Second! It Is Possible!

A colleague of mine was attempting to implement a heijunka system in his plant and wanted to know if I knew of anyone who had a sequencing box and utilized a person called a water spider. I remember laughing and saying that my company uses them everywhere. After some conversation, we set up a tour of one of these production lines that used a sequencing box and a water spider on a timed route. Initially, my friend was very skeptical that he would be witnessing anything like what he had read in some of his Lean books. When he arrived, we immediately went out to one of our production lines and reviewed the parts and sequencing box being used. After some quick questions and some disbelief, we couldn't possibly be consistently meeting a 10-minute pitch. I asked him to stand there for 30 minutes to an hour and watch for himself. Fortunately, he came prepared and proceeded to pull out a stopwatch to really verify if what I was saying was true. He started timing the process and was quite astonished to see every 10 minutes another container of parts was removed from the line and another one was started. His next focus was on the water spider that supported this line. Again, he started timing this person with his watch. The heckling really started when the water spider would leave the area and my friend couldn't see what he was doing (he was supporting another cell). My colleague had a pretty good time, and you can imagine all the joking-type comments which can be made within a 10-minute time frame. I just told him to focus on the time and start looking for the spider to be coming back into the area about 20 seconds before the 10-minute interval was up. Sure enough, around the corner pushing a container of parts was the water spider. He was right on time! Several more cycles revealed to my colleague that the water spider was on time every cycle within 10 seconds! He couldn't believe it and followed the water spider to see where he was going when he went out of sight. He thought he must have gone and sat down somewhere between his intervals, but after seeing the spider was supporting the other cell, my colleague was convinced that he had to implement this system back in his plant.

## Heijunka Box

We often use a heijunka or sequencing box as a visual control to know when or how we are doing according to the plan. These boxes generally have slots that represent time. It could be hours within a day or days within a month. The box is typically stored in the shipping area where the pull is started from finished goods. In the example in Figure 2.8, we see a box that has a specific part and quantity loaded into each time slot where each slot represents 11 to 12-minute increments based on the pitch. The night before, it is loaded with orders separated by product and scheduled shipping time. We immediately know by looking at the box if parts are late and how many are scheduled for that hour. Each slip contains spots to fill in process times so we can track the cycle time of each step and the overall throughput time.

The fact that companies, in general, do not level load their schedules create a tremendous amount of waste in their systems in extra labor and overtime costs. In many cases, this results in all their resources being needed at the exact same time. The level loading concept, while simple, is very important to making our Lean processes run smoothly. The goal in Lean is to staff the process based on data thus managing by fact. Then work to improve the process and layouts to take out costs. If you focus on the process (i.e., implementing pitch and scheduling leveling tools), instead of just cutting costs, you will realize the gains.

To effectively use these types of devices, we must have stability and some predictability in our production operations. If our FPY varies more than 15%, it may be quite difficult to effectively utilize the sequencing/heijunka box. Anything higher than this will result in chaos and

**Figure 2.8   Heijunka cards in slots by cycle 11–12 minutes.**

staff ignoring the box and doing whatever they think is best to get parts out. Another factor to consider is unplanned machine downtime. If one day the machine runs all day and then the next it is down for 3 hours, it will be very difficult to follow the sequencing box. Changeover times must also be predictable, and we often must standardize this process so we can have consistent times to complete the task. Whenever we do a heijunka/sequencing box, it is often precluded by a single-minute-exchange-of-dies kaizen. This helps to bring stability and standardization to the changeover process.

## Gotta Make the Numbers

Several years ago, we were working with a major automotive supplier who was having significant delivery issues. We were asked to help with one of their cells that was having difficulties. When we asked the production supervisor what was happening, he said that the material control department (who was responsible for setting up the sequencing box daily) didn't have a clue on how manufacturing works, and there was no way he could meet the production numbers the boss was asking for. He said that he must work overtime every day and still can't hit the numbers. "Everybody is breathing down my neck about our production numbers but I keep telling them there is no way we can meet their expectations in an 8-hour day. I have been working here for 3 years and I haven't seen it happen yet!" We then asked him how long he had been using the heijunka box and what involvement he had in the process. Quite aggravated, he responded by telling us that nobody really asks him how to do anything or what the problems are; he only hears that he needs to improve his numbers. We left the production supervisor and went to talk with the buyer/planner/scheduler for that production cell. This person told us the supervisor is very argumentative and that he used to visit the production floor to monitor the adherence to the sequencing box, but the supervisor would start verbally attacking him regarding the box and the expectations. We then asked to see how he calculated the sequencing box and what assumptions were made regarding FPY, machine uptime, and changeover time. After reviewing these data, we went back to the production floor (gemba) to see some of the data regarding how the production cell was doing. After reviewing the previous 3 weeks of FPY, machine uptime, and changeover times, it became quite evident where the issue existed. The changeover time used in the calculation was 10 minutes. When we reviewed the data out on the floor, the actual time spent to change over was running over 50 minutes on average for the past 3 weeks. We then asked the supervisor if he was having any issue with changeovers, and he responded by stating, "Well, actually, yes, I am." He said that the overhead crane used to change out the dies was broken, and there wasn't any money in the budget to get it fixed. He also said that it never did work right when they first launched the product, and due to money being tight, he would have to call for a forklift to lift and place the die whenever a changeover was required. Well, as anyone can imagine, the forklift driver was nowhere to be found when it came to change over the press. This resulted in wide variations in time to change over. Sometimes they would get lucky and find the forklift driver quickly, but most often, the driver was busy loading and unloading trucks so there was a long delay in getting to the press to assist them! We asked the supervisor if the forklift driver could meet the single minute exchange of dies (SMED) turnover time and he said "Yes, if he was immediately available." We suggested an immediate counter measure to implement an andon light notifying the forklift driver 5 minutes prior of an upcoming changeover. This gave the forklift driver time to complete whatever he was working on to be available for the changeover. Once we had this signal in place, the changeovers could consistently meet the expected times, and production was back on schedule with the sequencing box. Next, we had to work with the forklift driver to establish a "milk run" process for him/her. Eventually we were able to implement motorized die carts and side loaded dies to eliminate the need for the crane.

Lessons Learned:

1. Calculating the heijunka/sequencing box should be a team effort, and everyone should understand the assumptions regarding cycle times, changeovers, yield, and downtime.
2. A regular review of actual versus planned should be done at a minimum monthly with corrective actions or adjustments made accordingly.
3. Go to the gemba and see what is happening. If we would have simply listened to each one of the people complaining about each other without going out and seeing for ourselves, we would have gotten caught up in the us versus them scenario.
4. Consistency and predictability are a requirement if a sequencing box is going to be effective.

One of the important questions to consider when implementing a heijunka/sequencing box is where do we start? As with most companies and processes, parts typically get processed through several steps and travel quite a bit throughout the plant from one processing area to the next and even sometimes back and forth. As an example, for Company X's part,

1. It starts out on a machining center
2. Then goes to assembly
3. Back to another machining center
4. Assembly
5. Heat treat
6. Cleaning and then
7. Final assembly

Each of these pieces of equipment or processes has parts from other cells that run through them. The PC department schedules each one of these areas, and as one would expect, the on-time schedule attainment gets worse and worse the further upstream you look. When we use a scheduling box, we create a pull from the upstream processes. As a rule, we try to start the system in the final assembly area and make it the pacemaker. The reason for this is we typically use a replenishment pull strategy. That is, we are using the scheduling box to replenish the finished goods we have in stock (assuming we are not building to order). Quite often, these finished goods are in marked locations on the floor, and we can quickly identify which products are needed. Even if they are not in a dedicated space, we often see PC out on the floor verifying the amount of finished goods. Once this happens, they will load the scheduling box based upon the number of units pulled to go to the customer. The concept here is that the final assembly area is to build only those products with Kanban cards now loaded in the box. As we stated earlier, the box has several different slots based upon the pitch needed for each container. Each slot has a time associated with it, and at a quick glance, anyone can see the status of a job or when parts are planned to be run.

The integrity of the system is dependent upon the final assembly department following the sequence of the box and following their standard work (i.e., not skipping around). This system requires a significant amount of discipline and quick response leadership. Why is it important? It is important because there are calculations made regarding how long it takes to complete each pitch, and if, for some reason, the machine goes down or there is a yield problem, it must be corrected as soon as possible. As mentioned earlier in the book, that is why it is so important to have leadership as well as support staff engaged in this effort as it takes a collective effort to support an initiative like this. Maintenance needs to have someone available almost immediately to address equipment issues, quality also needs to have a quick response, as well as leadership to be able to react and respond to issues as they surface in real time. Because of this need, we often implement an andon light system. This enables the support staff to quickly recognize at a glance there is an issue and requires they respond immediately based upon the color designation used for each functional area. The colors to notify each functional area can be whatever the plant would like, but we typically see red used for maintenance or setup and yellow for quality, blue for materials handler (water spider), etc.

## What You Are Told Is the Problem, Normally Is Not!

We were asked to come into a particular plant to assist in resolving issues with short shipping the customer on a particular assembly line. When we arrived, we immediately asked to go to the gemba and see the finished goods/truck staging area. After walking out near the shipping dock, we could see remnants of what used to be a labeled holding area for finished parts. Unfortunately, what was in that location were other parts than what was labeled. When we asked the forklift driver where the parts were supposed to be, his response was "all over the place." He continued to add that there are so many finished parts coming off the lines and since they are short staffed in the material handling area that he just finds the closest spot to put things. If we want the parts in the marked location, go ahead and move them ourselves; he doesn't have time! After getting a pretty good picture of what was happening near the shipping dock, we walked over to the assembly cell. At first glance, it looked pretty good. There were parts moving from station to station, and people were keeping a steady pace of work. We also observed a heijunka scheduling system in place; but, after reviewing the box, we noticed that the process was over 2 hours behind. We then asked one of the assemblers if there was a problem causing them to get behind. To our amazement, her response was they weren't behind! She said: "We are actually right on schedule." After enquiring what schedule they were using, we noticed that there was a "hot parts board" the team was using to determine what to run next. The assembler went on to explain that the shipping department writes on the board what hot parts they need based upon the truck pickup schedule and what amount of finished parts he could find to fill the truck! Since they were the ones loading the truck and out in the area all the time, they knew how much inventory was on hand. We asked PC if they were involved in this and if they were the ones who arrange the heijunka box. The PC person said, "Yes, we are, but like the assembler told you, they don't follow it." He added, "Besides, I hardly ever go out there, but when I do I show them the paper documenting there is more inventory on hand than what the shipping department is telling them." We went back and talked to the assembler and she explained "Since Bob in shipping has been here for over 25 years and the planner is relatively new, we go by what Bob says. He knows what he is putting on the truck and is on a forklift most of the day so he can see what is in the plant a lot better than our planner who sits behind a computer all day." The cell supervisor finally showed up and introduced himself. He went on to apologize to us and told us that he was busy because he has another line, he is responsible for and it is a new product launch with many issues, and on top of it all, the customer is here today watching the process and "offering" assistance to him to ensure the parts arrive back at his plant on time. In the interest of his time, we quickly asked if he was aware of the two different scheduling systems being used in the cell we were evaluating. His response was, "Yes and the heijunka box hasn't been followed for a few months. When we first started using the box everything worked fine. Then maintenance got pulled all the time to set up the new lines, quality got pulled to the new launch, and I had to train all the operators on the new line so we were always delayed in responding to the andon light which caused us to fall behind. So now we just let shipping tell us what we need to run as he knows when the truck is coming and what we have on hand. The planner and the shipping guy are always arguing about how much inventory is here and I stay out of it!"

Lesson Learned: Standard work, roles and responsibilities, discipline and accountability are necessary if the heijunka box is going to work properly. If issues which arise aren't resolved quickly, the cell will simply do what they think is right (whether it is right or not) to get the job done. In addition, we discovered due to increased volume and new product launches; there wasn't enough storage space for all the finished goods parts, and often containers would be "lost" only to eventually show up a day or two later.

## Capacity and Load

When determining capacity and the load on the factory, there are certain calculations we must consider. Many times, the load is based on machining hours or percent of a work center that is scheduled. Our first calculation is of excess capacity.

$$\text{Excess capacity} = \frac{\text{Capacity} - \text{load}}{\text{Capacity}}$$

$$= \frac{160\,\text{hours}\,(8\,\text{hours} \times 20\,\text{days} \times 1\,\text{shift}) - 140\,\text{hours}}{160\,\text{hours}}$$

$$\text{Excess capacity} = 12.5\%.$$

What if load exceeds capacity? If load exceeds capacity, we must look at each machine and determine if we can offload to another machine, look at speeds and feeds, look at setup times and overall equipment effectiveness. We may also have to investigate adding a shift or working over lunches and breaks.

When we work on master layouts, we work to design cells to 50% capacity so we have additional room for growth. One of the master layout criteria is looking out several years to determine the customer's future anticipated demand to be placed on the machine, work center, or cell.

Tools we utilize for capacity are as follows:

1. Master schedule is used to forecast incoming production orders and materials.
2. MRP broadcast which goes to suppliers (planning document).
   a. They use broadcast to plan capacity.
   b. They use broadcast to plan raw material availability.
   c. They use broadcasts to schedule shop (for firm periods only).
3. Heijunka (level loading) is used to schedule floors based on sales mix.
4. Kanban is used as the "implementation tool."
   a. Supplier Kanbans are used to signal consumed purchased materials, triggering the replenishment cycle.
   b. "In-process" Kanbans are used to signal consumed manufactured materials, triggering the replenishment cycle. One-piece flow techniques are essential here.
5. World-class measurement tools (day by the hour and month by the day) and dashboard real-time KPI's are utilized to replace traditional variance and accounting efficiency reports.

## Shop Floor Scheduling without Using the MRP System

One of the first things we do is turn off the shop floor control sections of MRP when we implement Kanbans. In Figure 2.9, one can see a simple pull system installed at final assembly. This system was designed with no Kanban cards. Everything was triggered using visual controls (i.e., outlined squares on the floor, shelf gas gauges, and two bin systems). Once a unit goes to the final assembly, it pulls from the paint Kanban, the paint Kanban pulls from the welding Kanban, which pulls from the machine shop Kanban, which pulls from the raw material Kanban, which sends a signal back to the supplier to replenish. We also had 80% of their materials set up on VMI.

In Figure 2.10, at Ancon Gear, we set up a build to order scheduling system. The system started with receiving an order. Order entry filled in a card with the order information, and it was sent to planning. Planning consisted of one buyer/planner/scheduler who would check and order the materials if not on Kanban. The material and cards were placed in the heijunka box for each cell. The cell would pull the card at the designated hour and produce the parts and place them into the finished goods Kanban. The supplier would then replenish the Kanban material, and the order would ship to the customer. The order entry card would then go back into the file.

### *Peak Demand*

Since we cannot always level load our demand, sometimes we need to look at peak demand when determining capacity and how to set up the line. We need to make sure that we can handle peak demand whenever it occurs. We see this phenomenon more in hospitals, for instance, arrivals

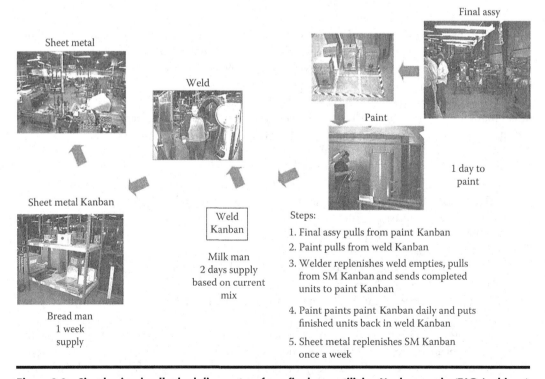

Steps:
1. Final assy pulls from paint Kanban
2. Paint pulls from weld Kanban
3. Welder replenishes weld empties, pulls from SM Kanban and sends completed units to paint Kanban
4. Paint paints paint Kanban daily and puts finished units back in weld Kanban
5. Sheet metal replenishes SM Kanban once a week

**Figure 2.9   Simple visual pull scheduling system from final assy utilizing Kanban cards. (BIG Archives.)**

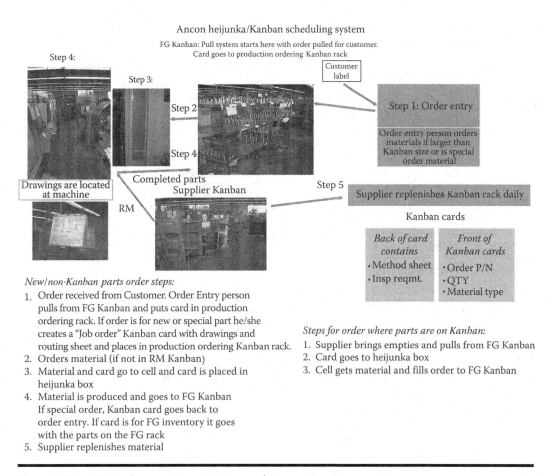

New/non-Kanban parts order steps:

1. Order received from Customer. Order Entry person pulls from FG Kanban and puts card in production ordering rack. If order is for new or special part he/she creates a "Job order" Kanban card with drawings and routing sheet and places in production ordering Kanban rack.
2. Orders material (if not in RM Kanban)
3. Material and card go to cell and card is placed in heijunka box
4. Material is produced and goes to FG Kanban If special order, Kanban card goes back to order entry. If card is for FG inventory it goes with the parts on the FG rack
5. Supplier replenishes material

*Steps for order where parts are on Kanban:*
1. Supplier brings empties and pulls from FG Kanban
2. Card goes to heijunka box
3. Cell gets material and fills order to FG Kanban

**Figure 2.10    FG Kanban system. (Courtesy of Ancon Gear.)**

by hour, but we also encounter it in factories and service industries. Internet-based orders peak at certain times during the day, or seasonality can affect demand as well. We generally look at peak demand either daily or hourly and determine the takt time and line constraints accordingly. Table 2.4 depicts an example of peak demand. Given: daily demand for part C is 7.5 units if it is level loaded, but in this case, peak demand is 10 units per hour. So, our takt time changes from 480 to 360 seconds. If our peak demand hits in the same hour, then our overall takt time changes from 60 to 42.8 seconds. We need to make sure that we don't have any piece of equipment that runs less than 42.8 seconds.

## *Setup and Number of Changeovers*

How do we determine the number of setups required per day on a given machine? We start with the capacity required for the machine (see Figure 2.11):

$$\text{Capacity Run} = \text{Time for the machine} \big( \text{total daily time required to run all parts for each model} \big)$$

$$+ \text{Time for changeovers}$$

**Table 2.4  Peak Demand**

| Product | Monthly Demand (Units) | Daily Demand (Units) | Takt Time (Seconds) | Hourly Demand (Units) | Takt Time (Seconds) | Peak Hourly Demand (Units) | Takt Time (Seconds) |
|---|---|---|---|---|---|---|---|
| A | 4,800 | 240 | 120 | 30 | 120 | 40 | 90 |
| B | 2,400 | 120 | 240 | 15 | 240 | 20 | 180 |
| C | 1,200 | 60 | 480 | 7.5 | 480 | 10 | 360 |
| D | 600 | 30 | 960 | 3.75 | 960 | 6 | 600 |
| E | 600 | 30 | 960 | 3.75 | 960 | 8 | 450 |
| Totals | 9,600 | 480 | 60 | 60 | 60 | 84 | 42.85 |

*Source:* BIG training materials.

We can then take the available time and subtract the time for changeover and divide by the time it takes for one changeover. This will yield the number of possible changeovers. Once the number of possible changeovers is known, determine how many different components you wish to always have on hand. These parts should be the high runners, which get used every day. Use Pareto analysis to determine the top 80% of the demand on the machine. Assuming the setup time is constant, divide the number of "high runners" by the number of changeovers possible in 1 day, and that will provide the inventory necessary to support downstream operations in the number of days.

$$\frac{20\,\text{high runners/day}}{20\,\text{changeovers/day}} = 1\,\text{day of inventory for each high runner}$$

Then, add in safety stock. For example:

- 1 day inventory/part + 1 day safety stock/per part = 2 days of inventory required for each part,
- 20 high runners/5 changeovers day = 4 days of inventory per part required (prior to safety stock)

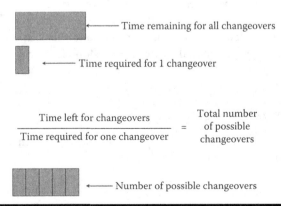

Figure 2.11   The impact of setups on scheduling. (From BIG training materials.)

An alternative to this method assuming the setup times vary would be to do the same exercise using setup times per part. Once we know the number of changeovers we can perform in 1 day, we can then determine the minimum amount of inventory that is required to sustain downstream operations.

## Implementing Planning and Scheduling Tips

- Implement in phases.
- Consider using finished goods Kanban if the factory or process cannot produce make to order.
- Develop level loading strategy, internal and external.
- Review sales strategies: does it make sense to offer a discount or price break anymore?
- Get sales/marketing on board. They must understand the system and the need for real information (i.e., no more "padding" delivery times).
- Whenever you make more than you need, it prevents you from making what is really needed.
- Eliminate buffers, reduce inventory, and change MRP lead time offsets after you have proven you can meet customer demand.
- Develop failure modes effects analysis or risk mitigation strategies for each process/machine.
- Keep scheduling systems as simple as possible or no one will follow them.
- Work the excess WIP off starting closest to the customer.
- Remember, if you dry up the line, you will lose output the next cycle.

Once you implement the Lean line, it pulls for changes in planning. For instance, now there are many work orders and many bill of materials (BOMs) changes needed. In the past, planning may have put an order into a subassembly area as a large batch so they had to cut only one work order at a time. Now we have put those areas together in line. This means that they must cut several work orders at one time since each work center is now producing at the same time in the line creating a lot of extra work for planning (as a planner in one of the plants we implemented stated, "I am only one man. How do you expect me to get all of this done?"). The goal now is to flatten the BOM.

## Lean Pulls Changes from Every Department

At Company X, the water spider kept missing the material replenishment at one of the workstations (it was a job shop environment so the parts were changed out for each order, which averaged 10–30 pieces). When we asked why, he explained that he only received the work order (which contained all the parts required) for one workstation. The paperwork for the other workstations was being delivered somewhere else and he wasn't sure where. We found that planning was delivering the paperwork to the operator and the operator was pulling the parts himself. When we explained we wanted the water spider to do this, he asked whether he could get all the parts required (Kanban and non-Kanban) on one sheet of paper from the planner. This meant we had to immediately start looking at flattening the BOM. This then created problems for accounting and scheduling. I explained to the team that this was a "good" problem because Lean should start to pull changes from planning, finance, and other parts of the organization.

## Chapter Questions

1. What is sequencing? How is it accomplished?
2. What is demonstrated capacity? How do you know if the area is using it?
3. Explain takt–flow–pull.
4. What is a build to order system?
5. What is a pull system?
6. Are all pull systems built-to-order systems?
7. Where should the heijunka box be located?
8. What is peak demand? How does peak demand impact line setups and capacity planning?
9. How would you schedule work in a process without using the MRP shop floor control system?
10. What is pitch, and how is pitch used in manufacturing planning?
11. What is a heijunka box?
12. What is level loading? Why is it important? How is level loading accomplished? How is it linked to Kanbans and the Toyota House?
13. What did you learn from this chapter?

### Discussion Question

If we are truly level loading, should we be pulling in orders from the next shipment month? Should there be an "end of the month" push?

## Notes

1. https://deming.org/a-bad-system-will-beat-a-good-person-every-time/
2. Furnished by Kenneth Hopper and reprinted with permission, e-mail personal correspondence.

## Additional Readings

Dolcemascolo, D. 2006. Improving the Extended Value Stream. Portland, OR: Productivity Press.
Hino, S. 2006. Inside the Mind of Toyota. New York: Productivity Press.
Hirano, H. 1988. JIT Factory Revolution. Portland, OR: Productivity Press.
McGuire, K. 1984. Impressions from Our Most Worthy Competitor. Falls Church, VA: APICS.
Ohno, T. and Mito, S. 1986. Just-in-Time for Today and Tomorrow. Cambridge, MA: Productivity Press.
Shingo, S. 1987. Key Strategies for Plant Improvement. Portland, OR: Productivity Press.
Smalley, A. 2004. Creating Level Pull. Cambridge, MA: Lean Enterprise Institute.

# Chapter 3

# Mistake Proofing

The causes of defects lie in worker errors, and defects are the results of neglecting those errors. It follows that mistakes will not turn into defects if worker errors are discovered and eliminated beforehand.

**Dr. Shigeo Shingo (1986)**

## Lean Goal Is Zero

Six Sigma tools are designed to measure, highlight, and eliminate defects with a focus on reducing errors to Six Sigma or 3.4 defects per million (see Table 3.1). But who wants to be one of the 3.4 people to get the defect? Many organizations use statistical process control (SPC). However, SPC will not ensure zero defects; since the defects are usually detected after they are made (historical data). SPC should be used as a preventive tool to identify patterns before an out-of-control condition happens.

Lean has strategies for control plans (see Figure 3.1), but in a truly Lean environment, they should disappear as any abnormalities should be clearly and immediately visible in the workplace and fixed in real time. Lean processes require defect-free processes to support a just in time (JIT) system so the goal of Lean is 100% defect prevention at the source. If this is not the case, then the system breaks down and delays occur. Mistake proofing, also known as poka yoke in Japanese, is a critical component of Lean and provides a mechanism to eliminate the errors so defects won't occur. The only way to get zero defects is to inspect 100% of the parts at each operation by machine, not human. This then leads us into the concept of jidoka.

The only way to get to zero defects is to eliminate the error before it occurs (see Figure 3.2). Therefore, it is important to understand the difference between an error and a defect. An error is a mistake that is made; a defect is a problem that occurs because of the error. Dr. Shingo often referred to this in his books as the importance of separating cause from effect.

An example would be as follows:

- (Cause) error—leaving the lights on in the car
- (Effect) defect—the car battery died

DOI: 10.4324/9781003185819-3

**Table 3.1  Sigma Levels**

| σ Capability | Defects per Million Opportunities with 1.5 Sigma Shift | Yield (No Defects) (%) | Cost of Poor Quality (COPQ) (%) |
|:---:|:---:|:---:|:---:|
| 1 | 500,000 | 50 | >40 |
| 2 | 308,537 | 69.1 | 30–40 |
| 3 | 66,807 | 93.3 | 20–30 |
| 4 | 6,210 | 99.4 | 15–20 |
| 5 | 233 | 99.97 | 10–15 |
| 6 | 3.4 | 99.99966 | <10 |

*Source:* BIG Archives.

*Note:* Six sigma assumes a 1.5 sigma shift.

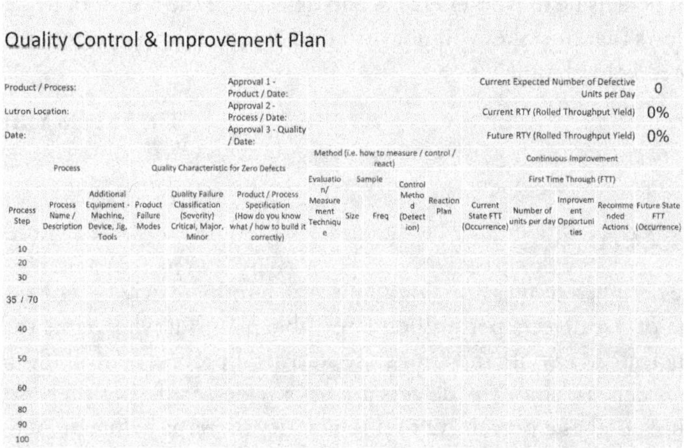

**Figure 3.1   Quality control plan.**

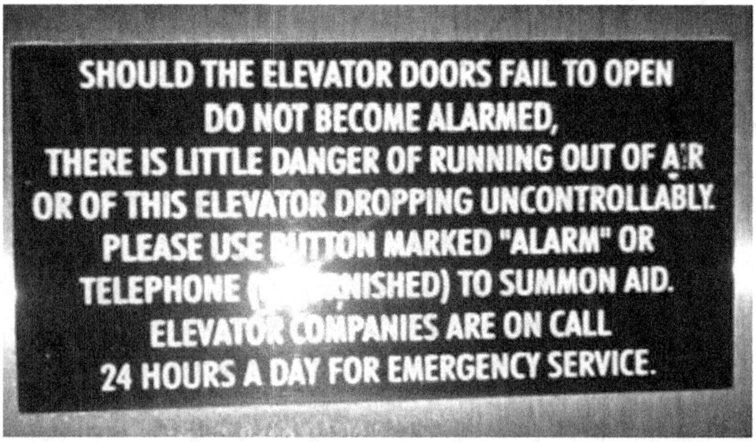

**Figure 3.2   Sign in a large hotel chain elevator that I got stuck in for 15 minutes. (BIG Archives.)**

The challenge is to somehow pick up on the fact that the error has occurred before the defect is created. Even with Lean, control strategies are needed as it is difficult to mistake proof 100% of the opportunities where errors can occur even though that is the goal. The goal of the engineer is to design the product to be error-free before, during, and after assembly beginning at the concept stage. This ties into Shingo's Plan, Control, Do, Check Act philosophy discussed earlier in the book.

## Three Types of Defects

Listed below are the three types of defects.

- Materials
- Processing
- Design

When we conduct the 5 Whys, we keep these categories in mind when looking for the root cause. Many times, we find multiple defects occurring. For instance, we may have a defect in materials but it is not caught in the supplier's process or in our inspection process. The worst types are those which are designed into the system. We see these defects all the time in test sets which result in false positives or negatives or where tweaking must be done either with a screwdriver or by changing out components until one works in the circuit or assembly.

## Special Cause versus Common Cause Variation

Whenever dealing with cause and effect, it is important to understand the difference between common cause and special cause variation. For example, if one were to drop a penny on the table, it will end up in one spot. If you drop it again from the same location, it will end up in another spot. This is an example of common cause variation. The penny is going to land within some range of different spots. If, however, we move the drop location, it will land in a different spot. This is a special cause action. Many times, in a process, we will see a result that is not the norm and assume it is a special cause when in fact it is within the normal range of variation. If we then take a special cause action, we will probably upset the norm. An example in life might be one person comes in late to work. The boss is so upset that he/she calls everyone together and says if anyone is late again in the future, he/she will dock their pay. This is a common cause action to a special cause situation. If everyone was late, then this might have been a reasonable reaction. This concept is since everything varies. That is to say that if nothing else changes, we can expect a certain amount of variation from a specific process. It should be noted that taking the wrong action given the type of variation can be worse than taking no action at all. This boss may have upset the whole team by taking this incorrect action. What action should the boss have taken? Right, a special cause action, like talking to that one guilty person in private to understand the root cause and work together to solve the problem.

# Is Six Sigma a Subset of Lean?

We found this question on a social networking board and found it somewhat intriguing and somewhat of a good way to start off this section. Lean and Six Sigma have been fighting each other as improvement implementation models in the United States since the late 1980s. Most Fortune

500 companies have at some point had struggles between the two approaches. At AlliedSignal (now Honeywell) during the 1990s, there was a vice president (VP) of Lean and a VP of Six Sigma. This resulted in quite a culture battle. Many companies have adopted a Lean sigma approach that attempts to combine the two concepts into one initiative.

Some Fortune 500 firms have chief executive officers (CEO) that may have started on the shop floor that are now in executive suites. But today, most companies use supervisor slots to rotate developing managers through as part of their training. So, the supervisors don't start on the shop floor and can't do the job they are supervising. The shop floor team members end up training the supervisors repeatedly as they rotate through this position. How does this policy impact mistake proofing?

From a historical perspective, the roots of Six Sigma as a measurement standard can be traced back to Carl Frederick Gauss (1777–1855) who introduced the concept of the normal curve. Six Sigma as a measurement standard in product variation can be traced back to the 1920s when Walter Shewhart showed that three sigma from the mean is the point where a process requires correction. Many measurement standards (CPK, zero defects, etc.) later came on the scene, but credit for coining the term Six Sigma goes to a Motorola engineer named Bill Smith. (Six Sigma is a federally registered trademark of Motorola.)[1]

Six Sigma was then packaged by consultants as a well-organized cohesive approach with standards for certification. Six Sigma was touted by Jack Welch, then CEO of GE, and Larry Bossidy, CEO of Honeywell, and adopted by hundreds of companies. Many companies and institutions launched their continuous improvement journeys with Six Sigma versus Lean because Six Sigma had such an organized rollout and was understood by the investment analysts and most of the corporate world. In essence, Six Sigma is a collection of quality tools. Most have been around for well over 100 years, and it is what the Civil Communications Section (CCS) and Deming and Juran taught to the Japanese after World War II.

One potential negative with Six Sigma programs is they are not generally rolled out with an overall continuous improvement philosophy and culture change (except within the bounds of total quality [TQ]). If it is implemented with no business management system defined, then management will not consider all areas of the business fair game for Six Sigma efforts, and it does not become part of the culture.

Six Sigma, in its original form, does not contain the tools to convert a batch process to a one-piece flow process. The tools do not drive a continuous improvement methodology or vision. In general, Six Sigma creates problem-solving black belt experts as opposed to the Lean approach that strives to get everyone involved in problem-solving. Six Sigma is a very data-intensive approach with generally a very specific project focus where green belts and black belts rigidly follow the define, measure, analyze, improve, control (DMAIC) problem-solving model. Many black belts will not deviate from the DMAIC framework, which can be difficult when implementing Lean, as the Lean tools do not necessarily fit directly with the phases of the DMAIC model. Many black belts we have encountered run through all the tools whether they need them or not. Again, we are speaking in generalities and there are Six Sigma black belts we recommend that have a different style and approach to black belt training and certification.

Ken Place[2] states:

"I feel the DMAIC framework is a good framework to stick with when improving a defined process using either Six Sigma. The problem I see is many processes are not even defined in the first place. If a process is not defined then there are other Design for Six Sigma approaches that can be used to define the process first such as Design, Measure, Explore, Develop, Implement (DMEDI)."

If you use Six Sigma to make an improvement in the middle of a batch process; but are still batching into it and out of it, where there is little to no documentation, and everyone does it a different way; how are you going to sustain any improvement in that environment? The problem with this approach, while it does get results, is like implementing Lean with just point kaizen events, where they become very difficult to sustain. Sustaining is managements' job and specifically the process owners. If the process has no owner, is it really a process? With no process owner, it is just pure variation. Doing a project with no owner defined is a failure from the start.

This has been the crux of the argument surrounding which do you implement first, Lean or Six Sigma, for years. Six Sigma proponents would argue, "how can you Lean something out when there is so much variation in the process." Lean would argue that you must stabilize the process first to get rid of the noise (variation) so the real variation comes to the surface and then one can apply the Six Sigma tools.

The Lean purest might say we don't need Six Sigma green belts or black belts because they do not have the right mentality.

Note: Toyota does not have Six Sigma green or black belts.[3] However, the Toyota Production System (TPS) incorporates Six Sigma tools, but they are utilized and taught as part of a total company-wide quality control (TCWQC) culture with an emphasis on using mistake proofing to reach zero defects versus Six Sigma's 3.4 PPM defect opportunities.

Defining how many opportunities exist with a part or product is very subjective and often gets inflated to make a process improvement look better than it truly is. What really makes it confusing today is when the Six Sigma camp learned they were not getting the results needed, they started including Lean tools in their roster of training materials and now terms like Lean Sigma are the norm. It has been our experience, with rare exceptions, that implementing Lean tools first and then Six Sigma tools work the best.

# The 3 Sigma Shift or the 3 Sigma Trick?[4]

## *When I First Heard of "6 Sigma"*

I first heard of "6 Sigma" when I was a manufacturing engineer working for Ford Electronics in 1990. I was a young engineer responsible for launching a through hole insertion process at a green field site in Lansdale, Pennsylvania. Basically, the equipment cut, formed, and inserted various resistors, capacitors, and diodes into printed circuit boards. These assembled boards were for the Electronic Engine Controllers which were then shipped to the Body and Assembly plants of Ford Motor Company. The volume was dual sourced with basically 2/3 of the volume being sourced to Ford Electronics and 1/3 being sourced to Motorola. I was part of a team that had worked hard in developing, accepting, and launching this process at what we believed were state-of-the-art insertion capability levels (i.e., 300 ppm). Based on the team's experience, competitive research coupled with the experience and guidance of the equipment manufacturer, we believed that 300 ppm (parts per million) defect level was Best In Class performance. Our goal to reach 300 ppm paralleled Ford's Q1 Quality effort to have all key Process Capability Metrics (i.e., Cpk & Ppk) at or above 1.33 which corresponded to "4 Sigma" quality levels or 32 ppm defect level (assuming a unilateral specification). So, we reached our goal of 300 ppm, initially felt proud but it fell short of our customer's 4 Sigma Quality goal of 32 ppm. Our initial sense of pride was quickly replaced by a sense of bewilderment as our customer contact at Ford reported that Motorola's equivalent process was running at "6 Sigma" quality levels. We quickly did the math and determined that

Motorola's insertion capability if truly at "6 Sigma" would have been running at 1 ppb (part per billion) defect level; yes—one part per billion. As one member of the team remarked, "we will have to wait on our grand-children to report back if that goal was reached." Little did I know at that time that I would later learn about Motorola's "6 Sigma" Quality Initiative and be privileged to become trained as one of Ford's early Six Sigma Black Belts.

## *Background on the Normal Distribution*

My aim is to keep the math simple as I don't wish for this to be a technical paper. My desire is that people will read this paper and develop a better understanding of the "Sigma level" process capability metric and ultimately ask the probing questions to uncover real breakthroughs in meeting customer expectations. Let me start by providing some background on the "Sigma level" calculations. First, they are based on an understanding of the Normal Distribution. The normal distribution is a data distribution that is very useful in modeling continuous data. For example, people's heights or weights and even exam scores can be modeled by the normal distribution. It is also commonly referred to as a "bell shaped curve." The normal distribution depicted in Figure 3.3 has a mean of zero and a standard deviation of one which is a special normal distribution titled the standard normal distribution. All normal data can be converted to the standard normal curve which was very useful in pre-PC (Personal Computers) days as lookup tables which were published for the standard normal curve. For the purposes of simplicity, the standard normal curve was selected for demonstrative purposes in this paper.

## *Process Capability with Normal Data Cpk*

Process Capability, as its name suggests, is all about determining if your process can meet your customer expectations. The assumption that your process data can be modeled by the normal distribution is a key underlying assumption for all the common process capability metrics and tends to be a valid assumption for many cases. Assuming that your process can be modeled by the normal distribution allows one to avail of certain properties unique to the normal distribution. By just knowing where your process is centered (i.e., the mean) and the variation around the center (i.e., the standard deviation), the probabilities associated with meeting customer expectations can be quickly and accurately determined.

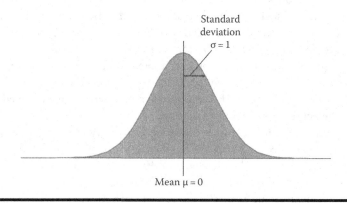

**Figure 3.3   Normal distribution.**

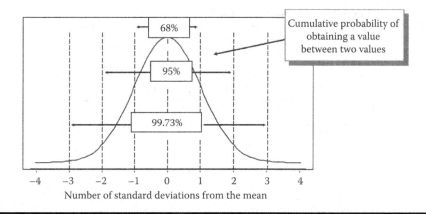

**Figure 3.4    Standard deviations.**

A review of Figure 3.4 illustrates that the area under the Normal Curve within +/– 1 Sigma of the Mean is about 68%, within +/– 2 Sigma is about 95%, and within +/– 3 Sigma is about 99.73%. A process capability analysis can be completed if one additional piece of information is known: which is, what are the customer expectations? Figure 3.5 depicts a process with all the data required to conduct a process capability study. That is, we know what the customer expects, we know where the process is centered, and we know how much variation there is around the center and we can also assume that the process data is consistent with the normality assumption.

Upon examination of Figure 3.5, one can see that the Customer Expectation lies about 2 Sigma from the Mean which means that the probability of not meeting the customer expectations is about 2.5% per the assumptions of normality. Or, in other words, how many sigma can fit between the customer expectation and the mean. This value is called the "sigma value" and is the process capability metric of interest for this paper. So, in summary, a sigma value of 2, often referred to as a "two sigma process," would be expected to have about a 2.5% defect level or

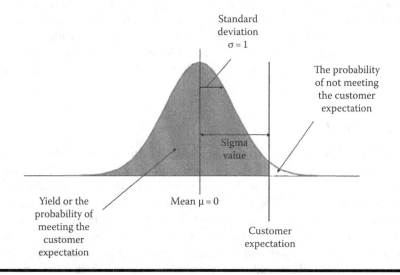

**Figure 3.5    Standard deviations and customer expectations.**

**Table 3.2  Sigma Value for Normal Data**

| Sigma Value | Yield (%) | Defect | Units |
|:---:|:---:|:---:|:---:|
| 0.0 | 50.0 | 50.0 | % |
| 0.5 | 69.1 | 30.9 | % |
| 1.0 | 84.1 | 15.9 | % |
| 1.5 | 93.3 | 6.7 | % |
| 2.0 | 97.7 | 2.3 | % |
| 2.5 | 99.4 | 0.6 | % |
| 3.0 | 99.865 | 1350 | ppm |
| 3.5 | 99.9767371 | 233 | ppm |
| 4.0 | 99.9968329 | 32 | ppm |
| 4.5 | 99.9996602 | 3 | ppm |
| 5.0 | 99.9999713 | 287 | ppb |
| 5.5 | 99.9999981 | 19 | ppb |
| 6.0 | 99.9999999 | 1 | ppb |

a 97.5% yield. Table 3.2 summarizes the exact yield and defect level for the sigma values from zero to six in 0.5 increments. An examination of Table 3.2 illustrates that the process defect level for a zero-sigma process is 50% (which one can see from Figures 3.3 to 3.5 must be true), a 3-sigma process would have a defect level of 1,350 ppm, a 4.5 sigma process would have a defect level of 3 ppm and finally a 6-sigma process would have a defect level of 1 ppb (part per billion).

Now go onto the Internet and then Google "Six Sigma calculator." There are numerous "Six Sigma calculators" available where one can enter the defect level and the calculator returns the sigma value. Start by entering a 50% defect level and most if not all calculators return a sigma value of 1.5; enter a defect level of 6.7% and the calculator returns a defect level of three. In essence, the results obtained report sigma values that are 1.5 higher over the ones presented in Table 3.2. So, what is going on?

## The 1.5 Sigma Shift

The concept of the 1.5 Sigma Shift was documented and introduced to the Quality world by Mikel J. Harry who at the time was working with Motorola Inc. Mikel was one of the patriarchs of the Six Sigma initiative developed by Motorola. Process capability studies are undertaken to determine how capable a process is of meeting customer expectations. In all cases, more capable processes have higher yields with reduced defects. We can determine from Table 3.2 that a process with a sigma value of 6, that is, a "6 Sigma" process, would have one defect per billion. Process capability studies are taken in a moment in time and typically have a limited sample size. Some quality practitioners refer to these studies as "short term" studies. There exists evidence that the capability forecasted from these "short term" studies falls short in forecasting what is going to happen over the life of a process. In other words, these "short term" studies represent the best-case answer but over time a process can degrade and thus the "long term" capability is rarely as good. This process degradation was aptly named by Mikel J. Harry as the process phenomena of "process shift and drift." His theory is summarized in a paper he published which was titled, "The Nature Of Six Sigma Quality." Personally, I buy off on the phenomena of process shift and drift as I have lots of personal experience that supports the evidence that processes do degrade over time. The question I am unable to answer though is by how much? Mikel J. Harry claimed that the process would degrade by 1.5 sigma and his claims are documented in the paper previously mentioned. Personally, it remains a theory and has not yet been proven. I am not interested in debating how much a process shifts or drifts; I agree that processes shift or drift and for this paper let's assume they shift or drift by 1.5 sigma.

## The 3.0 Sigma Shift

So, if an initial process capability is conducted (i.e., a "short term" study), we can expect that over time, the process will shift and drift and thus a "long term" study would have a lower sigma value and per Mikel J. Harry, it should be lower by 1.5 sigma. I have reviewed hundreds of process capability studies and never found one that I would view as a "long term" study. In every case, per Mikel J. Harry, the results should be offset by 1.5 sigma, if these studies are to be used to forecast what was going to happen "long term." However, in every case, where the sigma value was reported, it was offset by 1.5 sigma but in the other direction. In other words, every process with a sigma value of 1.5 was reported as 3.0 and every process with a sigma value of 4.5 was reported as 6.0.

When I would inquire, the errors would be from some software or Six Sigma calculators that have an automatic 1.5 sigma shift built into the code. In some cases, the more "enlightened" practitioners would claim that they had conducted a "long term" process capability study and thus were correctly adding 1.5 sigma to estimate the "short term" process capability. I still shake my head and wonder out loud, why would one ever do a "long term" study to estimate where a process will be "short term"; to me, it just makes no sense.

## Conclusions and Recommendations

I believe process capability metrics should be calculated and reported without any offsets. In other words, view all studies as "short term" and focus on making sure the data collected is representative of the process being studied. Let's focus our energy on making true improvements in the capabilities of our process as ultimately our customers will tell us if our improvements are on paper (e.g., via the 3-sigma trick) or if the improvements are in the field. The difference in meeting customer expectations is amazing – 1 ppb or 1,350 ppm by using the 3 Sigma trick. Which one do you want? I know which one our customers want.

**Andrew McDermott**

At Company X, they had a problem in manufacturing. They were supplying most of the top automotive companies. Their problem resulted in tens of thousands of defects. However, in their eyes, since it was only one problem, they negotiated with the customer to count it as only one defect. This enabled them to keep their "six sigma" or less than 3.4 ppm rating. We have seen this strategy used at other companies as well.

# TQM versus TCWQC

## *TQM*

Many companies have since struggled with Six Sigma implementation. The struggles started with the large TQ effort in the late 1980s and early to mid-1990s where TQ management (TQM) sadly became a fad. There are many reasons for this (see Table 3.3). Six Sigma picked up where TQM left off and some companies (like AlliedSignal) used TQM as an umbrella approach to roll out all their training initiatives. The United States failed with TQM because in most companies, it was launched as a shop floor initiative; compared to the Japanese which rolled it out as a company-wide initiative.[5] TQ's goals were the following:

■ To create a habit of improvement environment
■ Avoid setting static goals
■ Recognize all quality improvements pay for themselves
■ Shift the responsibility for quality to production
■ Recognize the next operator in the line as the internal customer
■ Refine and perfect our analytical skills
■ Focus and integrate management staff with strategy alignment, appropriate expectations and performance measures, meaningful meetings, and driving through employee desire

**Table 3.3  TQ versus Six Sigma Tools**

| *Generally Considered TQ Tools* | *Generally Considered Six Sigma Tools* |
|---|---|
| • Affinity diagram/KJ analysis | • SIPOC/COPIS |
| • Analysis of variance (ANOVA) | • Process mapping–very low level Xs and Ys |
| • Analytic hierarchy process (AHP) | • Capability indices/process capability CPk |
| • Brainstorming | • Design of experiments (DOE) |
| • Checklists | • FMEA |
| • Cause & effect—fishbone | • Kano analysis |
| • Graphical analysis charts | • Measurement systems analysis (MSA)/gage R&R |
| • Pareto analysis | • RACI diagram |
| • Empowerment models | • Regression analysis |
| • Communication models | |
| • Process mapping | |
| • Normality | |
| • Project charter | |
| • QFD/house of quality | |
| • Control charts | |

*Source:*  BIG Archives.

TCWQC (total company-wide quality control) operating practices included the following:

■ Establishing and maintaining excellent housekeeping standards
■ Maintaining equipment and tooling in excellent state of repair
■ Standardizing operations and insisting on compliance with quality standards
■ Scheduling performance at a rate of less than full capacity
■ Utilizing a well-defined problem-solving approach
■ Developing and implementing mistake-proofing devices throughout the organization

For years, we have argued for the reasons stated earlier that the Six Sigma tools are truly a subset of Lean thinking and Lean implementation tools, and they are included in the BASICS® model as such. Both Lean and Six Sigma begin with the voice of the customer (VOC). Both Lean and Six Sigma work toward quality improvement, through decreasing process variation, error, and defect reduction. However, frontline staff have a greater challenge with Six Sigma tools. Lean concepts and tools are better suited toward truly driving a cultural transformation. Lean encourages a different way of thinking, focusing on waste elimination, value-added activities, and process flow to achieve improvements.

The BASICS® model is a methodology utilized to help companies convert from batch to flow. It is then followed by the plan–do–check–act (PDCA) methodology. Improvement will never be complete as we will always invent and learn new tools. But the fundamentals of the improvement process will not change. We always say Lean is made up of two general pieces: people and tasks or one could say respect for humanity and scientific management.

## Root Cause Analysis: A3 Strategy

A great tool for root cause analysis is the tool Toyota uses called the A3 document (see Figure 3.6). It is a way to get all your information in one place on one sheet of paper. A3[6] can be used for problem-solving, for all types of proposals, and for statusing projects.

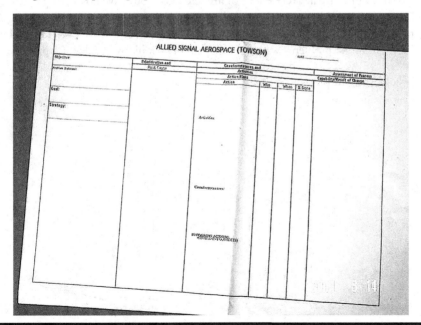

**Figure 3.6    AlliedSignal A3 document.**

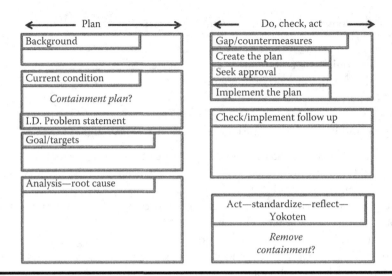

**Figure 3.7  A3 components.**

## A3s and Plan–(Control)–Do–Check–Act

The A3 report is a standardized report in a storyboard format. Its structure or layout promotes creative thinking using the PDCA methodology. The result of this thinking is placed in an A3 that may be referred to as a storyboard. The A3 organizes those thoughts to provide a shared understanding.

Let's walk through the PDCA model (see Figure 3.7). One should keep in mind that these are only templates. A3s should be utilized in whatever manner necessary to best tell the story (see Figure 3.8). A3s can be done by hand or on the computer. However, don't be fooled by a bunch of computer graphics which are not referenced or are referenced but have no bearing on the problem-solving. It is also assumed that one has a stable process prior to using A3s; otherwise, there will be no way to sustain the improvement when the A3 is completed. The first section is planning.

**(Plan)** Determine the problems with the current conditions and goals for a process:

■ Title/theme/issue/or problem and owner
■ Describe the background

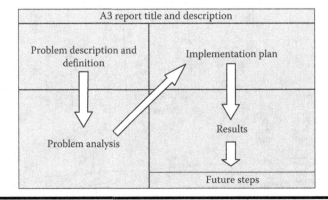

**Figure 3.8  A3 flow.**

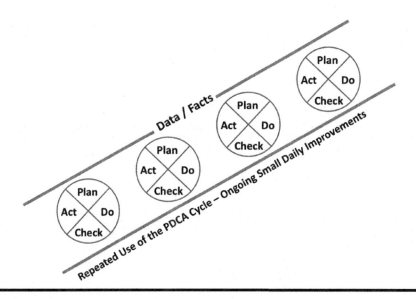

**Figure 3.9  PDCA cycles.**

- Identify the problem
- Current containment plan (if it exists)
- Analyze the current process
- State the problem and how it ties to the business condition
- Brainstorm goals/target condition
- Identify the gaps between as-is and target condition
- Develop countermeasures
- Create plan to refine and prioritize countermeasures
- Develop control plan to sustain the change with assigned owners

(**Do**) Give the changes or new process a one trial—look at it as an experiment:

- Implement plan

(**Check**) Evaluate the results—what did you learn:

- Follow Up

(**Act**) Incorporate the learning into the new process. Standardize and stabilize the change and go back to plan to repeat the process (see Figure 3.9):

- Update the standard work
- Review the process for learning and transfer to other processes or areas of the company.

Author's Note: Our experience is it takes about six or more attempts before being able to even begin to master the proper execution of an A3 (see Figure 3.10). Figure 3.11 is an example which is further down the learning curve.

There are two excellent books on this: Managing to Learn and A3 Thinking.

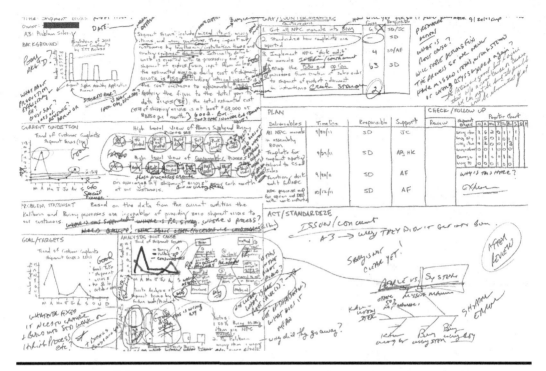

**Figure 3.10  Hand-drawn A3.**

## Problem Is Not a Bad Word

At Toyota, the word problem is not a bad word, contrary to most US companies. If we don't admit we have a problem or develop systems to expose problems, then we will never reach world class. If we continue to bury problems, they just get worse. After a long tour of a US plant by a team of Japanese executives, they were asked what they thought of the facility. The US executives were quite proud of all their improvements and indicated they had solved all their problems. The feedback from the Japanese was quite simple, "No problems, …are a big problem." A good analogy for this is the human body. If we have a problem, what do we do? We go to the doctor. What happens if we put off going to the doctor? In most cases, the problem will become worse or sometimes much worse. An undiagnosed case of a simple-to-treat strep throat can turn into a very-difficult-to-treat scarlet fever. By the time we go to the doctor, the condition may be much more complex and difficult to treat. This is true for organizations as well.

Lesson Learned: Make problems a good word. Find them, identify them, don't be afraid to call them what they are, and fix them so they don't come back.

## Knowing You Have Problems Is Good

One day at Toyota, a group of managers were being introduced to TPS. We were in an update meeting with our Lean sensei who posed the question: What are your problems today? One manager responded, "I have no problems" to which the sensei replied, "that is your biggest problem."

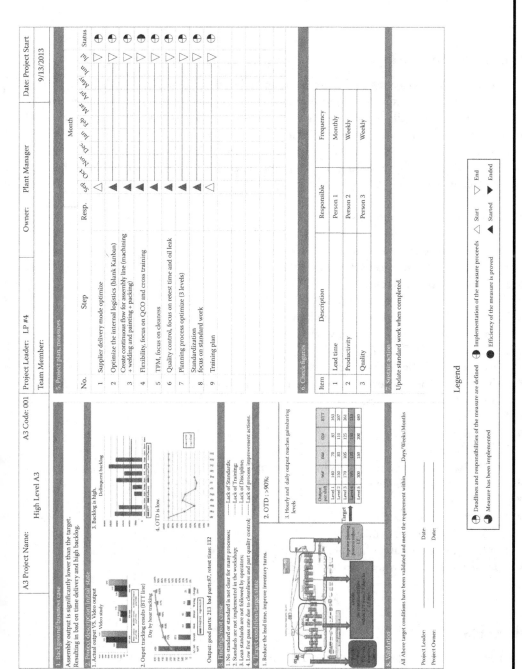

**Figure 3.11  A3 example.**

Lesson Learned: In a Lean environment of continuous improvement, there are always problems (opportunities) at all levels of the organization.[7]

## Problem Statements

Go to the floor or department and discover firsthand what the real problem is. Test (ask why) to see if the answer is a symptom of the problem or a true root cause. It is important to provide the necessary training to identify a good statement of the problem. A good problem statement should be an objective statement of the problem with any relevant data.

It should not include a solution and should not be prescriptive (ties in with Baldrige criteria). It should be verifiable. Clearly stating the scope and objectives of the project will help the team answer the following:

- Who is responsible for this issue?
- Who owns the process?
- Do we need a containment plan?
- How many parts are affected?
- Is the current standard clear?
- What is the business context and how did you decide how to tackle the problem?
- What do you know and how do you know it?
- Have you gathered and personally verified facts?
- Did you go to the Gemba?
- Have you engaged other people?
- What really is the problem—can you tie it directly to a business issue that is being felt?
- Does it address the business need?
- Is it concise?
- Is it workable?
- Is it measurable?
- Does it state a problem or process improvement (not a task)?
- Does it address consequences?
- Is it focused?
- Is it free of soft terms?
- Is it free of solution statements?
- Is it free of opinions about the problem?
- Has an appropriate owner been identified?

## Fishbones and Lean

Kaoru Ishikawa is credited with developing the fishbone tool (Figure 3.12). Today, this is known as one of the basic TQ tools. These tools are very applicable in companies. The fishbone is a tool to help identify root cause and is somewhat of a graphical 5 Whys' tool. It works by putting the problem at the head of the fishbone, then brainstorming and categorizing all the reasons for the problems (Figure 3.13). The first layer of problems, which are placed on the main branches of the fish, is normally only the symptoms of the problems we see. We then ask why? for each major

**Figure 3.12    Ishikawa Christmas Card sent to my grandfather, Charles Protzman Sr. in 1974.**

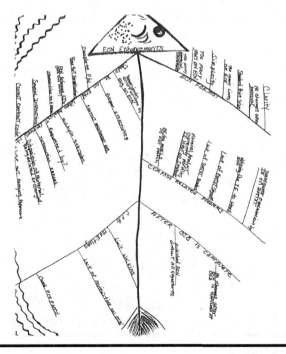

**Figure 3.13    Fishbone example.**

branch, which creates sub-branches. We ask why? until we get to the bottom branch or root cause. This tool provides a way to see all the problems in an area at a glance. Fishbones are a great tool for collecting, categorizing, and root-causing feedback from staff.

It is important to leverage tools to gain an understanding of the root cause of the problem. Identifying root causes allows for the correction of defects and is essential in working to prevent problems from reoccurring, which ultimately improves the overall process and quality of the result. If you don't know where you are going, any path will take you there.[8]

## Building Rework into the Cell

I once visited a McDonald's and noticed a sign in the parking lot. It said, "This Space RESERVED for Drive-Thru Customer 1 ONLY" (Figure 3.14). What is strange about this sign? Why would there be a parking space for a drive-thru customer? And yet a prime parking space right near the entrance at that! I could understand if this was a handicap spot. The spot is there for when we don't quite get your order right or done in time. Maybe we must brew a new pot of decaf coffee. So, you, as the drive-thru customer, must wait in a parking space! There are bigger hidden consequences to this sign, however. Once we put this sign in place, we have then admitted that we cannot solve the problem of getting the customer what they need when they need it. The process now has a rework or holding position, which takes the pressure off determining the root cause and implementing a corrective action. Now it is easy for the drive-thru server to say just pull up over there into the official drive-thru parking space. One day in May 2015, in Petersburg VA, I was asked to pull up to the reserved space. I assumed it was because I ordered 2 large cups of decaf coffee. When the person brought out my coffee, I asked her why I had to pull up since the other days prior to that was no problem. She said, "I don't know why because the coffee was sitting there ready." She said, "I guess it was because she didn't want to go over on the timer clock." When I first saw this sign, I bet my son who was with me that another sign will appear within the next six months for drive-thru customer 2. And so, it came to be. Only now the signs have the official McDonald's logo and wording on them. This means they have now

**Figure 3.14   Drive Thru Parking signs.**

**Figure 3.15    More Drive Thru signs appear—now up to five spaces at some McDonalds.**

standardized the rework and accepted it as part of their overall culture. This is called the embedded principle in systems thinking, which means that when you see a behavior or problem in one place or one situation, it is probably embedded in the culture throughout the company. Since that time, I have now even seen Parking space #5 (see Figure 3.15).

Authors Note: Drive Thru Parking is an example of within process storage.

## Poka Yoke

Poka yoke is a Japanese term that means fail-safing or mistake proofing. A poka yoke is any mechanism in a Lean process that helps your team members avoid (yokeru[9]) mistakes (poka). Its purpose is to eliminate product defects by preventing, correcting, or drawing attention to errors as they occur (see Figure 3.16). The concept was formalized, and the term adopted by Dr. Shigeo Shingo. It was originally described as baka yoke, but as this means fool proofing (or idiot proofing), the name was changed to the milder poka yoke.[10] The idea of mistake proofing started with Toyoda in the spinning loom factory.[11] Since then, the Toyota Motor Corporation has spent the last 60 years improving on the concept and always striving for perfection. In the example in Figure 3.17, when the cotter pin is removed, the shadow of it remains.

## Shingo's First Poka Yoke[12]

### *Problem*

While visiting the Yamada Electric plant in 1961, Dr. Shingo was told of a problem the factory had with one of its products. Part of the product was a small switch with two push buttons supported by two springs. Occasionally, the worker assembling the switch would forget to insert a spring under

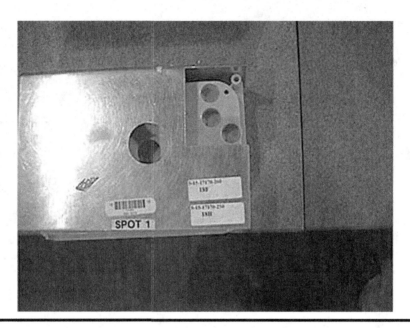

**Figure 3.16 Mistake-proofing device for assembly to make sure bottles are placed in correct holes in tray. (From BIG Archives.)**

each push button. Sometimes the error would not be discovered until the unit reached a customer, and the factory would have to dispatch an engineer to the customer site to disassemble the switch, insert the missing spring, and reassemble the switch. This problem of the missing spring was both costly and embarrassing. Management at the factory would warn the employees to pay more attention to their work, but despite everyone's best intentions, the missing spring problem would eventually reappear.

**Figure 3.17  Mistake proofing example—when the cotter pin is removed, there is a shadow left behind.**

## Shingo Solution

Dr. Shingo suggested a solution that became his first poka-yoke device: in the old method, a worker began by taking two springs out of a large parts box and then assembled a switch. In the new approach, a small dish is placed in front of the parts box and the worker's first task is to take two springs out of the box and place them on the dish. Then the worker assembles the switch. If any spring remains on the dish, then the worker knows that he or she has forgotten to insert it.

Lesson Learned: The new procedure eliminated the problem of the missing springs.

# Poka Yoke PDCA Steps

Poka yoke can be applied to any process whether shop floor or transactional. It can be used for any type of process error:

1. (Plan) Describe the defect or potential defect. Use observation, video, or statistics (i.e., Pareto chart) to identify the opportunity for a defect or, more important, for the cause (error) to occur. Show the defect rate. Operate where defect is or can be discovered. Identify where the defect is made.
2. Run the problem through the 5 Whys. Become the thing in the process. Detail the sequence of events documented in the standard. Watch the operation being done and detail the steps that differ from the standard. Understand the ways a process or a machine can fail.
3. Brainstorm solutions—involve everyone.
4. Decide the right poka-yoke approach. Identify the mistake-proof device required to prevent the error or defect.
   a. Control device (prevent an error)
   b. Warning device (highlight an error was made)
   c. A poka yoke can be electrical, mechanical, procedural, visual, human, or any other form that highlights or prevents errors during a process step.
5. (Do) Train the operator if necessary and implement the poka yoke.
6. (Check) To make sure it is working.
7. (Act) Update the standard work (if necessary) or process documentation. Depending on the device, determine if any preventive or predictive maintenance is required and add to the total productive maintenance (TPM) checklist.

# Self-Check Inspection

The first step to poka yoke is self-inspection. This is where each operator inspects his or her own work.

Definition—A self-check occurs when the operator who performs the work checks the work before passing it on to the next process (i.e., a push-pull check on an electrical connector to ensure the clip is locked as part of the process). This is self-inspection by the operator through sensory and visual cues.

**Pluses**

- Represents 100% inspection
- Makes instant correction possible
- Less psychological resistance to self-discovery than supervisor or even peer discovery

**Minus**

■ Operators may sometimes make compromises on quality characteristics or forget to perform checks.

The next level is called successive check inspection. This is where each operator inspects the work of the previous operators in addition to his or her own work.

## Successive Check Inspection

Definition

A successive check occurs after the previous operator has performed his or her work and that work is checked by the next (successive) operator downstream.

**Pluses**

■ Usually catches any mistake or defect overlooked by the first operator during self-check
■ Usually builds a spirit of cooperation between operators and teamwork in problem-solving

**Minus**

■ Successive checks and self-checks can function only as an informative inspection if corrective action occurs after the point of error, as compared to at the point of error.

The next level is 100% inspection at the source. This inspection is done by a machine, not a person. The only way to get to zero defects is to have 100% automated inspection at the source and catch the mistake (the error at the source), not the defect. This is the basic idea behind jidoka. In the example in Figure 3.18, there are two doors to a kitchen in a retirement home restaurant. The door on the right (with no handle) is IN and on the left is OUT.

## Example of Mistake Proofing (Poka Yoke)

Our house had an attached garage. The door from the garage to the house was right next to my office. When one of my children would come into the garage during the winter, they, like most kids, left the door open. The realization of the door being open was delivered by a cold blast and

Figure 3.18   In and out doors—mistake proof example in kitchen.

then a steady stream of freezing cold air into my office. Over the course of the next couple of months, I tried everything I could think of to get the kids to shut the door when they came in. We talked to them nicely. We explained why we needed the door closed when they came in and then moved to the frustration mode accompanied by shouting at them to close the door every time, they came in. The next step was looking at some type of punishment or negative consequences to get them to pay attention and listen to us. We made them come back each time to close the door. Even this didn't work. Then, one day as I was strolling through the local hardware store, I noticed an item called a self-closing hinge. I purchased the hinge and installed it immediately upon my arrival at home. Once installed, everyone's life in the house returned to peace and calm. When the kids came in, the door closed itself, no rush of air, no punishments, and life was good! Installing the hinge was such a simple fix; yet the first thought is normally to blame those in the system whom we perceive are creating the problems when in fact, the system is the problem.

Other poka-yoke examples are the following:

1. Fueling process of a car has six error-proofing devices:
   a. Insert in the gas tank keeps leaded-fuel nozzle from being inserted.
   b. Tether does not allow loss of gas cap. Some cars have eliminated the gas cap altogether.
   c. Gas cap has a ratchet sound to signal proper tightness and that prevents overtightening.
   d. Gas pump handle has automatic shut off.
   e. Computer on the gas pump checks your credit card by asking for a zip code.
   f. Gas gauge has an arrow pointing to the side where the gas tank is located.
2. New lawn mowers are required to have a safety bar on the handle that must be pulled back to start the engine. If you let go of the safety bar, the mower blade stops in 3 seconds or less.

## Corrective Action Request

Most companies have what we call the illusion of quality. Very seldom do we find a company that doesn't treat corrective actions as more than just going through the motions to check off the box. The most popular response to any corrective action request (CAR) is to add in another inspection. In many companies, they don't even bother getting to the root cause; they just add in inspection steps. Inspection is really a non-value-added process. Gilbreth and Dr. Shingo broke out inspection in the TIPS process just to identify it as a problem or step to eliminate. Our overall goal is to eliminate the need for inspection, which is somewhat of a paradox wherein the only way to obtain zero defects is to do inspection at every step, that is, poka yoke and jidoka—where one machine checks the previous operation to make sure it was done, then does the step, then double checks itself. The other secret to eliminate mistakes is to surface the mistakes. How do you create an environment where the worker can tell you about a mistake? Create an environment that celebrates people making mistakes and/or telling about it. This is a hard transition to make especially in the healthcare world. We need to work on creating the attitude of "how can we all work on fixing this together!"

### Negative Approach

These are inevitable

- People make mistakes.
- People place blame.

- We normally don't detect defects until final inspection.
- Sampling inspection.
- When some defects reach the customer, we call these "escapes."

## Positive Approach

How defects can be eliminated

- Create the environment where we surface mistakes and celebrate them.
- Ask why five times and use the 5W's and 2H's?
- Apply mistake-proofing devices for 100% inspection.
- Poka Yoke and Jidoka.
- Just do it.

Errors can be eliminated! Any kind of mistake people make can be reduced and even eliminated. People make fewer mistakes if they are supported by a production system based on the principle that errors can always be prevented. Remember, blame just hides defects and the root cause.

# Integration of Lean Tools

## A Hot Cup of Joe

What do you notice that is similar about the mugs Figures 3.19 and 3.20? Both are ceramic, and both are coffee mugs from a wonderful breakfast café known as the Blue Dolphin located in the Centre Shops and on St. Armands Circle in Long Boat Key, Florida. Notice, both cups have the same logo and picture on the front. The mugs come in two colors, white on blue and blue on white,

**Figure 3.19  Mistake proofing example for decaf cups of coffee.**

**Figure 3.20  Mistake proofing example for regular cups of coffee.**

and are for sale in their gift shop. However, there is something unique about these two cups other than the color. Can you guess?

What is unique is what the cups represent to the staff of the restaurant. The white on blue mug represents customers who ordered decaf coffee and the blue on white represents customers drinking regular coffee. We first stumbled on this observation when one of the staff noticed my cup was low and filled my cup with decaf coffee. I asked her how she knew I was drinking decaf when she was not our waitress. She said she knew because I had the (white on) blue cup. I immediately thought to myself, what a great system!

Jeanie, a waitress at the Blue Dolphin, states "We love it because we don't have to wait for customers to finish a conversation or interrupt them. Our goal is to fill their coffee cup before they ask for a refill and we immediately know if they are drinking regular or decaf." Brandon, another Blue Dolphin employee, in agreement states "I came up with this idea 15 years ago when I noticed how long it took one person to give coffee service to the restaurant. Not only were the customers not interrupted, but the whole process took 1/4 the time and everyone always had fresh hot coffee. It is such a simple system, makes it easier for us to do our jobs and we believe helps keep our customers coming back. They are always surprised that we know which type of coffee they are drinking, not to mention our coffee is good too."

The color of the cup allows the staff to work together as a team, and when any one of them is free, they can fill up coffee cups for everyone in the restaurant. The customers always get fresh, hot refills because they don't have to wait to tell their specific server to refill their cup or stop their conversation to remind them or another server which one to pour.

It later dawned on me how visual controls support mistake proofing. It doesn't mean they can't put the wrong coffee in the cup, but it certainly decreases the opportunity of mistakes while increasing the flexibility of the staff along with their customer satisfaction levels.

Lesson Learned: This is a simple example of how Lean tools can be easily and readily integrated to create simple, foolproof systems designed around the customer's needs. In this case, visual displays (i.e., the supplier's logo and name) that support their marketing or brand image are combined with the visual controls (i.e., blue on white vs. white on blue coffee mug), along with the level of the coffee in the cup, which triggers the need to be filled, to help mistake proof a process, increase the flexibility of the staff, and promote teamwork, who exceed their customer expectations, resulting in happy customers who keep coming back. Some of you may be thinking this is a silly example. Think about the next time you must ask for a refill, and then during a conversation at a critical business meeting, stop to answer your server's question about which type of coffee you are drinking, or if you are like me, interrupt your conversation to stop the server from pouring regular coffee in your cup to tell them you are drinking decaf not regular coffee. At Towson Diner in Maryland, they put a doily under the cup for the decaf coffees. At another Holmes Beach, Florida, local restaurant, Peaches, the orders are always taken from left to right starting with the first person on the left side of the table. This way, the servers never have to ask who ordered what (unless the patrons change seats).

## To Err Is Human

For those of you Six Sigma black belts out there, let us ask you a question. What is the sigma level of humans? If Six Sigma is 3.4 defects per million opportunities (with a 1.5 sigma shift), how many defects does the average human make per million? I have never been able to get a black belt or master black belt to answer this question, but I would guess there aren't many of us that didn't make a mistake today or yesterday or the day before. So, if humans on their best day might be one or three sigma, one can reasonably jump to the conclusion that if humans are involved in the process, there is a high probability that there is going to be a mistake found somewhere. This applies to inspectors as well. How many inspectors catch every mistake (see Figure 3.21)? In airports, even a well-trained highly skilled inspector is going to miss something. Have you ever gotten something

**Figure 3.21   Sign reminder.**

through the baggage inspection you shouldn't have? The only way to guarantee security at the airport is to have the machine catch the problem, not the operator.

Ten types of human mistakes[13]:

1. Forgetfulness
2. Misunderstanding
3. Wrong identification
4. Lack of experience
5. Willful (ignoring rules or procedure)
6. Inadvertent or sloppiness
7. Slowness
8. Lack of standardization
9. Surprise (unexpected machine operations, etc.)
10. Intentional (sabotage)

What is interesting about this list is when one extrapolates this to the business world, how many corrective actions are based on adding a human inspection element into the process? Adding human inspection may be a short-term fix but in the long run can't guarantee even 3 sigma quality.

Lesson Learned: Humans cannot physically inspect quality into a product or process.

# Types of Control and Warning Devices[14]

Warning devices alert the operator to a problem but don't prevent the error or the defect. Control devices shut down the operation or don't allow it to proceed until it is corrected.

Contact device: contact is established between the device and the product:

1. Plugs
2. House and car keys
3. Camcorder batteries

Fixed-value method: part must be a certain weight or it won't work:

1. Lot size
2. Egg carton

Motion step method: product must pass inspection before proceeding to the next step:

1. Bar coders
2. Garage door sensor beam
3. Motion detector lights

### Design-out defect

The goal is to eliminate errors by designing your products or processes Lean. Once you clean up the areas and standardize the work, then the variation sticks out. Six Sigma tools are designed to fix the variation. The Lean tools and Six Sigma tools integrate nicely. However, Six Sigma tools are only a steppingstone to zero defects.

## Design the Control Plan

Including the control plan (see Table 3.4) at this stage is consistent with Dr. Shingo's approach (vs. Deming) where it becomes part of the plan phase of P(control)DCA. The control plan is a spin-off of the block diagram. At this stage, we need to ask ourselves for each process box the following:

■ Who owns the process?
■ What is the process capability?
■ How do we make sure we are starting on a good part?

**Table 3.4  Control Plan**

| Characteristic (Y) | Critical Inputs | How the "Y" Is Set | How the "Y" Is Measured (Control) | What to Change or Fix if "Y" Is Unacceptable | What Parameter Is Effected if "Y" Is Unacceptable |
|---|---|---|---|---|---|
| Properly centered spring pin | Arbor press | Operator pushing pin with arbor press | Visual | Recenter pin in spring | Balance of motor |
| Properly retained pin | Adhesive Oven time Oven temp. | Apply adhesive and insert pin | Visual fillet of adhesive | Reapply adhesive | Balance of motor |
| Spring contained in rotor in correct direction | Spring gloves | Spring winding fixture 2387 | Visual | | Motor running direction |
| Endbell properly spaced from spring | Shims | Insert shims Press endbell against shims | Visual— four shims | | Motor balance Drift |
| Key flush with OD of arbor | Adhesive | Pressed in with tool | Visual | Reinstall key | Spring being kinked Balance |
| No adhesive on top of arbor | Q-tip Water | Wipe all excess adhesive off the arbor after installation of key | Visual | Remove excessive adhesive | Spring lay Balance |

**Table 3.4** *(Continued)*   **Control Plan**

| Characteristic (Y) | Critical Inputs | How the "Y" Is Set | How the "Y" Is Measured (Control) | What to Change or Fix if "Y" Is Unacceptable | What Parameter Is Effected if "Y" Is Unacceptable |
|---|---|---|---|---|---|
| Motor number on proper side | Direction of "C" hook | Diagram in work instructions | Visual | Put number on other side | Potential of motor being installed backwards |
| Motor with concentric bearings | Endbells Arbor Application of adhesive | Assembly fixture 11528 Preload weight Preload fixture | | | Balance Motor Speed |
| Motor with no cocked bearings | | | Fixture 11528 | | |
| Motor with endplay of 0.0001" to 0.0008" | Oven | Assembly fixture CC1156 | CC11556 endplay checking fixture | Flush bearings Tonk | Motor speed Kickoff speed |

*Source:* BIG Archives.

- ■ How do we know we are not passing on a bad part?
- ■ What is the output expected from the station (Six Sigma defines this as the Big Y)?
    - How do we measure it?
    - Can we measure it?
    - Do we have the right equipment and is it capable of measuring it?
    - Do we need to track the measure (SPC)?
    - Does it require operator judgment?
    - What are the critical inputs for the process box to obtain the Big Y (Six Sigma calls these Xs)?
- ■ How is the Big Y (output) set?
- ■ Are there little Ys (outputs) we must take into account?
- ■ How are the Ys (outputs) measured?
- ■ How are we going to control it?
- ■ Can we predict when it will go out of control?
- ■ Can we physically stop the process if it goes out of control?
- ■ Will the operators stop the line?
- ■ Will the machine shut down if it makes a mistake or crashes?
- ■ What to change or fix if a Y becomes unacceptable?
- ■ What parameters are affected if Y becomes unacceptable?

■ Do we have a review process as part of PDCA if the process goes out of control?
■ Do we have visual controls in place?
■ Will the process make itself immediately visible if it goes out of control?

The control plan is developed to get the product team including line personnel, team leader, and supervisor to think about how they are going to make sure they always produce a good quality product with a goal of zero defects. If we think back to the block diagram, the ideal line will involve designing an overall process to ensure we never pass along a bad part from one block to the next. This sounds easy but is very difficult to do. It is probably worthwhile revisiting our discussion of jidoka here. What would it take to mistake proof each step? How do we get the process to signal us if an abnormal condition appears? What changes to the equipment can be made to make it smart?

## Waterfall Chart

This is an example of the 5 Whys being applied from the Pareto chart to the root cause (see Figures 3.22a and b and 3.23).

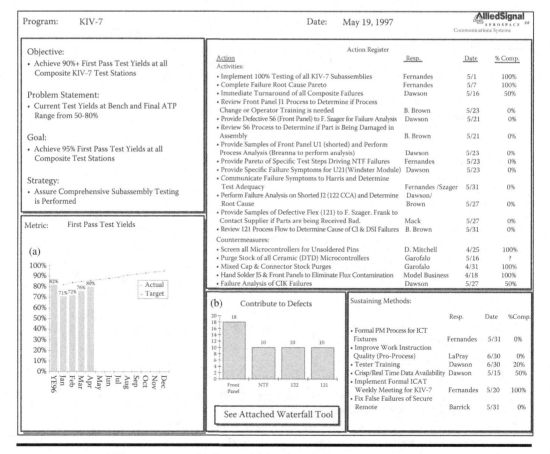

Figure 3.22 (a and b) Pareto waterfall example. *(Continued)*

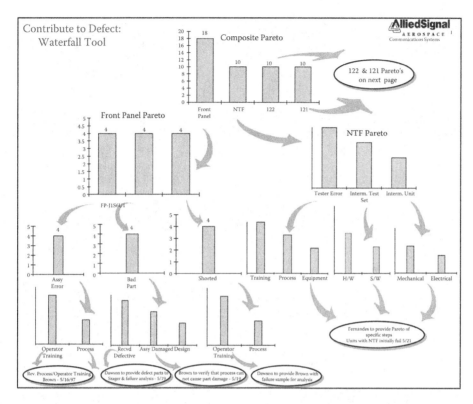

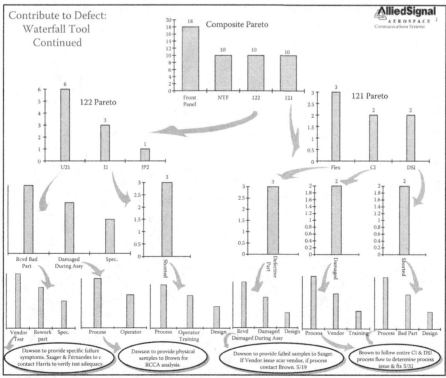

**Figure 3.22  Waterfall tool referenced in figure 3.22a.**

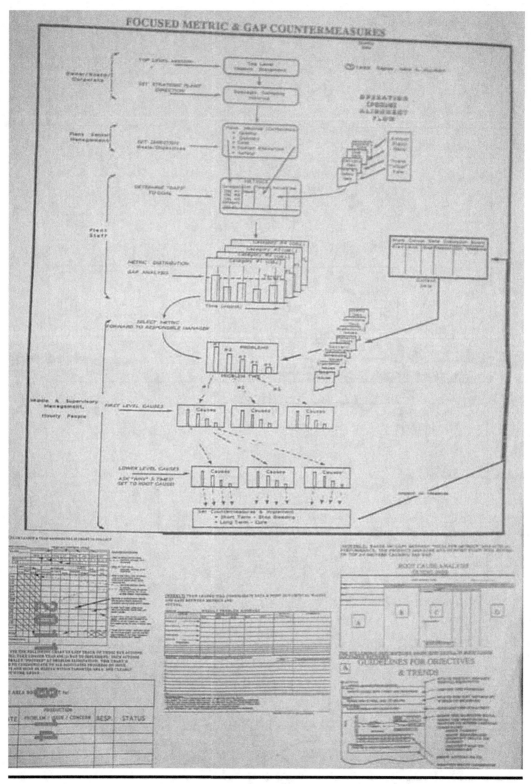

**Figure 3.23    Waterfall chart explanation. Includes 5 Whys gap and counter measure example.**

## Examples of Cause and Effect

1. Process: Car crosses over railroad track.
2. Defect: Train collides with car at railroad crossing.
3. Warning device: Use a sign and/or sound to warn the operator.
4. Control device: Put down gates to prevent the car from crossing.
5. Design-out defect: Design a bridge over or under to the railroad track, which prevents the error and the defect.

Lesson Learned: Goal is defect prevention at the source.

## Chapter Questions

1. What is a Pareto chart and how is it used to support root cause analysis?
2. Are Six Sigma and Lean different? How do they relate to each other?
3. How are warning and control devices used?
4. Is self-check inspection permissible? What are the benefits, if any?
5. PDCA is often an acronym in Lean implementation. What is the relationship to Lean?
6. How does poka yoke differ from PDCA?
7. How do Deming and Dr. Shingo differ in approach to quality?
8. Can poka yoke be used outside of manufacturing systems? If so, provide two examples.
9. Why is mistake proofing important?
10. What are some of the culture barriers to mistake proofing?
11. What is a waterfall chart?
12. What role do the 5 Whys play in mistake proofing?
13. What role do control charts play in mistake proofing?
14. What is the mistake proofing goal with Lean? a. Six Sigma b. 3.4 defects per million c. zero defects d. none of these
15. Are zero defects possible?
16. Name some mistake proofing devices which we use every day but probably don't realize it.
17. What are the three types of defects?
18. What is the difference between TQM and TCWQC?
19. What did you learn from this chapter?

## Notes

1. http://www.isixsigma.com/index.php?option=com_k2&view=item&id=1505:the-history-of-six-sigma&Itemid=156
2. Ken Place is a Lean Six Sigma master black belt full-time consultant with the University of Illinois Business and Industry Services. Ken has over 16 years of experience working in the auto industry supplying US and Japanese automakers. His experience comes from both manufacturing and quality capacities. Ken has worked with facilities throughout the United States, Europe, and Mexico to implement effective quality management systems compliant to QS9000, ISO 9001, and TS16949 as well as environmental management systems compliant to ISO 14001.
3. Talk to MWCMC by Gary Convis, April 2008, 1993; Jeffrey Liker, Toyota Way (New York: McGraw Hill), 2005.

4. White paper by Andy McDermott, Six Sigma Master Blackbelt, Master Lean Practitioner, Former Asst. Plant Manager at Lutron® Friday, February 14, 2014.
5. Based on the meeting between C. Protzman and Yoshio Kondo in 1996. Professor Kondo is the author of the book Company Wide Quality Control (Zenshateki Hinshitsu Kanri) (JUSE Press). Professor Yoshio Kondo—http://www.hk5sa.com/tqm/tqmex/kondo.htm
6. A book that highlights this approach is Understanding A3 Thinking: A Critical Component of Toyota's PDCA Management.
7. Story submitted by Professor James Bond.
8. David OKoren, Lean master black belt, AlliedSignal (Honeywell).
9. http://dict.regex.info Japanese to English dictionary, http://www.saiga-jp.com, http://thequalityportal.com/pokayoke.htm. Taiichi Ohno, Toyota Production System (Portland, OR: Productivity Press), 1988.
10. Harry Robinson (1997) Using Poka Yoke Techniques for Early Defect Detection, http://facultyweb.berry.edu/jgrout/pokasoft.html. Retrieved May 4, 2009. Shigeo Shingo and Andrew P. Dillon, A Study of the Toyota Production System from an Industrial Engineering Viewpoint (Portland, OR: Productivity Press), 1989, pp. 21–22. John R. Grout and Brian T. Downs, A Brief Tutorial on Mistake-Proofing, Poka Yoke, and ZQC, MistakeProofing.com. http://www.mistakeproofing.com/tutorial.html. Retrieved May 4, 2009. Poka yoke or Mistake Proofing: Overview. The Quality Portal, http://thequalityportal.com/pokayoke.htm. Retrieved May 5, 2009. Nikkan Kogyo Shimbun, Poka Yoke: Improving Product Quality by Preventing Defects (Portland, OR: Productivity Press), 1988, pp. 111, 209. Pokayoke. The Manufacturing Advisory Service in the Southwest (MAS-SW), http://www.swmas.co.uk/info/index.php/ Poka Yoke. Retrieved May 2, 2009.
11. Shigeo Shingo, Zero Quality Control (Portland, OR: Productivity Press), 1986.
12. Shigeo Shingo, Zero Quality Control (Portland, OR: Productivity Press), 1986.
13. Submitted by James Bond.
14. Charles Protzman Sr. and Homer Sarasohn, CCS Training Manual, 1948–1949 (prepared by Nick Fisher and Suzanne Lavery of ValueMetrics, Australia), p. 138.

# Additional Readings

Anderson, M.J. and Whitcomb, P.J. 2007. DOE Simplified. Portland, OR: Productivity Press.
ASQ. 1996. SPC Reference Guide. Milwaukee WI: Resource Engineering.
Beauregard, M.R. 1992. Practical Guide to SPC. New York: Vannostrand Rinholdt.
Gabor, A. 1990. The Man Who Discovered Quality. New York: Penguin Books.
Harbour, J.L. 1996. Cycle Time Reduction. New York: Quality Resources.
Hinckley, C.M. 2002. Make No Mistakes. Portland, OR: Productivity Press.
Juran, J.M. 1995. A History of Managing For Quality. Milwaukee, WI: ASQC Quality Press.
Kenney, C. 2008. The Best Practice, How the New Quality Movement Is Transforming Medicine. New York: Perseus Book Group.
McDermott, R.E. 2000. Employee Driven Quality. New York: Resource Engineering.
Nemeto, M. 1987. Total Quality Control for Management. Englewood Cliffs, NJ: Prentice Hall.
Shimbun., N.K. 1988. Poka Yoke. Portland, OR: Productivity Press.
Shingo, S. 1986. Zero Quality Control. Stamford, CT: Productivity Press.
Shinkle, G.A. et al. 2000. Transforming Strategy into Success. Boston, MA: Harvard Business School.
Shook, J. 2008. Managing to Learn. Cambridge, MA: Lean Enterprise Institute.
Sobek, D.K. 2008. Understanding A3 Thinking: A Critical Component of Toyota's PDCA Management System. Boca Raton, FL: Productivity Press.

# Chapter 4

# Lean +QDIP, and Huddles[1]

Most people spend more time and energy going around problems than in trying to solve them.

**Henry Ford**

## Huddle Meetings and +QDIP Boards

### Driving Good Business Behavior

The welder from the United Steelworkers (USW) union slipped between the focus factory's manufacturing engineer and customer service representative to speak with the focus factory's production planner. The focus factory's daily huddle meeting just ended, and he wanted to know why she had put two nozzles into work on the welding floor when all the parts for completion were not there. The welder would now need to set them off to the side. He added that bringing in the major materials for the build-to-order line two weeks in advance (too soon in his opinion) would not help their collective bonus payout, which was based on return on assets (ROA). His welding skills were considerably more practiced than his diplomatic communication skills (several choice adjectives of his encounter have been left out); however, several actions were on display for those who cared to notice:

1. Team members were starting to appreciate the waste of putting an order into work and then pulling it out of the line for lack of parts.
2. Team members were realizing there was visibility and transparency to these issues now that it was being measured.
3. Team members were taking ownership even at the cost of some disconcerting conversations and conversations were taking place.

A few days later, as the focus factory manager of another value stream in the same business unit kicked off the huddle meeting at exactly 9:15 am by announcing and recording yesterday's orders, a USW assembler inquired about the seasonality of the heating equipment since summer was over

DOI: 10.4324/9781003185819-4

and schools were starting up again. The cultural fly wheel[2] was starting to turn and was in step with the quantitative improvement seen in delivery, productivity, and inventory in the past 6 months.

## Visual Management

Visual management in the form of cell, focus factory, and business metric displays is critical to sustaining the continuous improvement cycle and gemba walks. The cycle starts with the following:

- An abnormality observed
- Root cause determination
- Analysis
- Implement the improvement
- Standardization
- Update the standard work (Sustain)

Metric displays and daily huddle meetings, at the gemba, help in each stage of the cycle and are critical to observing/identifying and eliminating the abnormalities. Metrics provide the quantitative data to drive behavior assuming there is relevancy and genuine interest shown by business leadership. Huddle boards along with +QDIP boards (Quality, Delivery, Inventory, Productivity + Safety/5S) are two great tools for visual management, communication, and—most importantly—continuous improvement.

> If nobody pays attention, people stop caring.
>
> **Jack Stack**[3]

## Out of Date Metrics May Be Worse Than No Metrics

While walking the floor at Company X in November with the plant manager, I noticed a total productive maintenance (TPM) board with an April date. I asked who is responsible for maintaining/validating actions on this board. Some moments passed and the comment was "I don't know who is responsible," replied the plant manager. After the tour, I went and asked the operators, who were responsible to complete the board, and their comment was "if management doesn't care, why should I?" Although not part of the Lean initiative, we got this back on track. I went over to the board on several of my following visits and confirmed the board was being used properly noting morale in the area improved significantly.

## Tiered Meetings Concept

Think of tiered meetings as the governance element of an operating system. It enables accountability (a core element needed for sustainment and driving culture) and culture change through the following principles:

1. Focus on the process.
2. Empowerment and engagement of those who do the work.

3. Standard work is in place and updated regularly.
   a. Operators
   b. Supervisors
   c. Engineers (quality and manufacturing)
   d. Managers
4. Follow Shingo's 1-3-10 rule.
   ○ Understand board purpose in 1 second
   ○ Understand current status in 3 seconds
   ○ Understand countermeasures applied in 10 seconds
5. Implement visual management everywhere.
6. Use gemba walks to link elements of the operating system together.
7. Utilize simple problem-solving as issues or trends arise with a focus on using the scientific method.
8. Quick escalation of bad news or misses to metrics.

The structure of tiered meetings is to allow the teams to focus on leading indicators at each level of leadership. It encourages the flow of communication from the floor to leadership and from leadership to the floor. The number of tiers will vary by company. Below is an example of a tiered stand-up meeting structure:

# Tier 1

This meeting is a 3-to-5-minute touch point with the manufacturing line or cell. The intent is to use open ended questions to engage the team to gain their input on an issue, recognizing someone based on the right behavior not a result, and informing the team of the plan of action for today. This meeting should happen at the start of the shift.

# Tier 2

This 10 minute meeting happens after the first hour of production is completed. This is done with the core team, ME, QE, planning, maintenance, and led by the supervisor and should be no more than 5–10 minutes. The intent of this meeting is to use the day-by-hour board to identify issues from the first hour and trends based on the last shift. The group leader identifies issues that will not be resolved by end of shift or issues that may or will prevent the shift from hitting their targets. These issues are then escalated to the Tier 3 meeting. The location of this meeting is important. It needs to be held at the day-by-hour board location so the actions can be tracked and the team knows their priorities. This will also allow the area leaders to follow up with coaching or resources when the leader performs their gemba walks.

# Tier 3

This 10 minute meeting happens daily and focuses on the daily trends based on the summary of all shift's performance utilizing the month by the day chart. The team is managing the daily trends to ensure that the weekly targets are being achieved. The attendees are the same as tier two but with the addition of the area manager. Daily trends that cannot be corrected by the end of the week are escalated to tier 4. The escalation may be an awareness, or it may be an ask for additional support needed to resolve the issue.

## Tier 4

This 5 minute meeting happens weekly with the area managers to include the engineering manager, quality manager, maintenance manager, and planning manager. Functional directors may attend to listen and observe at this meeting. This meeting is led by the Operations Director and the focus is to look at weekly trends that may impact the monthly performance of the site. The issues are prioritized for alignment on resources and actions are tracked to ensure issues are being resolved and understood. This is also where managers may adjust their standard work with regard to where and the theme of their gemba walks. Issues that will impact the month are escalated to tier 5 and decisions on priorities and support allocation is then shared with tier 3.

## Tier 5

This 30 minute meeting happens monthly with the directors and managers. The site's monthly performance and trends are reviewed. This meeting is led by the Site Director or Plant Manager. The issues are prioritized for alignment on resources and actions are tracked to ensure issues are being resolved and understood. This is where directors may adjust their standard work with regard to where along with the theme of their gemba walks. Issues that will impact the quarter are escalated to tier 6 and decisions on priorities and support allocation is also then shared with tier 4.

## Tier 6

This 30 minute meeting is held monthly by the Divisional Leader. The site directors, quality directors, and finance directors along with the divisional leaders' direct reports all attend. The focus of this meeting is understanding the constraints or themes the division is facing and what to prioritize and if additional resources need to be reallocated to resolve issues. The information and decisions are then cascaded to Tier 5.

The key thing to remember is that a red metric is the result of a process that is not yielding the desired outcome. How a leader reacts to this will drive the culture. If the leader is casting blame on people and not helping the team see the real issue(s) and help their approach on solving problems, the teams will shut down and no longer bring up issues or even assist in helping to resolve the issue. If the leader focuses on the process at the right level then the team will respond with engagement. Remember, all outcomes are the consequence of a process. It is nearly impossible for even good people to consistently produce ideal results with a poor process both inside and outside the organization. There is a natural tendency to blame the people involved when something goes wrong or is less than ideal, when in reality the vast majority of the time the issue is management's fault due to allowing an imperfect process. If you blame the people, you will never find the root cause.

## Huddle Boards and Daily Huddle Characteristics

The 5-to-10-minute daily huddle is the best way to start the day, communicate any necessary information, and share performance against business-critical metrics. At the beginning of the day, there should be a leadership huddle, which is led by the leader of the business. Managers, supervisors, and area leaders should all be present and participate. The huddle should be very tightly scripted and not be allowed to turn into a long-winded meeting. The leadership huddle should be a stand-up meeting held in front of the overall business (or overall site in the case of a multisite business) huddle board. The script for the leadership huddle should be a quick review of the daily metrics, a communication of any important announcements or visitors, a quick review of questions from lower level huddles, and then a *learning minute* given by someone knowledgeable about the topic.

## Daily Metrics Review

At the top of the leadership huddle board should be the five or six most important daily metrics, which will help drive the business to meet its yearly goals. The daily metrics commonly include the following:

- Daily sales (revenue)
- Daily bookings
- Safety
- Daily quality
- On-time delivery (OTD)

The metrics are purposefully broken down to the daily level to make the review meaningful and to allow the team to take corrective actions in their own areas when the previous day's metrics were not achieved. The huddle board should be designed to ensure the leader can quickly communicate the previous day's performance for each metric and should also be visual to show the performance trends for the month.

### Visual Means It Is on A Board Where Everyone Can See It, Not in A Computer!

Below each daily metric for the current month should be a graph of the monthly performance of the metric for the current year and an action tracker for actions to correct poor performance (Figure 4.1).

## Communication of Important Announcements or Visitor

This huddle is also the best way to communicate important information to the leaders of each team in the building. This info can be anything that is important for everyone in the facility to know such as upcoming events (i.e., company lunches, charity drives, open enrollment for benefits), upcoming audits, new hire announcements, or milestone employment anniversaries. The leaders, during the huddle, will pass this information on to their teams at their

**Figure 4.1 Tom Turton, Master Black Belt, Focus Factory Manager, formerly with ITT and Xylem conducting a +QDIP meeting.**

team-level huddle. The huddle leader should also ask everyone if there are any important visitors visiting the facility soon. The leader writes the name of the planned visitors on the huddle board in the visitors section.

## Questions from the Team-Level Huddles

The leader will also ask if there were any questions or concerns raised at the team-level huddles that the team leader could not answer or address. This practice lays the groundwork for open communication and greatly increases the chances that team members' questions and concerns are addressed. In general, there is more than one person who has the same question or concern, especially in a larger organization. If the leader can answer the question or concern immediately, they will ensure the answer is carried back to the team at the team huddle. If the question can't be answered immediately, the leader should give a date by which an answer will be given. This open communication builds trust and builds an environment where everyone feels they can openly ask questions and will have them answered.

## Learning Minute

The learning minute is an opportunity to hold a short daily training on a topic that is important to the business. The learning minute is a 1- or 2-minutes training session to teach everyone more about the business. Usual topics for these mini-training sessions are finance terms, product applications, safety talks, Lean concepts, or customer information. Topics are not limited to these categories and can be on any topic that would benefit everyone in the company. The goal of the learning minute is to spread knowledge with respect to the business, to enhance employee engagement, lay the foundation for accountable employees, and ensure staff is involved in the business.

Engaged employees are more likely to take on stretch objectives and make decisions that will be in the best interest of the business. These learning minutes are often delivered at the leadership huddle by a team member who is most knowledgeable about the topic, such as a subject matter or functional expert. For example, the controller may give the learning minute on any finance terms. The people who attend the leadership huddle then lead their own team huddle communicating the learning minute to their team at their huddle. This approach yields multiple paybacks as we not only disseminate the information but also encourage the leader-as-teacher concept—one of the pillars of a learning organization.

## Team-Level Huddles

Team-level huddles are very similar to the management huddle except the board contains metrics that pertain to the specific team. The team huddles are usually held at the focus factory level, department level, or sometimes even the cell level. Some examples of team-level metrics would be sales/shipments or OTD percentage for the focus factory or cell as opposed to the business or site-level metrics. This is important to maintain engagement as employees will generally lose interest or focus if they feel they do not have a direct impact on the metrics. It is also a development opportunity for the team leaders.

The team huddle leader is generally the focus factory/value stream leader, supervisor, department manager, or cell lead. Energy, motivation, and basic public speaking skills are more important than the consistency of hierarchy across the business in designating who conducts the meeting.

Lesson Learned: We worked with the team leaders (and eventually operators) and had them conduct several mock huddles before ever letting them present one to the floor. Not everyone is born with public speaking skills. Simple rules are as follows:

- No hands in your pockets while presenting.
- Make eye contact with everyone in attendance.
- Listen when people speak.
- Ask if you answered their question when questions arise—check for understanding.
- Speak loudly and clearly.
- No speeches.
- Make sure you are prepared—all charts updated and replaced daily.
- If you don't know an answer, admit it, and then follow up at the next meeting with the answer.
- Hold people accountable to their due dates.
- Always end the meeting asking if anyone has any new ideas on how to improve.

Attendees (see Figure 4.2) include all workers in the focus factory or cell, including the planner, manufacturing engineer, quality engineer, supply chain, and customer service representatives. If these functions are not co-located by value stream in your business, mandate they leave their offices and move to where the value is created, the factory floor, which is where the metric board and huddle should reside.

The huddle should be daily and at the same time every day. Over time, the huddle changed from kicking the day off at the start of the shift (generally 7:00 am) to after the first break at 9:15 am. Because office personnel did not start as early as the factory personnel, we saw more value in having the focus factory and other cross-functional office personnel present compared to the other advantages of starting it at the beginning of the shift.

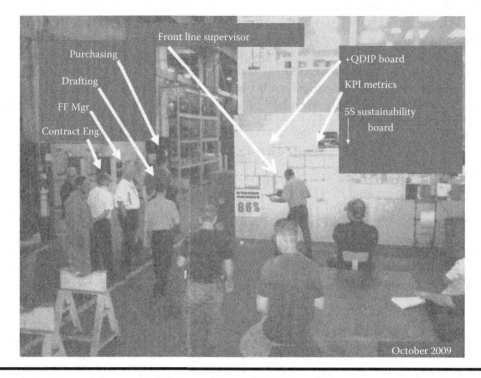

**Figure 4.2  Focused factory huddle attendees and area description.**

Some of the advantages of starting after the first break of the shift included the following:

1. Attendance of office personnel increased communication.
2. Material shortages are addressed immediately.
3. Machine maintenance is addressed immediately (a maintenance person is assigned to the cell).
4. Safety—near miss issues can be immediately addressed.
5. Through clear *day-by-hour* charts, the day's goals can be emphasized.
6. The office is now part of cross-functional daily meetings to help understand needs and floor issues.

## Introduction to +QDIP

The acronym +QDIP (see Figure 4.3) stands for:

- ■ Plus (+) stands for 6S (Safety + 5s)
- ■ Q = Quality (typically first pass yield but rolled throughput yield[4] has been used also)
- ■ D = OTD
- ■ I = Inventory (can also stand for Ideas)
- ■ P = Productivity

Other acronyms, such as QCD, SQDP, and SQDIP, are used where QCD stands for quality, cost, and delivery; SQDP substitutes S for safety instead of + for 6S and does not include inventory; and SQDIP includes inventory as well.

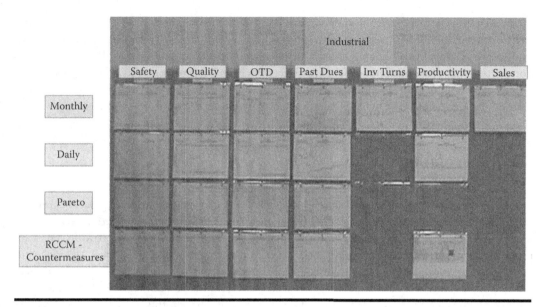

**Figure 4.3  Daily management metrics.**

## +QDIP Evolution and Journey at Company X[5]

The +QDIP metric boards and huddles were introduced years ago to Company X by a staff member from corporate headquarters who was exclusively dedicated to its rollout. The directive was that a +QDIP metric board must be at every cell with no exceptions. The business at the time was 60% built to order and 40% engineered to order by sales dollar. The company had approximately 45 cells, which we could identify and with several staffed by a single person. A person might be conducting a huddle for herself. We clearly did not have measurement capabilities to the single-cell level for 5S, clearly defined key to quality measurements, lead times for on-time performance by cell, standard inventory by cell, and productivity (day-by-hour) metrics by cell in this engineered business. Labor standards were old for 50% of the business. There were no batches of two let alone ten, unless the customer on the rare occasion ordered that many of the same products. Furthermore, the management team's gemba walk (which did not have a name when we started) evolved from the intended purpose of a cell communication process between management and the cell lead to a rote factory tour, which is not the intention.

Considering our business model, Lean journey maturity, and data acquisition capability, it was designed to fail under those circumstances. Could the management team really spend even 5 minutes at each +QDIP board (3 hours and 45 minutes per day) during the gemba walk?

## First Evolution

The first evolution was to take a step back and decide we needed to crawl before we could walk. We also balanced the purpose of the huddle more toward serving the employee with less emphasis on and moving away from the exclusive purpose of communicating to management.

Lastly, we opened the tightly scripted huddle to provide more macro-business information for all employees. Initially, +QDIP and key process indicator (KPI) boards were put in place for each major value stream, which numbered seven. The KPI board had prior MTD and year-to-date (YTD) metrics for OTD, inventory turns, and productivity. Productivity in this case was defined as standard to actual labor hours. This setup was now much more manageable. The data acquisition process supported this level of specificity, accurately and comprehensively. The +QDIP board provided day-to-day information, and the KPI board provided prior MTD and YTD for the three metrics just mentioned. The management team could manage spending 35–40 minutes per day.

## Second Evolution

In our second evolution, we had the employees develop their own metrics for +QDIP. This was most significant in terms of a cultural evolution. Now that the employees were educated on the business, we found they were losing some interest in the old meetings and the meetings tended to become very routine (i.e., same ol' same ol'). One of the employees suggested we change the board to represent problems not from management's view but from their (the employees) point of view. We took this as a great suggestion and then met to decide how to implement the board updates. We asked each cell to work together and determine what impacted them from the point of view of each of the quality, delivery, inventory, and productivity (QDIP) metrics. In one cell, this meant that productivity shifted from getting more units per hour metric to productivity being anything that kept them from being productive throughout the day. Each cell had different definitions for the +QDIP letter, but now they were *their* metrics not ours, and we obtained much more buy-in from the team members.

## Plus (+) = Safety/5S

Plus (+) still stood for 6S and our 5S and safety metrics of severity and frequency were agreed to and the team focused on the metrics. A highly visual, daily 5S standard work board existed in each value stream noting that any safety incidents that resulted in lost time had to be reported directly to the president of the division.

If all the 5S tasks were complete from the day before and there were no injuries or near misses, then the day was colored green (see Figure 4.4). If there had been a near miss or a 5S task was not completed, then the frontline leader switched markers real time in the meeting and colored the day's box red within the "+" month.

The day would be colored blue when the cell or value stream was not working due to a planned shutdown. If the shutdown was not planned (i.e., equipment down or short components needed for an order), blue would not be used.

## Q = Quality

Quality was the measure of the quality for the area. For a manufacturing cell, the day would be colored green, during the meeting, if there were no quality issues that day. If there was a quality issue that was caused by a nonconforming component or an assembly/machining error in the cell/area, the day would be colored yellow if the commitments for the day were still met despite the issue and red if commitments weren't met. A shop floor nontraditional definition was used for quality for +QDIP boards in support areas or departments. If anything inside or outside their cell impacted quality and they were able to install countermeasures and still meet the plan, it was coded yellow. For example,

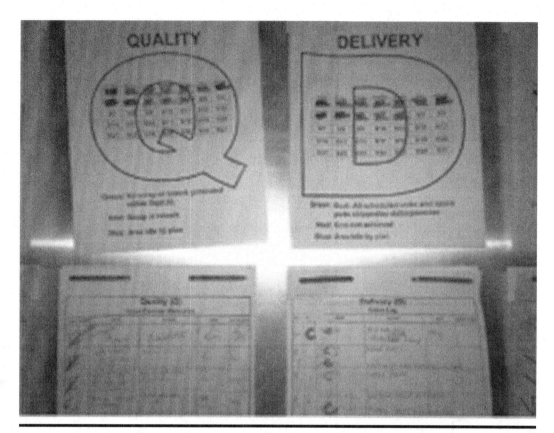

**Figure 4.4    +QDIP with supporting actions. The C means completed action. Teams had 24 hours to complete or it was escalated to the general manager. If the team met their daily goal, it was colored in green at the board during the meeting.**

a major change in the metric, in the spirit of the factory floor as a customer, happened; if all drawings and bills of material engineering produced and delivered to the shop floor were correct without errors, then the day was colored green for the engineering board. If not, the day was colored in red.

# D = Delivery

Delivery was a measure of the delivery from that area against their schedule. For machining or assembly cells, this was deliveries for the day either directly to the customer or to the next operation. For support departments, this would be a measure of the delivery of their service to their internal customer. For example, the receiving inspection +QDIP board would be green only if their inspections were all completed on time for the day, which allowed parts to go to the cells on time.

# I = Inventory

This metric changed from the number of inventory turns to a shop floor-based metric of whether all parts that were supposed to be available were available. If a work order was found to be short while building an order or short such that an order could not be started, the day would be colored red.

If a part was not the right revision letter or had quality issues (missed by receiving inspection), it would be coded red. If a part was missing in the bill of material (BOM) list, it was coded red. If a component inventory level was below the expected level in the cell but no orders required the parts were being built, the day would be colored yellow.

# P = Productivity

Productivity's definition (see Figure 4.5)evolved rapidly going from standard versus actual hours to a shop floor metric of:

■ Any unplanned machine downtime
■ Issues that caused the machine to operate at a slower speed
■ Any missing tools

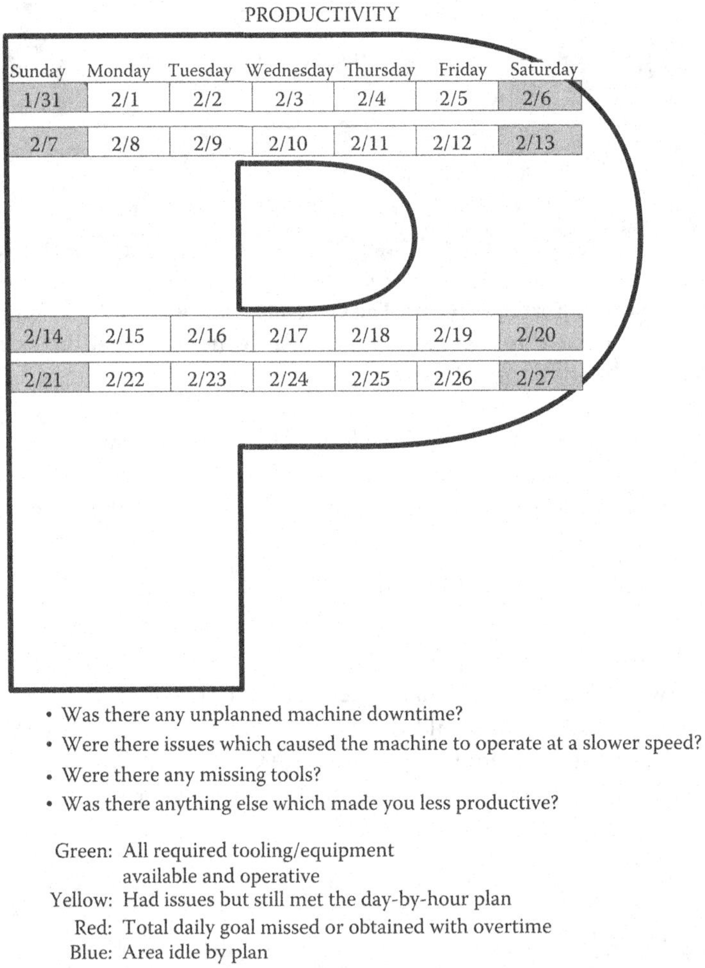

PRODUCTIVITY

| Sunday | Monday | Tuesday | Wednesday | Thursday | Friday | Saturday |
|--------|--------|---------|-----------|----------|--------|----------|
| 1/31 | 2/1 | 2/2 | 2/3 | 2/4 | 2/5 | 2/6 |
| 2/7 | 2/8 | 2/9 | 2/10 | 2/11 | 2/12 | 2/13 |
| 2/14 | 2/15 | 2/16 | 2/17 | 2/18 | 2/19 | 2/20 |
| 2/21 | 2/22 | 2/23 | 2/24 | 2/25 | 2/26 | 2/27 |

• Was there any unplanned machine downtime?
• Were there issues which caused the machine to operate at a slower speed?
• Were there any missing tools?
• Was there anything else which made you less productive?

Green: All required tooling/equipment available and operative
Yellow: Had issues but still met the day-by-hour plan
Red: Total daily goal missed or obtained with overtime
Blue: Area idle by plan

**Figure 4.5   Metrics converted by the team members to be meaningful to them.**

in which case, it would be colored red. Daily counters and the day-by-hour charts also fed into this metric. The color code is as follows: If the plan on the day-by-hour chart was met with no problems, then the day was colored green; if the plan was met but we had any of the issues noted earlier, it was yellow; and if the targeted plan output was not met on the day-by-hour chart, then productivity on the +QDIP board for the day was colored red.

## Daily Management +QDIP Boards versus Huddle Boards

Huddle boards and meetings tend to be higher level metric review and communication meetings, and +QDIP is a more detailed and tactical continuous improvement tool. The +QDIP board is generally created for each assembly and machining cell to record problems and to encourage root cause analysis and corrective action to fix the problem. For example, if a component part is short for building an order, the inventory block for the day would be colored red, but the specific part number would also be listed in the issues column in the inventory section. The team that is assigned to the board, to include supervisor, manufacturing engineer, quality engineer, buyer, and planner, would be responsible to check the board and assign their name as the owner of the issue for their functional area. In this case, the missing component would be owned by the buyer. The buyer would now be responsible for expediting the part to satisfy the order, determining why the part wasn't in the cell on time, and correcting the root cause. This forces issues to be dealt with properly to ensure items do not occur repeatedly on the board. This approach is used for all issues under each category on the board, so the teams spend less time firefighting and more time focusing on the problems and improvement opportunities. The successful use of this approach to identify root causes and develop corrective actions saves significant amounts of wasted resources and prevents a reoccurrence of the same issues.

The huddle board covers a larger portion of the business such as an entire focus factory, department, or sometimes the entire business. Huddle boards are used as a communication tool to engage people and show their performance against targeted metrics to guide behaviors toward improving the business metrics and to help employees think more like a business owner. +QDIP boards are more tactical and focus efforts on more specific tasks that cause daily problems in the cell or manufacturing area. The employees from all the different cells in a focus factory may all attend the same huddle in the morning, but they may each have their own +QDIP board for their individual cells. The huddle meeting will usually last about 10 minutes, but the length of +QDIP meeting depends on the status of the board when the team meets. If all categories on the board are green, the meeting is over in a few seconds, as there is no need to waste time. The team will only spend time discussing:

- Issues on the board that haven't been assigned an owner
- Issues where target dates to solve them do not meet expectations
- Very large problems that may need the focus of the entire team

# Results Focused on the Factory Floor as the Customer

Metric development should be evolutionary and focus on what the business needs and must be measurable when the metric is introduced. However, the emphasis on the factory floor as a customer has a profound effect on the culture and productivity. Drawing and BOM errors dropped precipitously as engineers did not want to explain what happened in front of 25 people on the factory floor.

The planners also did not enjoy the visibility associated with putting something into work, which then had to stop due to a missing part. This approach brings accountability into the organization at all levels. What became conspicuous besides the fact that sales per employee metric doubled over the course of 4.5 years is that everyone began to realize what they did made a significant difference. Everyone in the organization has a role, like a machine with many gears working together, to provide the desired product. All must do their part (role), so the machine provides the customer the value expected. The metrics were comprehensible, interesting, and relevant to them. It brought visibility to what they needed to do the job. It was also the beginning of developing a Hoshin environment where everyone on the shop floor saw how they contributed to the strategic goals of the business.

## Maintenance

Early in the process, a maintenance sheet was added to complement the follow-up action item sheets underneath each +QDIP monthly sheet on the board. The follow-up sheets had rudimentary issues (not root cause or Pareto which we would get addressed later), date assigned, action, who, and target completion date columns on them. Once completed, a big red "C" was written by the owner and the loop was closed.

We encourage team members to put anything that needed maintenance onto the log sheet. We assigned a maintenance person to each board and we totally neglected to appreciate how long it had been since anyone asked the employees on the factory floor what they needed fixed to do their job better. We were immediately overloaded with requests. Most maintenance log sheets were 2+ pages single spaced at each of the seven boards. It took 6 months to bring the requests up to date. The best practice we developed was assigning a maintenance person to each board and making it their responsibility to get the requests completed.

## Third Step in the Evolution: Open-Book Management

The next phase of the evolutionary process was adding daily and MTD orders and sales versus target. The actual delinquent backlog in dollars versus target was also shown. A magic marker was all that was used, and the daily orders, sales, MTD, and delinquent backlog were written in during the 10:00 am huddle in open space at the top of the white boards. This addition to the huddle drifts from the pure operations form of +QDIP daily management into the open-book practice of management as espoused in the book *The Great Game of Business.*[6] The management team had not heard of or read the book, however, as open-book management techniques continued, the results continued to improve. The results were heading toward excellence. Ignorance, speculation, rumors, and water cooler declined as employees were provided with daily facts and data concerning the business.

Some frontline leaders took poetic license and added comments on markets, competitors, and customer feedback that complimented the management teams' own huddles. These were not scripted notes for consistency across the huddles, a recommended practice for consistency of message. The information flow back and forth across the business improved dramatically. Educated employees on the floor began questioning the seasonal impact of school starting up on our heating equipment line mentioned earlier. An employee with business information and facts creates more value to the business. Something else occurs that is hard to quantify. Criticism and divisiveness went down, people helped each other more, and team morale flourished.

## Huddles and the +QDIP/Gemba Walk

The +QDIP or gemba walk has been described as a walking operations review with an emphasis on action. Those leaders of the business that can help solve issues the focus factories are having need to be part of the walk. For example, if errors in drawings are reaching the factory floor, then the engineering manager should be present. The purpose for attending is to understand the issues, know what is occurring real time, and to knock down any barriers to resolution. Like the huddles, the gemba walk should take place at the same time every day and the frontline leaders should be present to explain issues and make requests for help. The focus of the walk can be business dependent such as asset turns or safety, but customer satisfaction and productivity should be at or near the top. Each +QDIP board should be visited, but as mentioned earlier, the time spent at each board is dependent on the number of issues on the board that need to be addressed.

Businesses are like people in that there are some fundamental truths that apply to most and yet they are unique in their own ways. We don't subscribe to there being one right way for all businesses in all situations. However, each work cell should have the goal of having a +QDIP or KPI board (see Figure 4.6), a day-by-hour chart (see Figure 4.7), 6S fundamentals, standard work posted, and andon system. Good business sense and applicability need to be applied based on your business model, system data retrieval capabilities, and where the business is on the Lean journey curve. The important point is to start and let the continuous improvement begin.

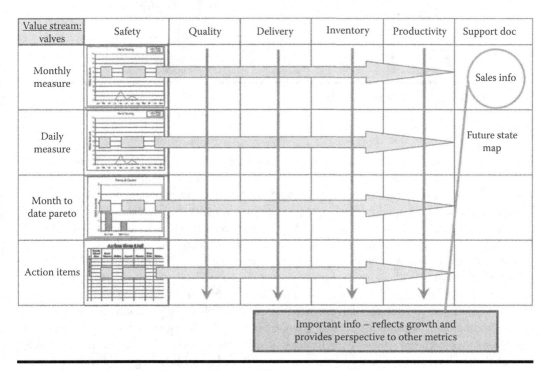

**Figure 4.6  KPI board with supporting countermeasures (actions).**

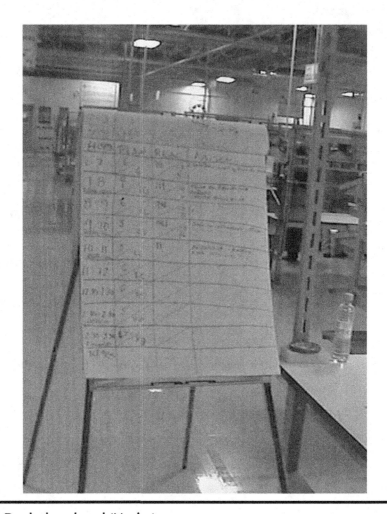

**Figure 4.7 Day by hour board (Mexico).**

## KPI Board

The KPI board and other value stream-related metrics (i.e., bookings, sales numbers, customer feedback) posted at the cell are another template that can be used as an alternative to the +QDIP template. It emphasizes root cause analysis through its Pareto sheets, which is advantageous from a Toyota Kata[7] (coaching) standpoint when indoctrinating the concept of root cause analysis (5 whys) into your culture. +QDIP focuses more on 6S as it reinforces safety and 5S adherence daily versus a once-per-week or -month 6S audit shown on the right-hand column of the KPI board. There are several other versions used in industry. Immediate business need should dictate specific data, and no information/layout will change and improve over time if the business is truly advancing.

In addition to the QDIP letters and countermeasures that are below the QDIP letters (see Figure 4.8), we also include the daily orders, delinquent backlog, and backlog (see Figure 4.9), which in some cases, we simply wrote on a white board daily during the huddle. It is important to share a quick high-level view of the health of the business to every employee. This should be done at the cell level and not just the focus factory level if a huddle is taking place at the cell level. The importance of this was highlighted when a member of the union asked during a huddle when

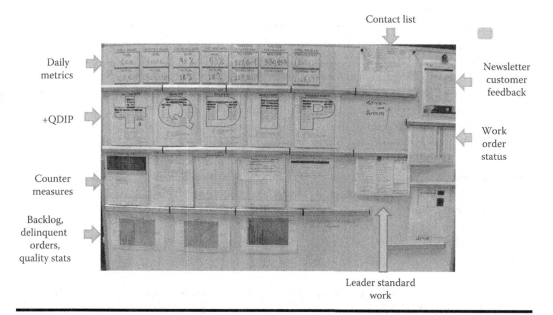

**Figure 4.8    Actions completed status.**

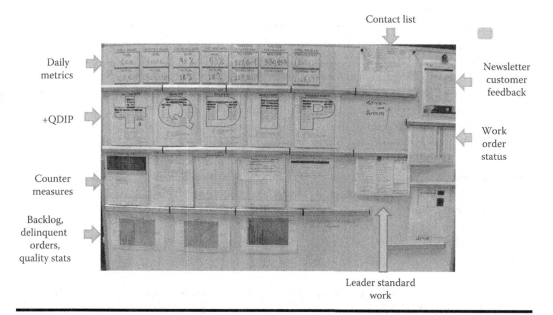

**Figure 4.9    KPI board with +QDIP.**

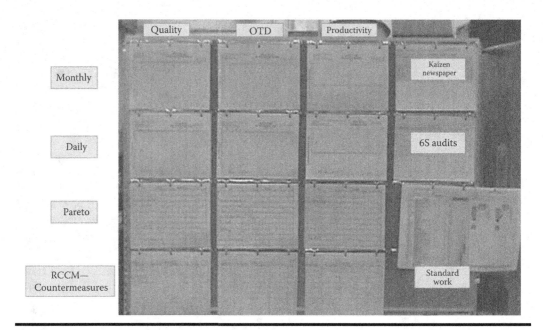

**Figure 4.10 KPI boards—value stream–related metrics posted at the cell. (From BIG Archives.)**

layoffs would be taking place in a particular focus factory. The operations, sales manager, and I had spoken about that exact subject the day before because of declining orders. We told everyone we had decided to wait another week to see if demand picked up before making an announcement. Note that, shown in Figure 4.10, the support document column has kaizen newspaper, standard work, and 6s audit. This can be modified according to the need to put a heijunka methodology sheet, TPM schedule, setup reduction time chart, or customer feedback note into the column. A team versatility summary that demonstrates the team's flexibility is also helpful.

The point is everyone who was paying attention at the huddle had seen our daily orders drop below budget or target for most of the previous three weeks. Additionally, the focus factory manager in this case posted a backlog bar chart for the immediate next four weeks by day at the bottom of the +QDIP charts. Everyone had a better understanding of cause and effect. Surprise, speculation, and suspicion were all greatly reduced. The data were visible, and there for the team to read, and for this example, orders picked up and layoffs were not needed.

The equivalent KPI board modified for the focus factory or value stream level is shown in Figure 4.11. Sample cell metric calculations are shown in Figure 4.11 and should be adjusted to align with your businesses' exact need and strategic goal deployment. The productivity and inventory turns are typically weekly or monthly at the focus factory level. This is particularly applicable if it is an engineered-to-order or large-dollar build-to-order business model as day-to-day measurement is too variable and thus not meaningful. To the extent that productivity can be meaningfully measured daily at the focus factory level, that is clearly preferred.

The following steps define how the KPI board works in Figure 4.10:

**Day**

■ Update row 2 (daily measure) of KPI board with daily performance results (day by hour).
■ Update row 3 (MTD Pareto) with the root cause of our misses of the day. Obtain data from the day-by-hour charts in the *issues* column.

| | Safety | Quality | Delivery | | | Cost | |
| --- | --- | --- | --- | --- | --- | --- | --- |
| | | | OTD | Past dues | Inventory | Productivity | |
| Metric | OSHA recordable incidents | Total yield | On time delivery to customer request date | Past dues | Turns | Productivity % | |
| Calculation | Data — Tracked | Total acceptable units/total units produced | Lines shipped OT to CRD/total lines shipped | Data — Tracked | COS/Total inventory | Total conversion cost (less materials)/total sales | |
| Data required | Recorded incidents | Daily defects | Lines shipped OT to CRD | Number of lines past due | Total cost of sales | Total conversion cost (less materials) | |
| | | Daily total units produced | Daily total lines shipped | Total past due $ | Total inventory | Total sales | |
| Goal | 0 | 98% | 98% | 0 | 4.5 | TBD (lower) | |

Daily | Weekly or monthly

**Figure 4.11  Cell metric calculations. (From BIG Archives.)**

- Update row 4 (actions) with actions linked to the Pareto—use problem-solving tools to determine root cause and effective countermeasures.
- Populate new day-by-hour charts and set the plan for next shift.
- The frontline supervisor is now ready for the daily gemba walk through the area.

**Month**

- Consolidate the row 2 data (daily measure) and transfer to row 1 (monthly measure).
- Aggregate row 3 (MTD Pareto) into a final Pareto for the month.
- Add a new blank month-to-date (MTD) Pareto and in front of the previous month Pareto on row 3.
- Update the actions on row 4 and put in front of previous month actions.
- Complete any required countermeasure plans for all monthly misses.
- The frontline supervisor now has all the information available for the monthly operations review.

## Cross-Functional Representation Is Important

Cross-functional representation makes the huddle process more responsive and sustainable. Figure 4.12 shows focus factory team members who were co-located on the factory floor waiting for the supervisor at the +QDIP board to kick off the huddle meeting. Staff cross-functional representation, at least intermittently, is valuable for the gemba walks. Lessons learned through the learning cycles in implementing factory floor metric boards, huddles, and gemba walks are numerous and listed in the following sections.

**Figure 4.12 Huddle meeting with focus factory team members led by Susan Canfield.**

## Metric Boards and Huddles

Early in the process.

- Expect a large increase of maintenance requests with a corresponding maintenance expense increase, which requires planning and budget development.
- Create a tight script for the huddle and practice it to ensure the team remains in focus and does not discuss solving world peace—delivers consistency of message/structure.
- Pick the huddle leader based on energy and public speaking skills, not necessarily hierarchy.
- Balance consistency with applicability when selecting metrics across and through (up and down) the business unit. The corollary to this later in the process is being aware of the check-the-box syndrome that points to a lack of a relevant metric.
- Metric board and the day-by-hour chart, if used properly, should enable any person to understand the issues and what is being done to fix them (Figure 4.13).
- Assign a maintenance person to each huddle.
- Informed and measured employees take ownership.

There is no perfect metric for all businesses under all circumstances. Use good business sense to keep metrics applicable and relevant to the desired audience.

**Figure 4.13  KPI board in procurement.**

## Gemba Walks/Watches

We were at a winery in Santorini, Greece, with Ritsuo Shingo.[8] He noticed they had several inspectors and Ritsuo asked what seemed like a simple question. "Why do you have so many inspectors?" The manager looked at him like he was crazy and said we must have inspectors. Their job is to make sure that no foreign particles get into the bottles.

The workers would pick up four bottles and hold them up in the air against a lighted back-drop to see if the bottles were clean. Ritsuo-san just sat there and spent almost two hours watch-ing and then he started to ask some more simple questions. Then he went to the machine and "got his hands dirty." He climbed the ladder (He was 69 years old at the time) and inspected the top of the machine. He asked why the lid to the machine was off as this could allow par-ticles into the machine. He also inspected the packaging and found problems there. When all was said and done, he found several problems and their root causes and suggested solutions. Implementing these solutions would eliminate the need for the inspectors. He explained by getting control over the process the results take care of themselves. This has always been his guiding philosophy. Ritsuo-san summed it all up by saying: "Gemba walks should be changed to Gemba watches!"

It is important that the management level guide the teams on a regular basis through their feedback and coaching. Without feedback, we cannot build on our strengths and work on our gaps. Genchi Genbutsu translates to go and see and refers to the management tactic of spending a good amount of time at the gemba or place of reality. Toyota Chairman, Fujio Cho said about going to the gemba…"Go see – ask why – show respect."[9]

## Leadership Development Walks

The term gemba walk that we now refer to as Leadership Development Walk has many meanings today and takes on various forms at every company. Gemba walks have really lost their original purpose in many factories. They range from just walking through areas to check on the daily management boards, if they even exist, to speaking with team leaders or group leaders etc. There are books written on them, but everyone has their own opinion on them. In our case, if you go to the floor (or office), it is a walk to the gemba. Gemba is where the action is going on. The common three aspects are to watch, eliminate waste, and learn. We conduct different types of walks that can be separate or combined and are not an inclusive list. They include:

1. Waste walks where we look for waste.
2. Process walks where we look at each workstation along with the tools and materials used to see what could go wrong and how to improve or mistake-proof.
3. Daily management walks where the manager should be able to look at the daily management board and know immediately if there is a problem. Depending on the severity of the problem, the manager may leave a note to be answered by the team leader or group leader (to see if they are managing the board) or they may use an urgent problem/gap on the board as a coaching moment to further develop their team leader's thinking.

## Waste Walk

A waste walk is a type of gemba walk used to teach others how to find and see waste. This was what is called the Ohno circle where Taiichi Ohno would make his managers stand in a circle he outlined on the floor. Waste walks offer a way to continually improve our ability to see waste in the process. Ritsuo Shingo says "You should not just watch their hands but also eyes and then ask why?" This concept dates to Frank Gilbreth's motion study process.

Taking a small group of your team members along as you continuously perform these daily walks will not only coach and improve the team member's ability to see waste but also will improve the plants ability to continuously improve. These walks are centered on the 8 wastes and require a leader with the knowledge and skill "to see" to be effective. That leader must coach and train the other team members and then allow them to identify and ultimately reduce the waste that is being found.

## Process Walk (Watch)

The first question we always ask on a process walk is: What is the standard? If there is no standard then we have an immediate gap and it means we need to do a job breakdown and develop the standard work. If there is a standard then we should be looking to see the actual condition. Are we meeting the standard? Therefore, creating and improving standards is part of Team Member Self Reliance. You can see how TSR now helps sustain the improvements.

## *Daily Management Walk (Watch)*

This walk reviews the daily management board. This is where we use Shingo's 1-3-10 tool. Are we ahead or behind schedule? Both are problems. If we are behind, we need to understand why and remember the problem is not the person. If we are ahead, we need to understand if we are following the standard. If we are and have figured out a way to better it, then we need to update the standard work to include the improvement.

The bottom line on it all is the gemba walk should be focused on teaching, coaching, and driving ongoing improvement toward your targets. This means you need to understand the gaps between where you are now and your target and then experiment using small PDAC cycles to overcome the gaps. Typical gemba-walk questions encourage problem-solving. Teaching and developing your people:

■ Problem identification—finding a gap or deviation from the standard
■ Problem-solving—watching and listening. One must touch and get their hands dirty.
■ Team—team leader and management coaching on how to watch and discover the root cause.
■ What improvements the team is working on now. Then we need to understand how and where they are in the problem-solving process. We need to understand the target they are shooting for compared to the baseline and if they have identified the root cause. The most important thing is to make sure they are not just throwing solutions at the problem.

Ritsuo Shingo[10] says "You cannot manage the floor or office area or fix a problem without going to the gemba, floor, or office, to determine what is really going on."

You cannot manage a plant from your office. Gemba watches are an important component of the Leadership Development Path and a sustaining mechanism if done properly. However, there must be visual displays and controls in place. If not, it just becomes a walk or a tour of the floor.

## Daily Management—QDIP Linkage

Figure 4.14 shows the QDIP linkage to the day-by-hour chart and month-by-day chart.

The day-by-hour board is designed to capture problems in real time. When the team leader (or operator) writes a problem on the day-by-hour chart, the team leader should immediately run through an informal plan–do–check–act (PDCA) cycle. The first question should be:

■ Do I need to stop the line? There should be a working document created (defined as the Lean line package) that includes criteria for when we stop the line. The criteria could be based on receipt of a nonconforming part, cleanliness issue, etc. Other problems may require quick countermeasures and do not cause the line to stop.
■ Is this a special cause or common cause problem? If it is a special cause problem, we need to determine why the problem occurred and implement a special cause solution. If it is a common cause problem, that is, within the normal variation, we may be able to keep the line running but capture the issue to address the root cause. For example, we may notice the parts are on the edge of a specification but still meet the specification. We may need to make sure a washer was cleaned at the proper time or an adjustment is needed in a machining parameter. If the parts are out of specification, we need to stop the line and find the root cause. Each type of problem requires a different solution.

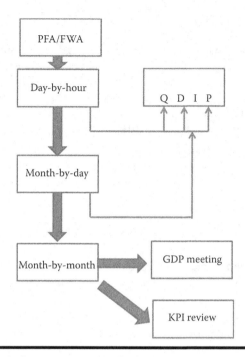

**Figure 4.14 BASICS® tools flow to KPI review linkage.**

- Next, is there a countermeasure required immediately to correct this problem and are other units impacted by the problem?
- If yes, implement the countermeasure and start the line.
- If we solve the problem, we should note that on the day-by-hour chart and update the standard work.
- If we implement a countermeasure but do not solve the problem, then the problem should be recorded under the appropriate letter on the +QDIP board and assigned an owner to follow up with a corrective action. As a rule, the owner has anywhere from one day to one week to fix the problem.

The day-by-hour chart production numbers are then transferred to the month by day and then month by month and reported to management at the desired frequency. All the problems need to be followed to a conclusion, which results in a change to the standard work. Most companies have a database where the problems and solutions are collected, so if a problem resurfaces, we have history and do not have to necessarily start over to acquire a solution.

## Chapter Questions

1. What should the format for the daily huddle look like?
2. Where should the metrics for the +QDIP board come from?
3. What are the advantages of a daily meeting?
4. What is a learning minute?
5. What is the linkage between the day-by-hour and QDIP board?

6. Why are gemba walks important?
7. Who should be involved in a QDIP meeting?
8. What is the advantage of having the QDIP information prominently displayed versus being in a computer?
9. Should we worry about customer's seeing the QDIP board?
10. Who should run the QDIP meeting?
11. What role does HR, Sales, or Engineering play in the huddles? Do they have huddle boards in their offices as well?
12. What did you learn from this chapter?

## Notes

1. Contributions from Joe McNamara, CEO at McNamara Manufacturing Holdings. and Ttarp Industries.
2. Reference is to flywheel mentioned in Good to Great, Jim Collins, ©October 2001.
3. The Great Game of Business, Jack Stack with Bo Burlingham, Doubleday, ©1992.
4. Rolled throughput yield looks at the first pass yield at each step of the process and then multiplies them together to get the actual yield of the overall process.
5. Contributed by Joe McNamara, Former GM or ITT Heat Transfer, Buffalo NY, (now Xylem), former VP of ITT CT Division, Now CEO of TTARP Industries, Buffalo NY.
6. The Great Game of Business, Jack Stack with Bo Burlingham, Doubleday, ©1992.
7. Toyota Kata, Mike Rother, McGraw-Hill, ©2009.
8. Ritsuo Shingo taught at the Lean Leadership Institute (LLI) conference, August 2017, hosted by George Trachillis in Santorini, Greece.
9. https://www.lean.org/shook/DisplayObject.cfm?o=1843
10. Ritsuo Shingo taught at the Lean Leadership Institute (LLI) conference, August 2017, hosted by George Trachillis in Santorini, Greece.

## Additional Readings

Besser, T.L. 1996. Team Toyota. New York: SUNY Press.
Covey, S.R. 1989. Seven Habits of Highly Effective People. New York: Simon and Schuster.
Crisp, M. (Ed.) 1991. Rate Your Skills as a Manager. Los Altos, CA: Crisp Publications.
Davis, B.L. 1996. Successful Managers Handbook . Minneapolis, MN: Personal Decisions.
Helfert, E.A. 1997. Techniques of Financial Analysis. Homewood, IL: Irwin Publishing.
Hindle, T. 1999. Reducing Stress. New York: DK Pub.
Jaworski, J. 1996. Synchronicity the Inner Path of Leadership. 2nd ed., Oakland, CA: Berrett-Koehler Publishers.
Pritchett, P. 1992. Team Reconstruction. Dallas, TX: Pritchette & Assoc.
Ryan, N.E. (Ed.) 1990. Taguchi Methods and QFD. Dearborn, MI: ASI Press.
Smiles, S. 2002. Self Help. Oxford, UK: Oxford Press.
Stephen, G.H. 1998. Systems Thinking and Learning. Amherst, MA: HDR Press.

# Chapter 5

# Visual Management

Visual Management – Everyone knows with no explanation.

**James Liu**[1]

## Visual Management System Components

There are several levels of visual factory management or visual management systems within a Lean enterprise.

Visual management systems are made up of the following components (see Figure 5.1):

1. 5S
2. Visual displays
3. Visual controls

## Management by Sight

Visual management is a work area that is where what is supposed to happen does happen, on time, every time. It is a capable repeatable system or process that is:

1. Self-explaining
2. Self-regulating
3. Self-improving

These techniques help us understand and make visible what's happening in our workplace so we can act on fact to achieve better results (Figure 5.2). It is known as Mieruka at Toyota, which means visualization or visual control. Mieruka has three main components: 5S—identification, visual displays—information, and visual controls—instructional and daily management planning which we call Sustain.

DOI: 10.4324/9781003185819-5

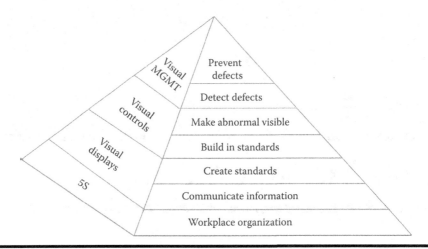

Prevent
defects

Detect defects

Make abnormal visible

Build in standards

Create standards

Communicate information

Workplace organization

Visual
MGMT

Visual
controls

Visual
displays

5S

**Figure 5.1 Visual Management pyramid.**

# 5S—Identification

5S has two major components—housekeeping and discipline. Housekeeping is not only about the old saying "a place for everything and everything in its place," but it is also about discipline. Discipline is putting things back in their place which is the most difficult part of 5S. We all need to be part of setting the standard at the highest levels if we are to be considered world class.

Whether or not 5S is implemented as a separate initiative, it becomes a part of every implementation. As we make changes to the layout and workstations, we implement 5S as we progress (see Figure 5.3). While some organizations add an S for safety and call this 6S, and others add a seventh S for satisfaction (employee), many use 5 because safety is a part of each of the 5S's.

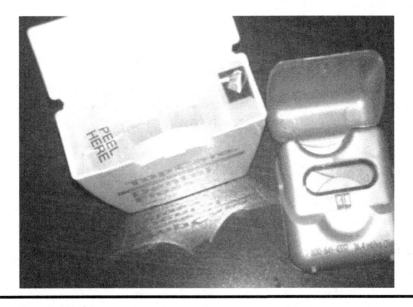

**Figure 5.2 Visual management examples.**

**Figure 5.3    Visual controls—the floss on the left has no real visual cue; however, the one on the right shows the level of floss available. (From BIG Archives.)**

5S is the beginning step and part of a larger whole, called a visual management system. The goal of visual management is to make problems visible so that action may be taken.

When a work area is neat, clean, and in order, it is a more efficient and safer work area. 5S is a method for creating and maintaining this type of work environment. Listed in the following are the definitions of each S with original Japanese words and different American definitions, depending on the source[2]:

1. *Seiri*: Proper arrangement, sort, cleanup, clearing up, or organization. The first step is to separate and consolidate those items necessary for the proper functioning of the work area (i.e., tools, fixtures, work instructions, parts, or office supplies) from the unnecessary items. Get rid of those unnecessary items.

   Note: We find "if in doubt, throw it out" to be a very dangerous and sometimes costly saying. Better to rephrase as "if in doubt, red tag it and use the disposition team or red tag auction process to determine its final location."

2. *Seiton*: Arrange, put in order and store, set in order, order, orderliness, organize logical order, or neatness. Arrange items so they can be retrieved immediately in the order required. Make a place for all the necessary items and put them in their place. Identify their appropriate place by outlining the area and/or labeling the space (see Figure 5.4).

**Figure 5.4    5S desk.**

**Figure 5.5  5S on the shop floor. Nurses Beth Lewis, Mary Ann Megimose-McClay, Amanda McNutt from Ohio Health System, Columbus, Ohio, and Scott Harris of Florida Hospital, part of the Adventist Health System, Orlando, Florida, participating in a 5-day seminar and 4 hour 5S kaizen event. (From BIG Archives.)**

Note: We prefer labeling to outlining as things tend to change quickly and you can end up scraping many pegboards that have permanent outlines.

3. *Seiso*: Neat, tidy, sweep, shine, cleanliness, cleaning, or pick up. Operators clean the work area daily. Sweep the floors, wipe off the machines, and keep a sanitary work area. Make sure everything is neatly in its place. This concept is often misinterpreted and misunderstood (see Figure 5.5).

4. *Seiketsu*: Cleanliness, standardize, neatness, or maintaining a spotless workplace. Find ways to keep the overall environment neat and clean. The white glove test is very applicable here. Are there ways to reduce dust, dirt, and debris that make the cleanup easier? How are old documents purged from the area? Are minimums and maximums identified and visible in storage? This makes visual management easier to maintain. Can we eliminate safety hazards? Make sure standard procedures and work standards are created to document the 5S process, including how 5S tasks are to be completed and visual photographs of what the area should look like when it is completed.

5. *Shitsuke*: Discipline, sustain, conduct, changing work habits, or training. Discipline and training. The most important step of all is to maintain/sustain the area once it has been created. Everyone must follow and update the standardized procedures for cleaning and organizing. Continue to look at the whole area, not just your workspace.

This is the most difficult S of all. To sustain, the 5S program must become part of the documented procedures and become part of the muscle memory of the company, monitored and audited (see Figure 5.6).

Time after time, we see companies start out with a 5S event because they think it is easy or an easy place to start. However, we have seen this stall or negatively impact many companies' Lean journeys as they find they can't even sustain the kaizen a week later. For example, Company X

| | 5S Daily Inspection | | | | |
|---|---|---|---|---|---|

Rank
A = Perfect score = 4 points
B = 1 or 2 problems = 2 points
C = 3 or more problems = 1 points
Maximum score in each category = 20 points

| Category | Item | A | B | C | Comments |
|---|---|---|---|---|---|
| Sort (organization) | Distinguish between what is needed and not needed | | | | |
| | Are things posted on a visual display board uniformly? | | | | |
| | Have all unnecessary items been removed? | | | | |
| | Is it clear why unauthorized items are present? | | | | |
| | Are materials inside cabinets neatly organized? | | | | |
| | Are passage ways and work areas clearly outlined? | | | | |
| | Are hose and cords properly arranged? | | | | |
| Stabilize (orderliness) | A place for everything and everything in its place | | | | |
| | Is everything kept in its own place? | | | | |
| | Are things put away after use? | | | | |
| | Are work areas uncluttered? | | | | |
| | Is everything fastened down that needs to be? | | | | |
| | Are shelves, tables, and cleaning implements orderly? | | | | |
| | Are all machine guards in their place? | | | | |
| Shine (cleanliness) | Clean and looking for ways to keep it clean | | | | |
| | Is clothing neat and clean? | | | | |
| | Are exhaust and ventilation adequate? | | | | |
| | Are work areas clean? | | | | |
| | Are machinery, equipment, fixtures, and drains kept clean? | | | | |
| Standardize (adherence) | Maintain and monitor the first three S's | | | | |
| | Is the area free of trash and dust? | | | | |
| | Have all machines and equipment been cleaned? | | | | |
| | Has the floor been cleaned? | | | | |
| | Are clean-up responsibilities assigned? | | | | |
| | Are all tools and gages within calibration dates? | | | | |
| (Self discipline) | Stick to the rules, scrupulously | | | | |
| | | | | | |
| | Are smoking areas observed? | | | | |
| | Are private belongings put away? | | | | |
| | Does everyone refrain from eating, drinking, and smoking in the workplace? | | | | |
| | Sub total | 0 | 0 | 0 | |
| | Total | 0 | | | |

**Figure 5.6  5S audit sheet.**

used to hand out a PIG award to the dirtiest area. The team members in the cell liked the stuffed PIG so much, they always kept their area dirty so they could keep it!

Note: Every reward system has its pros and cons.

The third and fourth S must be led by every executive, manager, group leader, and team leader. If you walk by a piece of trash and don't pick it up or see someone, not put a tool back and don't say anything, you have just rewarded that person's behavior!

Many areas audit themselves regularly to track their improvement. The area team uses the audit results to focus their improvement efforts and increase their score on the next audit. The area team should review the audit results, brainstorm suggestions for improvement, and take the necessary actions. In many companies, we have moved to audits with simply yes or no answers. Since the audits are conducted with the team leader, they get real time feedback on the opportunities. This keeps the focus on improvement and takes the pressure away "gaming the system" to just increase the score.

Lesson Learned: Sustain takes discipline and a system behind the process. What will happen when people don't follow the process or do their audits? If you want to sustain, then someone high up in the organization needs to audit. This means the site leader or top position at the plant or office where it is implemented. This is called a "layered" audit. This doesn't mean there can't be other audit teams but the Owner, CEO, Plant Manager, etc. set the standard!

The observation form can be tailored to the plant. A plant that does chemical processes will have some different items than a plant that only does assembly. Remember to include safety as part of your 5S audits.

Authors Note: In conversations with Ritsuo Shingo, son of the famous Shigeo Shingo, 40-year Toyota veteran, and the first president of Toyota China, he notes that he was always taught and always used a different sequence. The fifth S added in the west being unused, and not even recognized by him, or by those colleagues we know in Toyota in Japan. The sequence they are more familiar with is:

1. Seiri—Sort, arrange, organize.
2. Seiton—Tidy, Orderliness, Arranging Neatly, includes worker attire.
3. Seiketsu—Cleanliness or Hygiene.
4. Seiso—Shine, neat, and clean.

The first two are the responsibility of the worker and the last two the responsibility of the team leader. The most difficult part of 5S in our culture is the discipline necessary to maintain good housekeeping and worker attire.

## Benefits of 5S

- A cleaner workplace is a safer workplace (see Figure 5.7).
- Contributes to how we feel about and the pride we take in our product, process, our company, and ourselves.
- Customers love it.
- Product quality and especially contaminant levels will improve.
- Cleaning typically reveals problems and areas that need repair.
- Efficiency will increase.
- Good program to get everyone in the organization involved.
- Demonstrates an enterprise commitment to the Lean/5S program.

## Red Tag Strategy

You cannot save the goat and the cabbage.[3]

**Unknown**

Using red tags are helpful when establishing the 5S. Continuous improvement teams use red tags to mark unneeded items for removal. The red tag strategy helps us identify and separate out

*Presenting:*
*Sorting*
*Simplifying*
*Systematic Cleaning*
*Standardization*
*Sustaining*

**Figure 5.7 5S graphic. (Designed by Barry Rodgers and Dave Morrison, Lean practitioner/ facilitator; from BIG Archives.)**

needed items from unneeded items in our workshops. Items tagged are placed in a cordoned off area to be dispositioned later. The red tag strategy helps lay the foundation for improvement by making obvious which items are not needed for daily production activities.

## Lipstick Guy

At a company in Buffalo, NY, we had just converted a line from batch to Lean flow with the help of the team members. As we set up the new line, we created a place for everything, labeled it, and cleaned up the area. The area was swept, neat, and worked well. We implemented day-by-hour charts and line counters, and the line was up and running, meeting its hourly production goals. The team members worked very hard to get the line up and running in a day, and it was doubling the output of the previous line!

A week later, after several ongoing improvements were made to the line, the corporate Lean master (who was certified as a Lean master after conducting just seven kaizen events) came in and said to the team members on the line, "Boy, this line needs some work." We asked him what he meant after we explained how successful the implementation had been. He stated: "Well it might be running good, but it doesn't show very well." He continued, "It's kind of like the woman gets dressed up to go out but doesn't put on any makeup or lipstick! How come you haven't painted any of the work benches or machines? They should all be painted the same color. You all obviously don't know what 5S means!"

After this encounter, the team members' morale was deflated, and they were concerned they hadn't lived up to expectations. We met with the team and told them everything was fine, and we would discuss the issues with him. He later became known as lipstick guy.

Lesson Learned: Our primary focus with implementing any new line is to get it up and running, first making sure everything is in the right place for the operators and the line is safe to run. Initially this means organizing, labeling, cleaning the cell, and documenting the new 5S process and audits. The third S—Seiso—means to sweep and clean, not to paint and show off. 5S doesn't mean everything has to be painted and look brand new and 5S is not about the show. 5S is about housekeeping and discipline first, and it ties in with mistake proofing and visual controls by working to make the abnormal visible. Many companies have great 5S showcased lines that don't run very well but look pretty. We are not saying things should not be painted, but the top priority is to have them clean. Painting comes later and can be a great part of a follow-up kaizen event focused on total productivity maintenance (TPM) or machining/line upgrades.

## 5S Board

5S boards (see Figure 5.8) have the employee name or picture at the top and the days (and sometimes week, month, or quarter) on the side. The boards can be set up several different ways. Every employee is assigned a short 5 minutes or less task each day to complete. This can be expanded to include safety and TPM tasks as well. When the task is completed, its tag is turned over to show the complete side. These boards can be expanded to incorporate TPM and Lean audit-type tasks as well. The advantages of these boards are that they get all the employees in the area involved in the care and maintenance of the area and they are also useful to maintain audit compliance. As an example, one company added checking the fire extinguishers in the area as a task. Think of the benefits. As the task is rotated among the team members in the cell, each one learns where the fire extinguishers are located, how to check to see if they are pressurized, what to do in the event they are not pressurized and making sure the area around the extinguisher is clear. Now, when there is an audit, the team leader or supervisor never has to worry about the fire extinguishers passing the audit. There is always one task labeled to *reset the board*. This is assigned to an employee in the area to assign each task to an individual for the next week. If rotated, this ensures the tasks are rotated to everyone, so no one is unfairly always assigned a certain task.

A 5S board, if it covers all the 5S points, is somewhat self-auditing. If the person does not do their task, one knows in real time. A simple walk around the area to inspect the tasks provides the audit function.

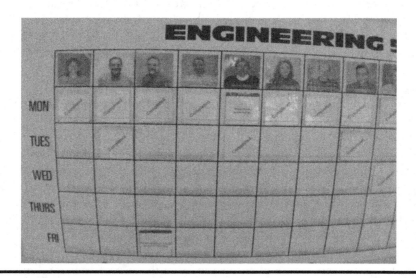

**Figure 5.8  5S daily management board in engineering office.**

## 5S Implementation Guidelines

1. Take pictures of the current situation. Use this for comparison after 5S is in place.
2. Eliminate unnecessary items from the workplace. Use the red tag system.
3. Find the source of dirt and grime and eliminate it! Tidiness reflects efficiency:
   a. Cleaning standards—who, what, where, and when
   b. Cleaning targets—storage areas, equipment, and surroundings
   c. Cleaning instructions—how to clean with designated cleaning frequencies, types of cleaners, and how much. Daily, weekly, and monthly schedules for cleaning
4. Visual one-step marking for organizing and returning things to their proper places.
5. Make 5S a habit—reinforce daily! Make and communicate 5S slogans to remind and encourage full participation.
6. Follow check sheets and audit your compliance through inspection tours.
7. Use 5S radar or other types of charts and checklists to establish a baseline and to measure improvements.
8. Find ways to improve. Kaizen your current 5S system. Create a proactive 5S mentality!
9. Discipline and training, training, training! 5S: make it a way of life!
10. Change your reward systems to demonstrate the importance of 5S.
11. Challenge each other to get better! Have fun doing 5S!

## Visual Displays—Informational

Visual displays are meant to communicate important information (see Figure 5.9) but do not necessarily control what people or machines do. Visual displays such as signs and bulletin boards do not suggest or enforce any action. They only communicate the name of an area,

**Figure 5.9   Visual display example. (From BIG Archives.)**

machine, or some other type of information. Visual displays can show what a bad part versus a good part looks like. They allow the factory to start to speak to you. This is the first step in establishing standards for storage, equipment, operations, quality, and safety. One big problem for most factories is keeping their visual displays updated. It is not unusual to see old charts and data hanging on the wall. One way to avoid this is to put the person's name and picture who is the owner of the display (to keep it updated) in the top right-hand corner with their desk or cell phone number.

## Visual Controls—Instructional

The analogy for visual controls is the human body.[4] When the body has a problem, it lets you know. It may be in the form of a fever, pain, bleeding, blister, etc. Once your body signals a problem, it needs to be taken care of right away or it tends to get worse. The goal is to make every problem immediately visible so it can be fixed right away. This sounds easy to do but is very difficult. Visual controls communicate information in a way that helps everyone identify or prevent a problem and they build in standards and make defects (abnormalities) obvious.

As you walk around an area, the factory or office should talk to you and communicate its condition as you walk around it (see Figure 5.10). Think about an airport. Everything is visual, even the tarmac (see Figure 5.11). Signboards communicate the status of the flights; each gate is labeled and contains a signboard of which flights are leaving the gate and when. Restrooms, handicap areas, safety issues concerning strollers on escalators, and a speaker above saying "caution, the moving walkway is ending" are all visuals and *talk to you* as you walk through. You immediately know the status of your flight and what is going on around you. Does your factory communicate to you the same way the airport does? What happens when the airport does not communicate

**Figure 5.10 Visual control—when a tool is missing, you know immediately. (From BIG Archives.)**

**Figure 5.11    Visual controls on the tarmac. (From BIG Archives.)**

to you? Your flight gets delayed, but they don't tell you why or how long. We all tend to get very frustrated. The same holds true in the factory.

Visual controls are different from visual displays because they go a step further to suggest some action be taken or they help remind us to do something but usually can't force certain actions to be taken. For instance, a red light, stop sign, and RR signal (see Figure 5.12) are visual controls versus displays because they tell the driver to stop but can't force the driver to stop. We can still go through the red light, RR crossing, or stop sign at some risk to ourselves and others. The driver stops because they know if they continue, there may be some negative consequence, like an accident or a ticket.

In the example shown in Figure 5.13, the water level on the pitcher controls how much water to put in the coffee maker.

They are communication tools to help the systems within an area respond to customer demand and changes within the environment. These controls come in many forms, but the common

**Figure 5.12    Visual controls Stop sign, RR signal, and Red light. (From BIG Archives.)**

**Figure 5.13 Visual controls Water level on pitcher. (From BIG Archives.)**

denominator among them is they cause an appropriate action when a visual signal occurs. The following is a list of examples:

- Kanban (see Figure 5.14) is an information signal that communicates when to replenish. This is also a visual control process.
- Mistake proofing often contains visual controls and displays to prevent the action from occurring again.
- Level loading is done using visual controls and Kanban.
- TPM uses visual controls to trigger preventive or predictive maintenance.

**Figure 5.14 Visual signal for replenishment, also visual displays in pricing and signage, etc. (From BIG Archives.)**

**Figure 5.15   Day-by-hour board. (From BIG Archives.)**

A day-by-hour chart (see Figure 5.15) is a visual control in that it does more than tell us how we are producing to plan by suggesting action be taken in the event we don't meet the plan. Visual control examples are numerous. I'm sure you can find some anywhere you look even at home, for example, on your coffee maker, there are indicator lines on the pot itself as well as the water reservoir:

- Sight and sound alerts warn or describe process status.
- Gauges have colored areas indicating acceptable ranges.
- Road signs and railroad switch markers.

## Andon

Andon is a form of signaling device. It can be visual or a noise in the form of an electronic counter (see Figure 5.16), clock, buzzer, or even music.

Prior to installing any type of andon or visual control, a prerequisite is to create a sustainable system behind the andon signal. This may involve some type of quick response and escalation process. One needs to create standard work and establish the positive or negative consequences in the event the standard is not adhered to. One must make sure there is a fix-it mentality, so it never comes back and creates poka-yoke devices where necessary. For andon to work, one needs to establish one-piece flow, 5S, procedures for stopping the line, and the proper signaling devices (see Figure 5.17).

## Examples

- When a dryer is complete, the cycle buzzes.

**Figure 5.16 Andon—counter. (From BIG Archives.)**

- When a Kanban card is placed in the post-office box, it triggers the right number of parts to be made or replenished (see Figure 5.18).
- On a line when an andon light is turned on, it may signal to a material handler that parts may need to be collected to be washed, or to a team leader or supervisor that a machine is down.

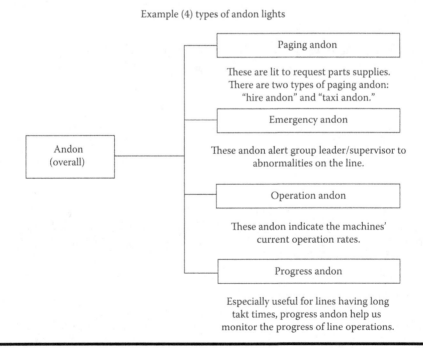

**Figure 5.17 Types of andon. (From The Visual Factory.)**

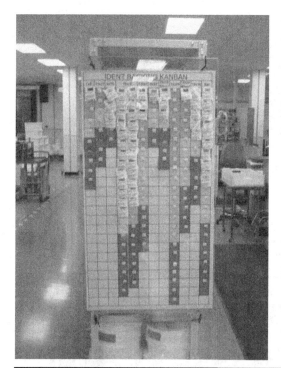

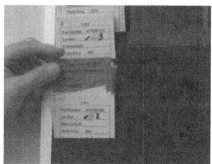

**Figure 5.18 Kanban boards. (From BIG Archives.)**

## *Make Sure You Have a System Behind It!*

The goal is to create a visual management system so anyone can walk around the area and know exactly what's going on and how the area is doing without asking anyone. The area should be constantly speaking to you. For example, the second color tissue (see Figure 5.19) shows the box needs to be replenished. The key is having a system behind it to recognize the signal and replace it (Figure 5.20).

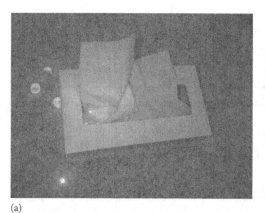

(a)                                        (b)

**Figure 5.19   (a) Tissue box and (b) Simple, inexpensive andon lights. (From BIG Archives.)**

*Change is ever constant: a way of life and Lean*
Valerie Lager, Educator

Flow production: Describes how goods, services, or information are processed one piece at a time. Depicted here is Stacy Huth RN, reviewing the acute care chart process with Mary Ann Snyder UC. Together they are trying to determine what is necessary or value added, not value added but necessary, and not necessary.

Stacy Bauer Rood RN is demonstrating a visual control board. This visual control board allows for visual management of the Lean care track for RNs, registration and patient care providers. *At a glance* we know who is being cared for; where they are; and what has been ordered, what is being completed, or is completed for our patient care items. This simple *tracking board* of sorts has been improved many times by those that work in the Lean care track. A visual control compels someone to take action but may not necessarily force the action (i.e., a stop light).

Another visual control, represented above, and recently created is the completed and discharged bins for patient charts. This system has also been changed several times by those in the Lean care track to help our care providers move patients through the flow efficiently.
Visual management system example
Visual controls are part of an overall visual management system. Visual management systems are composed of

1. 5S
2. Visual displays
3. Visual controls
4. Begin to integrate elements of poka yoke (mistake of fool proofing)

An example of a visual management system with which we are all familiar is fire safety. The fire safety plan has many components of a visual management system. The goals of a true visual management system are to rapidly expose any abnormal conditions, i.e., the

**Figure 5.20   Visual controls—ACMH hospital newsletter. (Reprinted with permission from ACMH Hospital.)**

# What Do 5S and Surgery Have in Common?

When we create our Lean environment in factories, we use the emergency room as an example. We ask 5-day training class participants the following questions regarding creating a Lean environment:

1. Does every second count?
2. Do I need all my tools and supplies at point of use (POU)?

3. Do I need standing/walking operations?
4. Does everyone need to know their jobs and have standard work?

The answers are a resounding *yes* to each question. Then I go on to explain and ask what the difference is between a factory and an emergency trauma room:

1. Does every second count? Yes.
2. Do I need all my supplies at POU? Imagine the doctor says, "Scalpel," and the nurse says, "Wait a minute doc, it's in the cabinet over there!" After searching, she can't find it and says, "It must have been moved out of the room to the 'core' supply area!"
3. Do I need standing/walking operations? Imagine they wheel you into the emergency department and all the doctors and nurses are sitting down on chairs.
4. Do we need standard work? Imagine if all procedures were not standardized.

## Visual Management System—Daily Management Planning

Implementing a good visual management system means one must eventually integrate the following Lean tools:

■ 5S
■ Visual displays
■ Visual controls
■ Mistake proofing
■ Level loading
■ Kanban
■ TPM
■ Standard work
■ A3—PDCA
■ FMEA
■ Control plans

Visual management is a system that supports daily management planning and leader standard work. When integrated with mistake proofing, devices may be installed to detect or prevent defects or injury from occurring. The goal of a good visual management system is to make abnormal conditions immediately visible using the tools referenced previously, 5S, visual displays, and visual controls, and taking the premise one step further by incorporating root cause, countermeasures, andon, risk mitigation, TPM, and mistake proofing. A good visual management system allows problems no place to hide and prevents defects from occurring in the first place. The goal of the system is to prevent or mitigate the defect.

Another goal is to eliminate the need for checking. Most supervisors spend their time in their office or walking around the floor checking on this and that to see if anything is wrong. Why? Because it's not visible. If we can make machine cycle times versus their standards visible and alarm when there is a mismatch, then the system is telling us about the problem. This means we no longer must check. Eliminating checking will free up a significant amount of time each day for any supervisor/group leader.

Visual control is the principle of making production activities, processes, and results visual and clear, so they are self-apparent and obvious to all. Visual control begins with making the factory's abnormalities and forms of waste so clear that even a beginner will recognize them:

■ By learning to distinguish promptly between what is normal and what is not
■ By making abnormalities and waste obvious enough for anyone to recognize
■ By constantly uncovering needs for improvement
■ By eliminating the need for the group leader/supervisor to check
■ Visual control can be applied throughout all facets of manufacturing

An example of each component can be found in automobiles. Let's say you leave the headlights on in the car. What happens? The car has a light that shows your headlights are on (andon). If you take the key out of the ignition, it makes a noise (andon) to make you aware your lights are still on. The next level is where it mistake proofs it by turning off your lights for you after a preprogramed length of time. The lights going out is the final signal of the visual management system. The car now prevents the defect by mitigating the error and preventing the defect (dead battery). We discuss visual management from a supervisor's perspective later in this chapter.

Notice we said visual management system with an emphasis on system. Prior to implementing 5S or any type of visual system, one must create and document the *system behind the system* with standard work to make sure the new system will work properly. Everyone should have roles and responsibilities tied to this new system so that when an andon light or audible is triggered, people know who should respond and when.

## Day-by-Hour Chart

Measurements of the process in the area are visual controls updated by team members and are used to drive improvements. Day-by-hour charts are a simple form of an area metric. When the area is performing to the takt time (TT) or planned cycle time, it is meeting its target metrics. When the area misses, comments are noted on the chart to help the teams follow up with countermeasures. The charts are used to facilitate team meetings (huddles, quality circles, etc.) and become the primary communication tool.

The day-by-hour chart (see Figure 5.21) displays the planned production for each hour, considering breaks, meetings or huddles, and exercise times. There are many variations of this chart depending on the line or area in which it is utilized. Each hour, the team lead or one of the operators enters the actual amount of product (or paperwork) produced. If there is a variance for the hour, the team lead or operator enters in the variance and the explanation for the variance and whether any containment actions or countermeasures were required. The real value in the chart is twofold. First, it shows the team members how they are doing against the plan (which originally comes from the workflow analysis [WFA] and subsequent standard work). The second is to assess the reason for the variance. If the variance is negative, there should be some type of action taken by the team lead or supervisor to begin to root cause and take counter measures to correct the variance. If the problem can be corrected right away, that is noted on the sheet. If it cannot be corrected right away, it should go to the +QDIP board (Quality, Delivery, Inventory, Productivity, +Safety/5S) under the appropriate heading and then root caused by the team or supervisor. The key is to flush out all the problems in the line.

When the line first comes up, the problems would normally be so many that we only fill in the plan column of the day by hour and keep a separate list of items that need to be fixed and we allocate them to a quick fix team or rapid response team (which is normally the team implementing

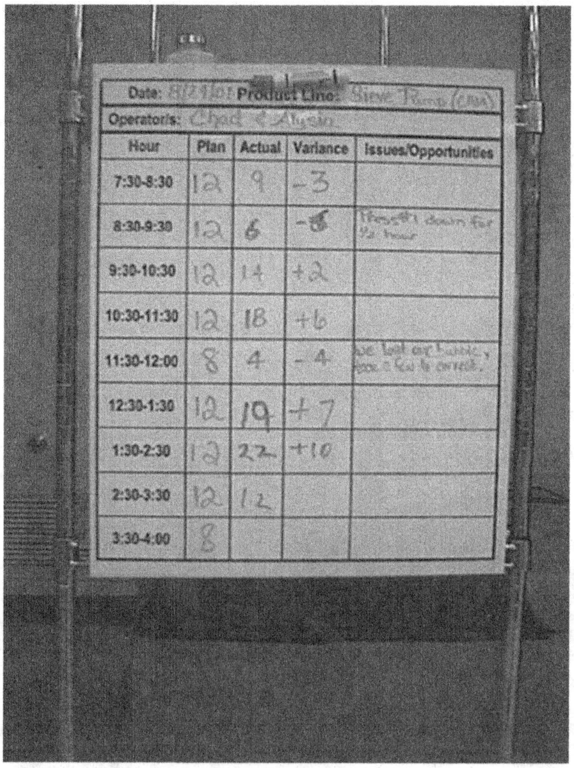

**Figure 5.21   Day-by-hour chart. (From BIG Archives.)**

the line). If the line can produce more an hour than the plan, we need to put as much effort into investigating as well to ensure, first off, that the standard work is being followed correctly, team members aren't rushing, and no shortcuts are taken. If they continue to beat the plan, we need to film, analyze why (with the team member), and update the standard work. This tool should also be one of the items monitored in daily management gemba walks.

Some lines have so much variation or have so many models produced we don't know what the plan should be initially. Since the WFA is generally performed on only one model or sometimes two or three models, there may still be several models or options yet to be determined. In this case, we set the plan based on the times for the average model by assessing whether the current model being produced has inherently more or less labor time and adjust up or down from the average output each hour accordingly. Eventually we study and record the times for each model and create a mixed model total labor time (TLT) chart.

This chart will also give the operators something to shoot for each hour since they know from sitting in the analysis sessions these times are more than achievable. When we first set up the line, we normally don't require the supervisor to put in the plan, but we do get them used to recording the actuals each hour. The reason for this is when we put the plan up immediately, the team members (operators) think we want them to rush to meet the numbers. Nothing could be farther from the truth. So, we let them get used to the line and work our way down the learning curve, and normally a week later, we will start entering the plan by hour. We also have a spreadsheet designed to aid in filling out the day-by-hour plan that is especially helpful for supervisors when doing mixed model lines. Figure 5.22 shows the weekly and daily metric priorities.

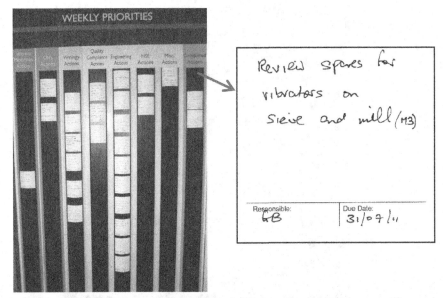

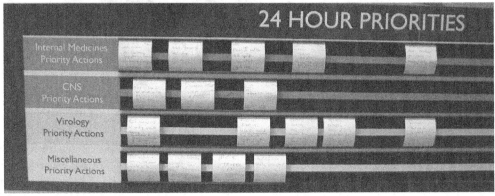

**Figure 5.22 Visual metrics priorities—to ensure priority actions that are to be closed out within 24 hours.**

## Team's Territory[5]

*Team's area (see Figure 5.23)*

1. Identification of territory
2. Identification of activities, resources, and products
3. Identification of the team
4. Markings on the floor
5. Markings of tools and racks
6. Technical area
7. Communication area and rest area
8. Information and instructions
9. Neatness (broom)

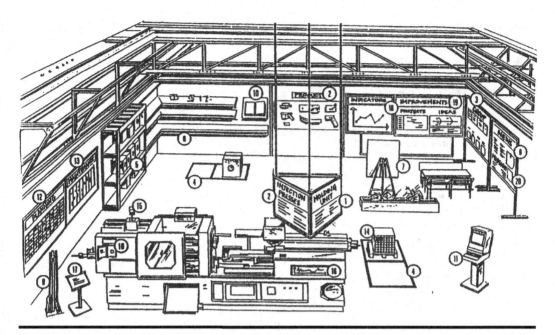

**Figure 5.23   Visual factory. (From The Visual Factory.)**

*Visual documentation*
  10. Manufacturing instructions and technical procedures
*Visual production control*
  11. Computer terminal
  12. Production schedule
  13. Maintenance schedule
  14. Identification of inventories and work in process (WIP)
*Visual quality control*
  15. Monitoring signals for machines
  16. Statistical process control (SPC)
  17. Record of problems
*Displaying indicators*
  18. Objectives, results, and differences
*Rendering progress visible*
  19. Improvement activities
  20. Company project and mission statement

## *Why a Visual Factory*

- Surfaces problems quickly
- Reduces search time by 50%
- Improves safety
- Increases productivity
- Easier for new employee to learn
- Enabler for standard work

- Management by sight—limited or no technical knowledge of area needed to assess the current condition
- Improves safety, increases audit compliance for HS&E
- Can sometimes lower insurance rates
- Enabler for high-performance work teams
- Reduces meetings to discuss work issues
- Sees if you are on target to meet requirements
- Identifies flow and roadblocks
- Communicates to everyone what performance measures are in place
- Demonstrates all elements for safe and effective work
- Provides real-time feedback to everyone involved
- Can positively influence the behavior and attitude of team members
- Customers love it
- Shows everything has a place and everything is in its place
- Controls inventory
- Indicates performance
- Indicates nonconformances
- Indicates when help is needed
- What are goals/targets, key measures, roadblocks to success?
- Most importantly, how do my individual efforts contribute toward the success of my organization?

## Chapter Questions

1. What is a visual display?
2. What is a visual control?
3. What are the three components of a visual management system?
4. Does visual management apply to office environments?
5. What are the benefits of a visual management system?
6. What are the 5S's?
7. Which S do you think is the most important?
8. Where do you see 5S being most useful for you?
9. How is 5S implemented in the office environment? Are there unique challenges?
10. What challenges do you see in using 5S?
11. What is management's responsibility with 5S?
12. Why should management embrace a visual management system?
13. Who sets the standard?
14. How do you sustain 5S, visual controls, and visual management systems?
15. What are tangible benefits of a 5S factory?
16. What is a day-by-hour chart? How is it used?
17. What did you learn from this chapter?

## *Homework*

1. Create a 5S audit sheet
2. Take a gemba walk. Does the factory talk to you?
3. Put on a white glove and see how long it stays white.

## *Exercises*

- What are goals/targets, key measures, roadblocks to success?
- Most importantly, how do my individual efforts contribute toward the success of my organization?
- Give an example of a visual display and control at work and at home.
- Create a visual display for your workplace or classroom.
- Create a visual control for your workplace or classroom.

## Notes

1. James Liu 刘 伟, Engineering Manager, China.
2. Nelson, Mayo and Moody, Productivity Five S Series, Powered by Honda; Shimbun, The Five S's, Visual Control Systems; Hirano, Putting Five S to Work; and Ohno, Workplace Management.
3. Source unknown.
4. Taiichi Ohno, Toyota Production System (New York: Productivity Press), 1988.
5. Michel Greif, The Visual Factory: Building Participation Through Shared Information (See What's Happening in Your Key Processes—At a Glance, All) [Hardcover] (New York: Productivity Press), 1991.

## Additional Readings

Galsworth, G.D. 1997. *Visual Systems*. New York: American Management Association.

Greif, M. 1991. *The Visual Factory: Building Participation Through Shared Information* (See *What's Happening in Your Key Processes—At a Glance, All*) [Hardcover]. New York: Productivity Press.

Hirano, H. 1993. *Putting 5S to Work*. Tokyo, Japan: PHP Institute.

MCS Media. 2008. *The Five S for the Office User's Guide*. Chelsea, MI: MCS Media.

Nikkan, S. 1995. *Visual Control Systems*. Portland, OR: Productivity Press.

Osada, T. 1991. *The Five S's*. Tokyo, Japan: Asian Productivity Association.

Rubin, M. and Hirano, H. 1996. *5S for Operators*. Portland, OR: Productivity Press.

Smith, W. 1998. *Time Out—Visual Based System*. New York: John Wiley & Sons.

# Chapter 6

# Total Productive Maintenance

"Maintenance should be looked at as a capacity generator."[1]

## TPM: Definition

TPM stands for total productive maintenance and is a combination of the following:

1. Preventative maintenance—completing routine tasks at set intervals to prolong the life of the equipment and to prevent breakdowns from happening in the future.
2. Predictive maintenance—performing tasks based upon a historical pattern of breakdown or wear. Often companies have several similar machines, and lessons can be learned based upon past breakdowns or wear patterns that can be incorporated into routine tasks, which should reduce the risk of breakdowns.
3. Participative management/employee involvement results in a productive maintenance program carried out by all employees. TPM is, in effect, equipment maintenance performed on a company-wide basis, and there are five goals of an effective TPM plan:
   a. Maximize equipment effectiveness (improve overall efficiency)
   b. Develop a system of productive maintenance for the life of the equipment
   c. Involve all departments planning, designing, using, or maintaining equipment in implementing TPM—to include engineering and design, production, and maintenance
   d. Actively involve all employees—from top management to shop floor employees
   e. Promote TPM through motivational management (autonomous small group activities)

The word total in TPM has three meanings related to three important features of a good TPM program that is composed of the following elements:

1. Total effectiveness (pursuit of economic efficiency or profitability)
2. Total PM, including maintenance prevention and activity to improve maintainability in addition to basic preventative maintenance
3. Total participation with autonomous maintenance by operators and small group activities in every department and at every level

DOI: 10.4324/9781003185819-6

TPM involves everyone in the organization, from top management to the team member on the floor. With TPM, the staff members share in the maintenance and upkeep of the equipment and complete day-to-day checklists (adding oil to a machine, changing over reagents), and the maintenance team ensures the complex items are completed to support operation schedules. The analogy is taking care of your car. You wash it, check the fluids, and put gas in it, but when there is a big problem, such as a transmission overhaul, you take it to a mechanic. As the car owner (process owner), you still own the timely completion of the maintenance or repair. TPM has many applications in industry. There are machines throughout the operation, but we often don't think about them. All this equipment needs to be maintained if it is to be available when needed. In a Lean enterprise, the team members, whether working on the shop floor or in the office, become the front line for maintenance when reporting problems or making minor fixes to machines.

## What We Typically Find[2]

As a consultant, I have visited clients where previous Lean initiatives have not been successful. I remember visiting a potential client, and as we were walking around the plant, I noticed a TPM board. We walked over to it and I noticed signatures and information missing and the date was from four months ago. I asked members of the senior leadership team a question. Does anyone check this board? No was the reply. Why not? was my next question. No one told us we had to check the board. Would checking this board be of any value to you? A comment from one member of the senior leadership was yes. I then went to the floor and asked several questions about the TPM board that included the following: who checks? How frequently? Does anyone from the leadership team check the board? How do you feel about that? The replies to these questions included the following: we do, daily, no, and the consensus was unanimous—nobody cares. Again, I asked the same question about the value of the TPM board. Most of the floor personnel did not understand the purpose of the board but rather they just followed the instructions given to them—only one-way communication!

I explained to the senior leadership team that the TPM board was a visual management tool and the tool must be managed. Indeed, any system or process being created and developed must include leadership management and accountability to ensure sustainment. In addition, I explained that all employees responsible for completing this board must understand the purpose of this board as well as why they are being asked to complete this TPM board. Understanding requires a good flow of information through communication in a two-way direction.

At another Company X, I was visiting a potential client, and as I introduced myself to the leadership group. One of the members immediately became very defensive and said, "we already do Lean and especially TPM." I replied, "Please show me." I was taken to an area and shown the TPM activities wall. To the untrained eye, it looked ok, but to the trained eye, it was a mess. The TPM cards were out of date, the checklists were 2 months past due, neither the operators nor the maintenance team could explain the system.. Management was convinced TPM was working as it looked great and showed well, however, the sustainability portion (accountability) for TPM as well as the two-way communication of this activity to the group on floor was absent.

## Can This Equipment Be Saved?

While the pictures below (see Figure 6.1) may look disastrous, they usually fall under the boiled frog syndrome (see Figure 6.2). We pass the equipment every day, without even giving it a thought, except to complain about how old it is and constantly ask when they are going to replace it. But if you can't take

**Figure 6.1 Equipment pictures. (From BIG Archives.)**

care of the existing equipment, why should we replace it? The process owners need to ensure the equipment is maintained in their areas. If not, it reflects their ability to truly lead and own their area. They must remove all roadblocks to the successful completion of the assigned TPM tasks by their employees.

Discipline is necessary to implement and sustain a TPM program. Consider painting the floors with light gray or white color to show any oil leaking from machines and then have someone not just fix the leak but find out the root cause of the leak. Dr. Shigeo Shingo would sit for hours watching and listening to machines. He would tell you that the machines talk to you, and if you study them long enough, you can normally figure out the root cause of any problem. The goal is always to fix the problem so it never comes back otherwise we can assure you that it will rear its ugly head again when you least expect it. Unfortunately, taking the time to get to the root cause or standing there listening to a machine run for hours are not actions looked at favorably in most companies, because there is pressure to just get the lineup and running or to always appear busy.

Like cars, most of us know when the car is not idling properly, has a miss or is knocking, or is pulling to the right. Many of you with automatic transmissions can feel when the car is ready to shift and often release the accelerator pedal to make it shift. You become the machine. We can use the same process in our factories by installing sensors and andon signals to warn us before something goes wrong.

**Figure 6.2 With sign—boiled frog syndrome at work—"Please do not Lean on the sink's edge. It is pulling away from the wall." Hmmm. (From BIG Archives.)**

Accountability and pride are required to ensure the machines are operating as planned and designed. It is not just the company's machine; it is your machine! We should clean our machines daily and check the gauges to make sure the fluid levels are proper and look for opportunities to improve the machine. If we do not, it should be quickly evident to the process owner, and swift, appropriate, corrective action should be taken. If we allow bad behavior to become a habit, a standard if you wish, it is hard to break.

Many companies have been successful at revving up the machine like over boring your pistons in an engine block and having the machine exceed its original design specifications. If you have the need to decrease the cycle time and can do it safely, it can be a much cheaper alternative as compared to purchasing a new machine. Similarly, if you can improve the machines, build in jidoka, etc., it can be a barrier to entry to your competition as those features won't be available commercially.

## Total Productive Maintenance Goals

1. Eliminate unplanned machine downtime
2. Increase machine capacity
3. Incur fewer defects (scrap or rework)
4. Reduce overall operating costs
5. Allow for minimum inventory
6. Increase operator safety
7. Create a better working environment
8. Improve environment and sustainability
9. Eliminate breakdowns
10. Reduce equipment start-up losses
11. Faster more dependable throughput
12. Improve quality

## Six Big Losses (in a Factory)

The six big losses in a factory (see Figure 6.3) are listed below:

1. *Availability*
   a. Equipment failure (breakdown losses)—This refers to downtime resulting from machines breaking down.
   b. Setup and adjustment (setup losses)—This refers to downtime caused by setup times.
   c. Idling and minor stoppage—This refers to losses that result from uneven workflow or short stoppages due to detection of defective products.
2. *Operating Rate*
   a. Reduced speed—Machine is running slower than it was designed to.
3. *Defects Produced: Quality*
   a. Defect in process (defect losses)—This refers to waste that occurs when defective products must be thrown out or reworked.
   b. Reduced yield (yield losses)—These are the results of constant stopping and starting of equipment, including the loss from start-up to stable production.

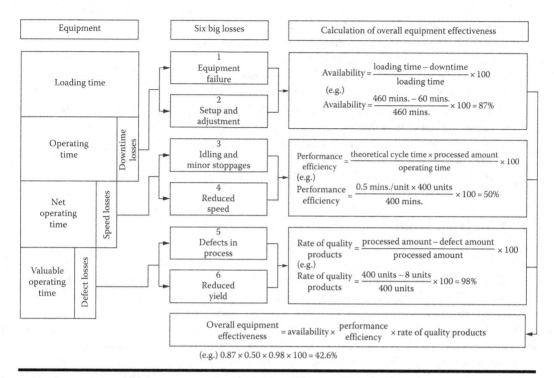

**Figure 6.3 TPM six big losses.**

Listed below are factors resulting in Machine losses:

4. *Factors Leading to Machine Troubles[3]*
   a. Dirty machine
   b. Dirty oiler
   c. Flooded oil pan
   d. Oil leakage
   e. Empty oiler
   f. Overheated motor
   g. Uncontrolled vibration
   h. Scattered chips
   i. Difficulties in inspection
   j. Dirty floor
   k. Lack of organization

5. *Factors Related to Operators[4]*
   a. Not concerned about dirty machine
   b. Make mistakes in operation, changeover, and maintaining
   c. Have no knowledge of inspection
   d. Incapable or unwilling to conduct easy maintenance
   e. Lack of knowledge of the machine itself—oiling, tool change, parts change, adjustment, etc.
   f. Do not ask for help even when a problem exists
   g. Consider production more important than good machine maintenance
   h. Do not have control over machines

These factors, by definition, are all controllable by the process owner.

6. *Factors Related to Mechanics/Maintenance Crews*[5]
   a. Replace or repair parts, but do not question why trouble occurred or the root cause of the problems so they never come back
   b. Do not train or work with operators on basic/easy maintenance task
   c. Do not effectively communicate with operators
   d. Focus efforts on major urgent troubles and forget about dealing with quality-related problems and loss of machine speed
   e. Consider machine deterioration as unavoidable
   f. Seek solutions in new machines or new technologies rather than in available resources
   These factors and behaviors are all owned by the maintenance process owner.

## TPM Metrics Goals

### *Zero Breakdowns*

TPM is just-in-time (JIT) for machines. The machine must be ready when you need it and for however long you will need it. If not, we cannot support one-piece flow goals and meet production targets. Part of this JIT strategy for TPM dictates the creation of a spare parts list and on-call contact lists located at the machine, which include in-house and supplier contact information for repair and service, as well as timing (escalation protocols) based on what is happening on the machine or in the area. The spare parts list is generally available from the manufacturer as well as maintenance recommendations. Almost everything today is available on the Internet. An interesting concept here was undertaken by Snow Jiang. Because spare parts can be very expensive, it doesn't normally pay to have every part for the machine available. If one does a failure mode and effects analysis (FMEA) and a break-even analysis, one can determine the optimum level of spare parts to carry on hand. The break-even analysis compares the cost of the part and carrying the part to the cost of the machine breaking down for the length of time it would take to replenish the part (Figure 6.4).

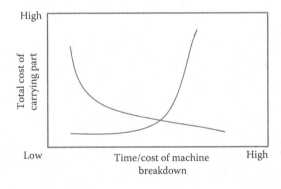

Hand drawn explanation
from Snow Jiang

**Figure 6.4  TPM break even analysis—one must consider the total cost of the machine being down. On a Lean line, a machine being down means the entire line is down. As a result this analysis may be different in a Lean vs. batch environment. (Courtesy of Snow Jiang, Plant Manager.)**

## Zero Defects

The machine should be processed and capable of making zero defects, and in the event, it has a problem; it should shut itself down and signal the shutdown with an andon light to make the problem immediately visible. This is one of the principles of jidoka. In some cases, we configure the machine to text the person responsible when the machine goes down.

## Process Capability

Process capability is the measure of the inherent reproducibility of the product produced by a process. The most widely adopted results for process capability (Cp) are as follows:

■ Cpk > 1.33 = more than adequate
■ Cpk ≤ 1.33 but > 1.00 = adequate, but must be monitored as it approaches 1.00
■ Cpk ≤ 1.00 but > 0.67 = not adequate for the job
■ Cpk ≤ 0.67 = totally inadequate

# Overall Equipment Effectiveness

The goal of overall equipment effectiveness (OEE) is to take metrics that individually might look good and review them together (see Figure 6.5). The metrics are the following:

1. Scheduled available time (any unplanned downtime or changeover time counts against this)
2. Operating rate or speed at which the machine is designed to run
3. Defect rate—the percentage of parts manufactured per specification

Many companies do not have the discipline to accurately collect the needed information for OEE on an ongoing basis. If one is going to utilize OEE, it is imperative that the proper data are

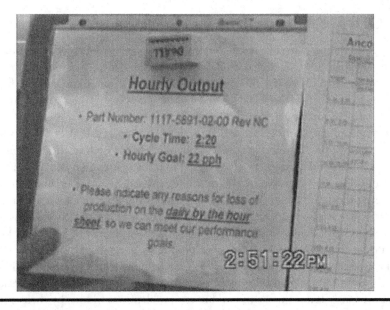

**Figure 6.5   Hourly output and machine cycle time goals.**

collected and proper data collection procedures exist; otherwise, your OEE analysis is based on faulty data. Many times, companies' interpretation of scheduled available time is incorrect or the data are skewed to make the process owner look good. The other question is, "Is everyone measuring each of the categories the same way?" The purpose of the operating rate metric is to determine if an operator is slowing the machine down due to a problem, or where they just want more overtime.

> At Company X, they were measuring operating rate by comparing their output to the standard. When I asked them how they arrived at the standard, they said it was based on demonstrated performance. Their demonstrated performance had been going down each year so the operating rate metric improved each year compared to the declining standard. The standard was not based on the machine cycle time, or speeds and feeds. Therefore, the operating rate calculation was useless and hid any chance of improvement.

Lesson Learned: Operating rate should only be based on the manufacturer's recommended speeds and feeds for the machine. It should be a cycle time–driven metric not based on actual output compared to some standard that hasn't been updated in years.

Other pitfalls are encountered when OEE is applied to a cell or overall area. The metric was designed to be used for one machine as there could be different challenges at each machine in an area. This is not to say an operational definition cannot be created to apply OEE to an area, but it is important if you want it to be actionable, to understand what you are really measuring.

### *OEE Formula/Calculator*

Here is an example of applying OEE (See Table 6.1) to a machine that overall looks pretty good. It was available 61% of the time, was running at 96% of its original cycle time, and 99% of the parts were good! Not too shabby, but the overall OEE is only 58%, right? So, let's go step by step through our OEE Equation.

## Improper OEE Measurement

> Company X was a highly automated facility. They had a multistage piece of equipment for which they measured scheduled available time to run time. They told me they did not need to measure OEE and their measure of run time was more than sufficient. They claimed that the operating rate could not be changed by the operator and the defect rate was included in their output per hour.
>
> As we got into the setup improvement activity, we noticed that at times, several holders on the equipment were not running or filled. Since each of these stages contained a part (or should have); in effect, it meant that the operating rate of the machine was not at 100%. For example, if the machine had ten holders but only five were working, even though the run time was 100% and it was running at the speed it was designed to run, the actual operation rate was 50% and that is assumed it was running at the speed it was designed to run. This meant the machine had to run hours longer to make up for the holders, which were not producing parts. However, the scheduler included the additional run time required in the scheduled time essentially hiding the problem. In addition, we found they were averaging about 5% defects. So, their capacity was significantly lower than standard but the problem was hidden by their existing metrics or scheduling methods.

**Table 6.1 TPM Calculator Example[6]**

| | | | |
|---|---|---|---|
| *Overall Equipment Effectiveness (OEE) Calculator* | | | |
| *OEE Is a Measure of the Value Added to Production through Equipment* | | | |
| A | Working minutes per day | 480 | Actual time per day or per shift |
| B | Loading time per day = available time (minutes) | 420 | Actual time less time taken for meetings, breaks, and lunch |
| C | Total output per day (good and bad units) | 15,300 | Actual output per day from day-by-hour chart |
| **Types of Downtime** | | | |
| D | Setup | 90 | Time from last good piece to first good piece |
| E | Breakdowns | 60 | Any time equipment is stopped due to breakdown |
| F | Adjustments | 15 | Any time equipment is stopped due to adjustments |
| G | Total downtime per day | 165 | (D + E + F) |
| H | Defects | 153 | # defects in total output per day from day-by-hour chart |
| I | Actual cycle time | 0.0200 | Measured at the machine via watch or video |
| J | Ideal cycle time | 0.0160 | Cycle time the machine should be running per manufacturer's specs or speeds and feeds |
| K | Operating speed rate | 80% | Ideal cycle time/actual cycle time (J/I) |
| L | Net operating rate | 120% | [(Output per day × actual cycle time) ÷ (loading time − downtime)] [(C × I) ÷ (B − I)] |
| M | Availability rate | 61% | [(Loading time − downtime) ÷ loading time] [(B − G) ÷ B] |
| N | Performance rate | 96% | Net operating rate × operating speed rate (L × K) |
| O | Quality rate | 99% | [(Total output − defects)÷total output] [(C − H)÷C] |
| P | OEE | 58% | (Quality rate × performance rate × availability rate) (O × N × M) |

# OEE Equation

Given the following:

## *Scheduled Availability*

Ten percent of the time, we had planned for the machine to be down for normal maintenance.

## Operating Rate

We had to slow the machine down due to a service issue, so its operating rate was at 90% of what it was rated.

## Defect Percentage

We had 95% good results, that is, 5% had to be retested. These numbers by themselves look pretty good, but they hide the true utilization of the machine. The true utilization is 0.9 × 0.9 × 0.95 or 76.95%. It turns out the process capability of the machine is just below 1.0. So sometimes it produces bad parts.

OEE multiplies these percentages of available time, operating rate, and % good parts together (0.9 × 0.9 × 0.95) (see Figure 6.6) to determine the true capacity (77%) of the machine (see Figure 6.7). OEE has become somewhat of a controversial metric, and in his book, World Class

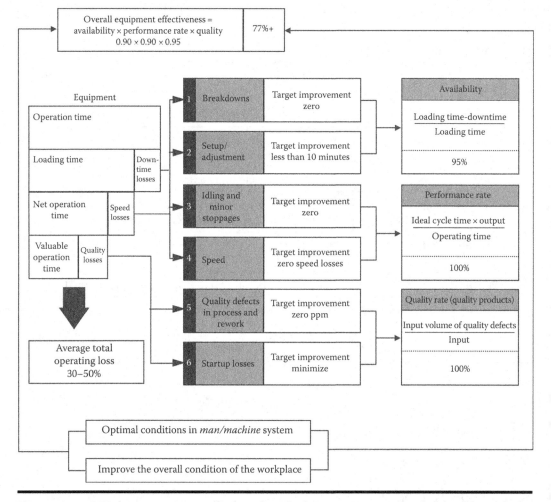

**Figure 6.6 OEE improvement goals for chronic losses. (From TPM development plan—Nakajima with some modifications in targets.)**

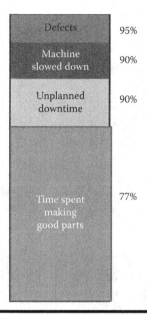

| | |
|---|---|
| Defects | 95% |
| Machine slowed down | 90% |
| Unplanned downtime | 90% |
| Time spent making good parts | 77% |

**Figure 6.7   Overall equipment effectiveness (OEE) results percentages.**

Manufacturing,[7] Richard J. Schonberger argues it should be abandoned. However, we feel OEE is very useful if utilized properly. It is important that available time be equal to the time the machine is scheduled to be running. In some cases, we choose to have the machine idle for many seconds a cycle. This should be counted against us even though we know the reason why we keep the machine working at this rate.

## New Maintenance Paradigm

Consider the quote at the beginning of the chapter. When it is time to cut heads, where do we normally start? We normally start with indirect labor. The first indirect labor target in operations or manufacturing is normally maintenance. Financial teams and management often ask, "What do they really do?" We can outsource maintenance if we must, right? Sometimes this perception is warranted, but quite often the response is due to poor management of maintenance resources, lack of understanding of the maintenance processes, or lack of discipline and accountability within the maintenance department itself. Laying off maintenance workers first is easy to do because it is quick money on paper, but what does it cost in the long run? When we reduce maintenance resources, the day-to-day problems don't get fixed or, sometimes, even worse, well-intentioned but untrained people try to fix them. Over time, our equipment shuts down or stops running.

Strict and honest management reviews, performed on a regular basis, should be what prevents a management team from doing something like this to themselves. This can be measured by the percentage of PM tasks completed to schedule and the percentage completeness of spare parts inventory. The review of metrics that define a healthy maintenance process should show green, yellow, or red. Reality is that this often leads to a Jack Nicholson moment for management where we find they can't handle the truth, so they stop doing management reviews.

Lesson Learned: Maintenance should not be looked at as a cost center but as capacity generators.

**Figure 6.8** Rick Mangone, director of global quality, STR solar, demonstrating a WORKSMART® flexible two-bin workstation (http://www.worksmartsystems.com) installed in AlliedSignal 1996. The stations are like erector sets and can be easily modified. (From BIG Archives. With permission from Rick Mangone.)

## Lean and Maintenance in Factories

We are constantly asking maintenance to fix machines, remove doors on cabinets, install flexible workstations (see Figure 6.8), remove walls, change workstations, fabricate point of use (POU) locations, and produce mock-ups for pilots. In essence, maintenance really wears two Lean hats. One is helping the factory with Lean changes and the other is considering that maintenance, itself, can be leaned out.

> At Company X, we needed some major layout changes to support Lean. We determined that major changes were needed to overhaul the venting and filtration systems. These changes were not necessary for our project but were overdue to the company's ongoing maintenance. Instead of budgeting for maintenance needs, the company waited for major projects to add to these large-dollar tasks. The ventilation added about $2 million in cost to our ROI. Fortunately, management chose to look at these improvements as ongoing maintenance of their system versus tying it to our project. The capital improvements weren't required by Lean, but it was the only way maintenance could get money to fund the changes.

## TPM Development Plan

### *Where to Start?*

Again, start with a TPM pilot. Select a machine that everyone agrees will result in a successful implementation. One can develop simple checklists posted on the machine (see Figure 6.9). Develop the OEE measurement and restore the machine to like new condition. Determine the

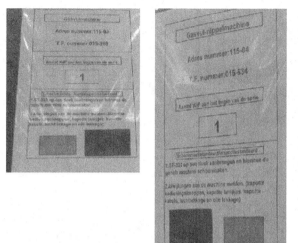

**Figure 6.9    TPM cards—green is complete/red is pending.**

operating rate and post it on the machine. Make sure the operators can't slow the machine down without escalating the problem to the team lead. Then measure the defects and calculate the after OEE and compare it to the before OEE. This program will increase the capacity of machines and in many cases can prevent the purchase of new machines due to the productivity gains realized. TPM should be very visual and not just in someone's computer (see Figure 6.10). One can install simple visual boards to capture and document problems, trigger, track PMs, etc. (see Figures 6.11–6.13).

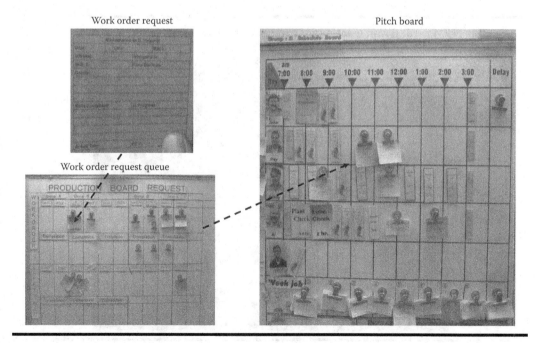

**Figure 6.10    Visual control for TPM. (From BIG Archives.)**

**Front of card**

| MACHINE OR LOCATION | SHIFT (circle) | FREQUENCY OF PM (circle one) | | Original Date | Revised Date |
|---|---|---|---|---|---|
| | 1  2  3 | Weekly  Bi-Weekly  Monthly | | | |
| | | Quarterly  Semi-Annually | | | |
| | | Annually Other (note in comments) | | | |
| Description of Task     ☐ PM | | ☐ 5-S | | Special Comments | |
| | | | | | |

**Back of card**

| | 1 | 2 | 3 | 4 | 5 | 6 | 7 | 8 | 9 | 10 | 11 | 12 | 13 | 14 | 15 | 16 | 17 | 18 | 19 | 20 | 21 | 22 | 23 | 24 | 25 | 26 | 27 | 28 | 29 | 30 | 31 |
|---|---|---|---|---|---|---|---|---|---|---|---|---|---|---|---|---|---|---|---|---|---|---|---|---|---|---|---|---|---|---|---|
| Jan | | | | | | | | | | | | | | | | | | | | | | | | | | | | | | | |
| Feb | | | | | | | | | | | | | | | | | | | | | | | | | | | | | | | |
| Mar | | | | | | | | | | | | | | | | | | | | | | | | | | | | | | | |
| Apr | | | | | | | | | | | | | | | | | | | | | | | | | | | | | | | |
| May | | | | | | | | | | | | | | | | | | | | | | | | | | | | | | | |
| Jun | | | | | | | | | | | | | | | | | | | | | | | | | | | | | | | |
| Jul | | | | | | | | | | | | | | | | | | | | | | | | | | | | | | | |
| Aug | | | | | | | | | | | | | | | | | | | | | | | | | | | | | | | |
| Sep | | | | | | | | | | | | | | | | | | | | | | | | | | | | | | | |
| Oct | | | | | | | | | | | | | | | | | | | | | | | | | | | | | | | |
| Nov | | | | | | | | | | | | | | | | | | | | | | | | | | | | | | | |
| Dec | | | | | | | | | | | | | | | | | | | | | | | | | | | | | | | |

Year

◣ Down      ◪ PM Complete      ⊠ Problem Identified      ▨ Problem Repaired

**Figure 6.11   TPM card. (From Continuous Progress Archives.)**

**Figure 6.12   This a visual display communicating updates for the TPM program along with a visual control of the annual PM schedule. (Courtesy of MarquipWardUnited, a division of Berry-Wehmiller Inc.)**

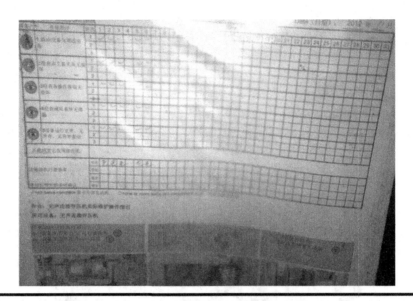

**Figure 6.13    TPM checklist posted on the machine. (From BIG Archives.)**

## *TPM Daily Checklist*

The best way to start TPM is by creating simple checklists for just one pilot piece of equipment. Next, add TPM-related metrics to its processes to ensure they are being carried out properly (see Figures 6.14 and 6.15). As more confidence is gained and sustained, then add the next piece

**Figure 6.14    Total productive maintenance (TPM) daily checklist example. (From BIG Archives.)**

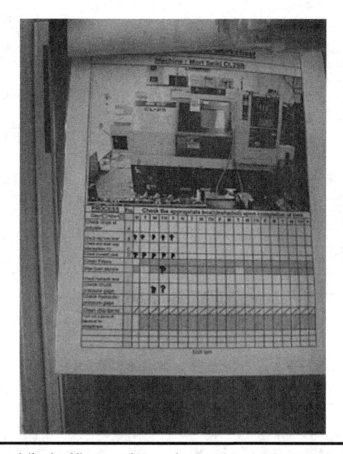

**Figure 6.15  TPM daily checklist (over the month). (From Ancon Gear.)**

of equipment. There must be a written process tied to ISO or QS9000 or some other formal standard documenting the process like a TPM card. The TPM card describes how the machine is to be maintained and documents the maintenance of the machine. One used to see similar cards inside Xerox® machines or large printers.

## Role of 5S, Jidoka, and Visual Controls with TPM

5S is involved when cleaning up the machine and restoring it to its original condition. You will be surprised what problems you find when cleaning a machine or any surface (even at home). Jidoka is the process of improving the machine and updating it so it stops if it makes a mistake. When the machine stops, it should signal the operator with either an andon light, music, or buzzer. This is the linkage with visual controls. Every line, whether water, air, gas, or electric should be labeled with the appropriate data and flow arrows. Electric boxes should be labeled as to voltage and what equipment it supports (see Figure 6.16).

### Andon

Uptime or downtime clocks (see Figure 6.17) can be very helpful when working with machines to include TPM and daily production activities. The andon system and clocks can easily be tied to CNC controllers to show when the machine is cutting and when it is idle.

**Figure 6.16    TPM/5S labeling of circuit boxes.**

## TPM Communication

It is important with TPM as with any other program to create a communication plan. Newsletters, bulletin boards, and informational meetings are good vehicles to communicate the vision for the new TPM system and the roles each person will play (see Figure 6.18).

## Construction Challenges

When implementing Lean, there will be construction challenges: regulatory agencies, permitting bodies, and government regulations impacting construction projects. Maintenance and compliance team members should be on the team and involved early and trained in Lean principles, be always in the communication loop, and be part of the planning process.

**Figure 6.17    Downtime clock wired into PLC. (From BIG Archives.)**

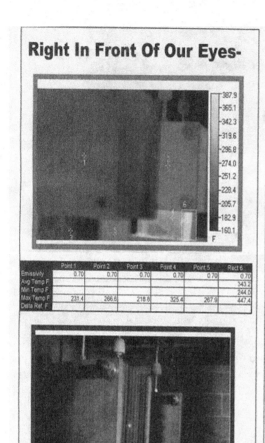

## Right In Front Of Our Eyes-

| | Point 1 | Point 2 | Point 3 | Point 4 | Point 5 | Rect 6 |
|---|---|---|---|---|---|---|
| Emissivity | 0.70 | 0.70 | 0.70 | 0.70 | 0.70 | 0.70 |
| Avg Temp F | | | | | | 343.2 |
| Min Temp F | | | | | | 244.0 |
| Max Temp F | 231.4 | 266.8 | 218.8 | 325.4 | 267.9 | 447.4 |
| Delta Ref F | | | | | | |

*You couldn't ask for a better example for the value of Predictive Maintenance and the advanced technologies than this episode captured on our infrared camera. This occurred on EAF #2*

On Friday August 26th at approximately 10:00 AM melt shop maintenance personnel noticed that the internal oil temperature in the #2 EAF transformer had reached 176° F. This is the maximum recommended allowable oil temperature for this model of Electromelt transformer. Cooling water flow changes were made throughout the day to no avail.

At 6:00 PM the transformer was inspected using infrared thermography and revealed that two of the three secondary bus bars on the transformer were significantly warmer than the third one. Maximum temperatures between the bus bars varied from 268°F on the center phase to 448° F on the pit side phase. This large temperature rise between phases indicated an electrical fault in the connections. The infrared image can be seen alongside the visual image in figure 1 below.

Close visual inspection of the pit side bus and the floor side bus revealed that the insulation boards had been cracked due to bolts coming loose and causing excessive temperatures as a result of decreased electrical resistance. Continued use of the transformer in this condition would have resulted in imminent failure in a short period of time. Estimates from electrical consultants are that the transformer would have failed completely within two days.

Total downtime to make the needed repairs was 14 hours, which is much shorter and less expensive than the 4-5 days that it would take to change out the transformer. Also, the backup transformer at the Kansas City plant is 6 MVA rather than the 7.5 MVA it would replace. This would have resulted in lost production of several million dollars.

The Kansas City facility is implementing an IR electrical inspection program that will help to identify electrical faults before they cause downtime. Using infrared to look for loose bolts also decreases employee exposure to arc flash and electrical shock hazard since the bolts don't need to be checked as often by manually tightening them. IR and other predictive maintenance technologies are proving to be a

**Figure 6.18 Company X newsletter from 2006. With permission. (from BIG Archives.)**

## *When You Have to Move Equipment …*

The other paradigm set for maintenance is if you need to move it once, and figure out how to make it at least 50% easier to move the next time. Some maintenance staff take real pride in this challenge. At one company, a machine had to move to another floor. The machine wouldn't fit on the elevator and the only way to move it was to remove a window and crane it to the next floor. The head of maintenance, Larry, figured he could cut the machine in half and then move it up the elevator shaft and weld it back together. Crazy right? That is what they did. A new paradigm some companies have adopted is if they (the maintenance people) are not working, the company is not making money. The company feels if they are not working, the machines will not run and running machines is what makes money for the company. The goal of this paradigm is to change the thought process. Though this means maintenance workers should never be idle. Even if there are no machines down, they can always be working on the next improvement. This means continuous improvement must be part of the mission for maintenance. Again, maintenance wears two hats, one is staying engaged with Lean by training operators to perform maintenance tasks, fabricating feeders, poka yokes, material transfer mechanisms, etc., while the other is continuously improving the maintenance department itself, i.e., implementing standardized troubleshooting procedures, 5S the maintenance area, streamlining response times to failures, and helping to reduce downtime by fixing problems so they don't return. Believing that being idle at any time is a positive thing, it is headed down the path to failure.

At another plant, we had to move a machine that had a separate electric panel console, hard drives, and hydraulic system. The machine had been moved several times in the past and maintenance dreaded it. Each time they had to disconnect all the cables to the electric panel, all the hydraulic lines to the hydraulic system and then move it as three separate pieces. During a 2-minute kaizen event (brainstorming session), maintenance figured out they could purchase a steel plate and mount the electric panel and hydraulic system to the steel plate and move it as one big unit. The next time we went to move it, we installed air cushion panels under the steel plate and moved the equipment in less than a couple of minutes.

Lesson Learned: We need to budget for predictive and preventative maintenance. Maintenance should not be looked at as a cost center but as a capacity generator.[8]

## When You Must Purchase New Equipment

### Capital Equipment Checklist

Use the capital equipment checklist (see Table 6.2) prior to purchasing new equipment. Make sure new equipment is installed in the proper place according to the product flow. Don't just put it wherever it will fit!

**Table 6.2  Capital Equipment Checklist**

| *Cost* |
| --- |
| Is the equipment relatively low cost? |
| Do the return on investment (ROI) and ROA justify the cost? |
| Would last year's model satisfy your needs and cost less than this year's model? |
| Could some other type of equipment be used that is less expensive? |
| Is used equipment available? |
| Do we currently have another machine or stand-alone piece of equipment that can do all or a portion of the job? (i.e., stand-alone drill press, gear machine) |
| Was there an attempt to build or modify equipment using in-house resources? |
| Would it make more sense to lease instead of purchase? |
| Is it costly to upgrade to meet future needs? |

*(Continued)*

**Table 6.2** *(Continued)* **Capital Equipment Checklist**

| |
|---|
| Do we really need all the "bells and whistles"? |
| Is the equipment "right sized" for the job? |
| Can existing equipment be modified to eliminate the need to purchase new equipment? |
| Can the equipment support multiple models? Can the equipment be used or modified to be used on other lines? |
| Question the need for 6 ft. or 12 ft. bar feeders. Bar feeders should only be required if the machine is going to produce completed parts by itself (lights out) |
| Have you done a tips and workflow analysis on the machine? |
| Will purchasing this equipment reduce a true bottleneck? |
| Will purchasing this equipment reduce the number of operators? |
| Is it possible to eliminate the operation that the equipment is being purchased to perform? |
| What is the cost of consumables (coolant, tools, filters, wear parts, etc.)? |
| *Safety* |
| Is special personal protection equipment (PPE) required to operate the equipment? |
| Are safeguards built-in? (i.e., wire caging, splash guards) |
| Does it require two hands to operate? Can it be safely modified to operate one-handed? |
| Can I operate it without any PPE |
| *Setup* |
| Will the equipment support one-touch exchange of dies (OTED) or single-minute exchange of dies (SMED)? |
| Is equipment setup video available? |
| Are parts within the equipment standardized so no special tools are required for setup? |
| Can the machine be set up without any tools or using a single tool? |
| Is the equipment mobile? Can it be modified to be mobile? |
| Can the equipment be programmed from a remote location and in the background memory? |
| Does it have unlimited settings? If so, can it be modified to use only the required settings? |
| *TPM Ready* |
| Does the equipment require periodic calibration? How often? |
| Is there easy access for periodic maintenance? |
| Does the supplier provide good product support? |
| If the equipment is used, are repair records available? |

**Table 6.2** *(Continued)* **Capital Equipment Checklist**

| |
| --- |
| Are schematic and equipment drawings provided? |
| Are replacement parts readily available? How fast can I get them? What is the cost of the inventory for the spare parts? |
| What is the anticipated cost for maintaining the equipment? |
| Do we have the skills necessary to perform periodic maintenance? If not, does the supplier provide training? |
| Does the equipment require periodic maintenance? How often? How long will it be down for maintenance? |
| *Cycle Time* |
| Does the equipment support one-piece flow? |
| Can it be used in-line? |
| Is the equipment cycle time capable of producing parts at less than 50% of the takt time (TT) for intended use (will allow for future growth and surges)? |
| What is the cycle time and throughput time of the machine? |
| Can we have Standard WIP at the machine? |
| Am I creating isolated islands with fractional labor? |
| Can the operators control the cycle time? If so, can we design it so they cannot! |
| *Installation* |
| Can I put the equipment side by side with another machine? If not, can we redesign the access panels to support this? Is the chip conveyor in the rear? |
| Does the equipment require any special installation? |
| Will the equipment fit through existing openings? |
| Do the existing facilities provide the power resources required to operate the equipment? |
| Can the equipment be moved easily and safely? |
| Does it require extensive work after being moved? (i.e., calibration, leveling) |
| How can I install the equipment so it can be moved quickly if necessary to another location? |
| Can I install it without a PIT or footer? |
| Does it come with a conveyor system? Does the conveyor store or transport? |
| Is special training or skills required to set up or operate the equipment? |
| Have you seen the equipment in operation? If no, do you have feedback from someone who has? |
| Does the machine may need to be mounted in an isolated slab, or a pit? |

*(Continued)*

**Table 6.2** *(Continued)*   **Capital Equipment Checklist**

| *Autonomation/jidoka* |
|---|
| Can the equipment run without the operator having to stand and watch it? |
| Can the equipment load and unload itself? |
| Does the equipment support hanedashi? (auto-eject) |
| Does it perform self-diagnostics? |
| Does it warn when tools need replacement? |
| Does it make sure the part it is working on was good before it started? |
| Does it stop itself if nonconforming product is produced? |
| Are the warnings audible or visible (andon)? |
| Will the machine stop before it crashes |
| Will the machine always produce a good part? |
| Is 100% inspection built into the machine? |
| Can the machine call someone if it is down? |
| Does the machine have a downtime clock built-in? |
| *Equipment* |
| Are you aware of a new technology that will make the equipment obsolete? When? Can you visit a site where the equipment is being used? |
| Is it automated or CNC controlled? |
| How many operators do I need to operator the equipment? |
| Can one person operate it? |
| Does the equipment support waist high, elbow deep work areas? |
| Is the equipment less than 5′ tall to support visibility in the work area? |
| Can it be operated standing up? |
| Can the equipment be adjusted to support different heights of operators? |
| Can it be used in-line? In a clean room environment? |
| Is vibration an issue? |
| Does it operate within allowable noise restrictions? |
| What is the equipment's capability? |
| How will material be fed into the work cell to optimize operator movements in the cell? |
| Is the width of the machine no larger than needed (reduce operator travel)? |

**Table 6.2** *(Continued)*   **Capital Equipment Checklist**

| |
|---|
| Is it repeatable? |
| What is its reliability in mean time between failure (MTBF)? |
| Does it require frequent adjustments? |
| Does it use standard jigs and fixturing? |
| Is it compatible with existing equipment? |
| Is it modular? |
| Does it have an open architecture or is it proprietary? |
| Will it be operating at approx. 50% capacity (surge capacity support)? |
| Does it have two-button switches that are BAD! Can it be operated with a one-button switch by hand or thigh? |
| Does the machine let you know if a bad part has been produced? |
| How does this equipment improve or at least support the existing flow? |
| Does the equipment need a specific humidity range to operate |
| Will the machine warn of low level of materials (i.e., injection molding, printing statements) |

*Source:* Mark Caponigro, Dave O'Koren, Charlie Protzman, BIG Archives.

## Too Many Bells and Whistles

Many machines have many more options and features than required for the work at hand. Not only does this make the machine more expensive but also more costly to repair and maintain. Many household machines (appliances) fall into this category. A simple washing machine virtually never breaks down, and when it does, it needs a new belt or chain for the motor. A newfangled electronic washing machine with 14 cycles and 10 speeds with the works generally breaks down more frequently and requires an expensive electronic module or assembly that must be ordered. Ironically, most of us may only use one or two of the hundreds of possible permutations and combinations of features available. This can lead to more complex and expensive repairs for features never utilized. Sometimes machines must be modified (see Figure 6.19) to implement the preventative maintenance, especially when we move the machines literally next to each other when setting up the cell.

## Who Should Own TPM?

Most companies tend to have maintenance own TPM, but this is not necessarily where it belongs. TPM belongs with the senior leadership team or even better, the Board of Directors. It should be considered a company-wide initiative. Maintenance, like quality, needs to be seen as part of everyone's job. While there is an owner of the company-wide preventive maintenance activity, there is also local ownership of the completion of the daily tasks by the workshop or office department. The process owner, where the machine is located, owns the timely completion of these tasks. The operators are the ones who perform the tasks. If they do not perform the tasks well or schedule,

**Figure 6.19 Machine modified in order to fix a recurring problem. (Courtesy of Ancon Gear.)**

the process owner should perform an analysis of why they are not doing their activity and take the proper action.

The senior leadership team ultimately owns the performance of the TPM SYSTEM. The system performance is really a culmination of how all the processes of the business are functioning together, as a system. The metrics of each process should be chosen specifically to drive achievement of the system goals. This will help get companies away from their past silo-based behavior. Senior leadership should remove any roadblocks to the success of the maintenance process owner in daily operations and monthly management reviews.[9]

TPM is a system whose objective is to maintain the overall delivery's system process capability and minimize total costs. Failure to do this has far-reaching effects on an organization in terms of operations, reputation, profitability, customer reputation, products, and employees. For TPM to be successful, every employee must be involved, and maintenance must create robust procedures that will drive and improve equipment performance and reduce unplanned downtime and losses. In the end, this will help reduce inventory and improve both quality, which customers will see, and capacity that will enable company growth.[10]

## TPM Is Not a Cost Reduction Program

TPM requires that up-front costs be budgeted to provide the team with cleaning supplies, spare parts, paint, and whatever is necessary to restore the machine to original condition. Maintenance costs do increase with a TPM program, but it is in the form of either preventive or predictive maintenance. A total life cycle costs analysis (or total cost of ownership) will show a small front-end investment will reduce recurring maintenance costs, thus lowering total life cycle costs. Think of the costs incurred when a machine goes down or is not operating properly or is making bad parts. Human nature is to wait until it breaks to fix it. TPM counteracts this philosophy.

In the long run, TPM helps to reduce equipment operating rates, improve costs, and minimize WIP inventory resulting in increased labor productivity and capacity. TPM programs are not created in weeks and typically can take a year before they are functioning well.

## TPM versus Reactive Maintenance

One would assume that reactive maintenance programs are much more costly than TPM, which utilizes predictive and preventative maintenance. The theory is we don't have time to shut down the equipment for planned maintenance; yet somehow, we have time for unplanned downtime. Most companies that transition to TPM find their costs initially increase, but their unplanned downtime decreases significantly, and overall, the costs offset each other. Yet, their customers are happier because they can now plan their downtime versus a machine going down during a critical order creating tons of scrap. Companies that are on hourly delivery schedules, like in the automotive industry, could incur severe penalties with unplanned machine breakdowns, which domino into shutting down their customers' assembly lines. There was one company that was virtually totally automated, with coffers of inventory stored at their distributors, who told us, based on their in-house study, it was cheaper to live with and deal in the reactive maintenance environment versus TPM. Which is more costly, distribution chains with tons of inventory or a good solid TPM program that can support JIT deliveries?

### *Reactive versus Preventative versus Predictive Maintenance*

Preventative maintenance can keep you up and running but predictive maintenance should be the goal. A good analogy might be the following considering your car tires. You can wait for your tires to fail (worst-case scenario) but that is how most companies work. This is called reactive maintenance. You can replace your tires before they fail but you may give up many miles of travel (this is called preventative maintenance). Or you can use a technology solution to predict exactly when the tire is going to go bad. This is called predictive maintenance. Many technologies exist in the marketplace today that were not available 20 or 30 years ago. These technologies are utilized by NASA and the military. They include ultrasound and sonic testing, infrared thermography, and vibration testing. In many cases, the technology can tell you if a motor bearing needs just lubrication or is going to fail in the next 30 days. In some cases, this is like another analogy. Consider hurricane warnings. The more warning you have, the more you can get prepared for it. If I know a bearing is going to go up, it gives me time to purchase it versus carrying it in an expensive spare parts inventory. In many parts, it can eliminate the replacement cost altogether. For instance, if there is a problem in an electrical panel and I catch it right away I can just replace a simple breaker versus suffering a major downtime problem at some point in the future. The overall goal of preventative coupled with predictive maintenance should be to eliminate your unplanned downtime completely. Jeremy A. Watts, Regional Accounts Manager for US and Canada, states:

> There are many tools available today for predictive maintenance, also known as condition-based maintenance. For instance, CTRL Systems Inc. manufactures the UL101, an ultrasound tester capable of finding air leaks in a plant's compressor system, down to pressure levels of 2 PSI. With many utility companies offering energy incentives for decreasing consumption, simply locating, and repairing leaks can translate into

millions of dollars of real savings for some companies. In addition to its benefits for leak detection and energy savings, the UL101 can provide an earlier and more accurate indicator of motor bearing problems, leading to corrective action which can prevent catastrophic failure and extend the life of the equipment. Except in instances when it is unsafe to do so, the simple and expedient testing process can be performed while the machines under test are up and running. The equipment can also be set up to do ongoing monitoring which will signal maintenance technicians before a problem occurs.

## Centralized versus Decentralized Maintenance

We have seen this issue debated at many companies, sometimes resulting in shouting matches. The goal of centralizing maintenance is to ensure maintenance team members are not idle and to expand cross-training within the maintenance team. Decentralizing involves dedicating a maintenance team member to a product line, family, or value stream. The best model we have seen is to merge these two and have each maintenance team member dedicated to a product line as their first responsibility, and when their task is complete, they are available for the next centralized task in the queue. It is also a good idea to have the maintenance team member start out working on the floor prior to ever working in the maintenance department. This will help them gain an understanding of how a Lean line runs and how the equipment should perform. The next step would be to work with them to develop ideas on how to improve the equipment or maintenance of the equipment.

Regardless of how maintenance is broken up, the various processes owners need to make sure and justify with data, if they have the right number of people and associated skill levels in place to meet the agreed-upon metrics. Either strategy can work, but there needs to be enough trained people in place so areas are not fighting over the limited number of maintenance people trained to do certain things. Otherwise, this allows excuses as to why metrics were not hit and begins to erode the system effectiveness.[11]

## Benefits

Implementing a TPM program will yield the following benefits:

- In the long term, maintenance costs will stabilize (and usually decrease) and machine uptime will increase.
- A reduction in overtime caused by improved equipment reliability.
- Reliable equipment, improved productivity, and increased manufacturing capacity with no capital outlay.
- Operators have more input into their jobs, improved skills, and increased job satisfaction.
- Maintenance function has time to work on correcting chronic problems, improving reliability, and time for planned maintenance.
- Maintenance function can help in the design and fabrication of Lean concepts for machines and cells, including material transfer and poka-yoke devices.
- TPM does not eliminate operators or maintenance people.
- TPM builds trust and respect between operations and maintenance, enhancing teamwork.
- Pride in the equipment condition and uptime.

# Chapter Questions

1. What does the acronym TPM stand for?
2. Is TPM a cost reduction program? Please explain your position.
3. Who has responsibility for TPM?
4. What are the factors used when calculating OEE?
5. What are the goals of a TPM program?
6. Why have some TPM programs failed?
7. What are some of the costs to consider when considering TPM at your plant?
8. What is the new Lean paradigm for maintenance?
9. How does your company handle maintenance issues and what do they do to prevent small issues from becoming large expensive repairs?
10. Should maintenance teams be centralized? What approach supports Lean best and why?
    a. What are the six big losses?
    b. Is setup part of unplanned downtime?
    c. Should OEE be used for entire cells? If your answer is yes, please explain under what conditions.
11. What did you learn from this chapter?

# Notes

1. In the productivity series entitled TPM. Productivity Press TPM Video Series.
2. Submitted by James Bond, College Professor, Toyota retiree, and current international Lean consultant personal correspondence, December 5, 2012.
3. TPM, Productivity Video Series©. TPM Video Tapes Productivity Series.
4. TPM, Productivity Video Series©. TPM Video Tapes Productivity Series.
5. TPM, Productivity Video Series©. TPM Video Tapes Productivity Series.
6. Based on Nakajima, *TPM Development Program* (Productivity Press), 1982
7. World Class Manufacturing, Richard J. Schonberger, Free Press (January 24, 2008).
8. TPM, Productivity Video Series©. TPM Video Tapes Productivity Series.
9. Personal e-mail correspondence with Ken Place January 21, 2013, Ken Place is a Lean Six Sigma master black belt full-time consultant with the University of Illinois Business and Industry Services. Ken has over 16 years of experience working in the auto industry supplying US and Japanese automakers. His experience comes from both manufacturing and quality capacities. Ken has worked with facilities throughout the United States, Europe, and Mexico to implement effective quality management systems compliant with QS9000, ISO 9001, and TS16949 as well as environmental management systems compliant with ISO 14001.
10. Professor James Bond, based on person correspondence and chapter review, February 10, 2013.
11. Personal e-mail correspondence with Ken Place, January 21, 2013, Ken Place is a Lean Six Sigma master black belt full-time consultant with the University of Illinois Business and Industry Services. Ken has over 16 years of experience working in the auto industry supplying US and Japanese automakers. His experience comes from both manufacturing and quality capacities. Ken has worked with facilities throughout the United States, Europe, and Mexico to implement effective quality management systems compliant with QS9000, ISO 9001, and TS16949 as well as environmental management systems compliant with ISO 14001.

# Additional Readings

Campbell, J.D. 1995. Uptime. Portland, OR: Productivity Press.
Kennedy, M.N. 2003. Product Development for the Lean Enterprise. Richmond, VA: Oakley Press.
Nakajima, S. 1988. Introduction to Total Productive Maintenance. Cambridge, MA: Productivity Press.

Nakajima, S. 1989. TPM Development Program. Cambridge, MA: Productivity Press.

Nihon Puranto Mentenansu, K. 1997. Focused Equipment Improvement for TPM Teams. Portland, OR: Japan Institute Productivity Press.

Smith, P.G. and Reinertsen, D.G. 1998. Developing Products in Half the Time. New York: Reinertsen Thomson Publishing Inc.

Tajiri, M. and Gotoh, F. 1999. Autonomous Maintenance in Seven Steps. Portland, OR: Productivity Press.

Wheelwright, S.C. 1992. Revolutionizing Product Development. New York: Free Press Simon Schuster.

# Chapter 7

## Applying Lean to Accounting

There are so many men who can figure costs, and so few who can measure value.

**Author unknown**

Any intelligent fool can make things bigger, more complex, and more violent. It takes a touch of genius—and a lot of courage—to move in the opposite direction.

**E.F. Schumacher[1]**

Accounting is unable to either set or attain ideal standards.

**Harrington Emerson**

This chapter is divided into three parts:

- Part 1 Hidden Wastes: The Sixth Level of Waste
- Part 2 Lean and Collecting Costs
- Part 3 Lean Accounting by Jerrold Solomon[2]

## Part 1: Hidden Wastes: The Sixth Level of Waste[3]

### Paying the Price: Understanding What It Costs to Run Your Business

We contend that more money is lost in companies from measures not tracked than from measures tracked. What do we track? We often track direct labor and direct material and supplies, but we don't always track excess and obsolete inventory, supplies opened but not used, restocking supply labor, rework labor, retention/retraining costs, staff impact by IT issues such as slow response times, cost to keep the business systems fed, cost of inaccurate data and centralized printers, centralized departments, machine downtime, cost of being late from breaks or lunch or lining up at the time clock early, poor office area or cell designs and layouts, not having the right tools to do the job, time spent on work-arounds, or time searching for equipment and supplies. These costs play a role in productivity as well as costs to operations, asset management, capital, and cash flow. What is your cost per minute in the office or on the floor? Again, none of these costs are

DOI: 10.4324/9781003185819-7

normally tracked. If a company doesn't fully understand and track the costs of doing business, then opportunities to improve may go undetected and are lost. Occasionally, we are asked to review new layout designs for departments or companies.

> During a project at a company located in Pennsylvania, we followed an office employee for 25 minutes looking for a person to approve a change to an order. She finally found the person she needed who told her to leave it on the desk and she would get it back to her later that afternoon. How much time do we lose seeking approvals? How much time do we lose every time we walk to the printer and wait for another job to complete? How much time do we lose with social chatter in the office or on the floor?

At a large hospital group in Florida, the office architects created several isolated spaces because this is what they thought the lab department wanted. Eventually, every architect seems to get into the mode of "we can't put it there, so let's put it over here," with no regard to process flow. Materials are normally centralized, creating lots of walking for the staff, which is waste. Something as simple as an inefficient layout "can double or triple your labor costs," and it's all hidden. Does your finance team ever review the layout from a waste versus a cost perspective?

## Results-Driven Management

The CEO and CFO are typically proponents of results-driven management. Our goal with this chapter is not to bash or undermine the accounting or finance profession. The people in these roles are highly skilled and talented, noting there are rules and laws, such as internal, external, and government audits, that must be followed. Yet, the philosophy that changed the role of finance from a reporting body to one of finance driving results is now ingrained in our organizations from the teachings of our leading business schools. In the past, we have found that this philosophy can lead to destructive behaviors such as Enron, Bernard L. Madoff Investment Securities, LLC Ponzi scheme, Fannie Mae and Freddie Mac, subprime mortgages, and subsequent bank and government company bailouts like General Motors. Our goal is to highlight the systemic problems inherent in the traditional accounting approach and highlight some of the pitfalls that exist. We hope that the following will provoke thought and will be taken in the spirit of the need for continuous improvement.[4]

## How Will Your Organization Define Lean Savings?

> Not everything that counts can be counted and not everything that can be counted counts.
>
> **Cameron**[5]

When an organization is in the early stages of Lean adoption and the cultural transformation has not yet occurred, management finds itself in a position to financially justify the Lean initiatives. At this stage, Lean is not embedded in the way they do business. The expected results will depend on how Lean is brought into the organization. In most cases, we have found that the early expectations are always viewed in terms of labor reduction. To illustrate, let's review the expected Lean results we discussed earlier in the book. Each result is qualified in as to whether one could easily translate the results into hard savings, defined as bottom line to budget labor savings; soft

**Table 7.1   Expected Savings**

| Expected Results | Hard | Soft | Cost Avoidance |
|---|---|---|---|
| 20%–80% Increase in productivity | X | | |
| 50%–90% Reduction in WIP | | X | |
| Increased customer satisfaction | | X | |
| 75%–99% Throughput time reductions | | X | |
| 20%–50% Reduction in space | | | X |
| 75%–95% Reduction in distance traveled | | X | |
| 10% or more reduction in process imperfections | | X | |

savings, which contribute to but may not yield a direct quantifiable bottom line budget reduction; and cost avoidance. In an organization, cost avoidance is a real savings but not accounted for as such and again is not an operational bottom line reduction; however, it is generally a significant capital savings.

Most finance leaders repeatedly ask how Lean will impact the bottom line and what can they remove from the budget at the end of the project. This is due, in part, to the fact Lean is normally brought in at a time when the organization has a compelling need to change and is most likely in need of bottom line savings. The savings listed in Table 7.1 are beneficial and will result in service and operational process improvements and will ultimately contribute to the financial success of the organization. In our experience, however, most financial leaders especially in the initial Lean implementations only want to know the bottom line labor reductions they will receive and when it will directly impact this year's budget. It is critical when starting on a Lean journey to define what will be considered Lean savings prior to starting the journey.

A hospital in Florida was considering a large expansion of its facility. After learning about Lean, they embarked on an initiative to determine if they could streamline processes, eliminate waste, and decrease (avoid) costs during this capital project. Their CFO initiated the Lean program but left the company midway through the project. The area management fully supported the endeavor, and the Lean initiative continued, ultimately proving the new expansion was not needed, and the organization saved millions of dollars in capital outlays. In addition, the metric improvements outlined in the beginning of the initiative were met, and several hundred thousand dollars in labor savings were identified. Near the end of the initiative, the Lean team gathered to present its final results. Several of the executives in attendance had not been on the journey, and the CFO who had resigned never briefed his superiors or peers on the Lean initiative's original deliverables or subsequent progress. The area management, team members, consultants, and those who had been on the journey clearly understood the progress made. The key deliverable originally assigned to the team was to determine if this sizable expansion and millions of dollars were needed. The team was very excited about presenting the results.

By the end of the project, the management team, who once believed the expansion was needed, was convinced they could do the same amount of work in less space by eliminating waste and streamlining processes. This produced a multimillion dollar cost avoidance. As the team reported out, many executives nodded in approval of the management and teams' accomplishments. However, during the report out, a new "CFO" unschooled in Lean, whose primary focus was "labor/labor savings" did not care the original project goals were cost avoidance, shunned the team and the millions saved by concluding there were not any "real" savings here. He then continued to attack the Lean consultant saying that any Lean consultant worth their salt should have labor savings of at least 10 times their costs, and he saw no value added in this project.

**Lessons Learned:**

- Monitor and update new participants and key stakeholders on the progress of the Lean initiative and have action plans to address engagement and buy-in to align goals and objectives. Ensure alignment with key stakeholders, especially the executive sponsor.
- Clearly outline the line-of-sight wastes and how they will impact organization of soft and hard dollars, and tangible and intangible benefits that will aid in the Lean cultural transformation.
- Decide up front how to define Lean. Understand the type of savings the organization deems valuable, and how and by whom they will be calculated. Will cost avoidance be considered? How will material savings be defined?
- Make sure that these savings assumptions and expectations are included in the team charter.
- Viewing only labor savings as the only bottom line savings is a very dangerous, shortsighted, and misleading approach to process improvement and Lean.
- There are many hidden costs and savings that are not included in traditional finance reports.

## The Value of a Group Tech Matrix

A tier 1 automotive company located in Chicago had a bottleneck in their heat-treating area where they had four ovens working around the clock. The heat-treating ovens were constantly breaking down because there was significant time lost changing the oven profiles for each part, there was no time for preventative maintenance (PM), there were containers of parts everywhere in the area, and they were constantly behind on their delivery schedule as a result.

While this was not the focus of the Lean project, we were asked if we could review the process. There were already requisitions written and vendors being solicited to purchase another oven at the cost of over $1 million and the installation also near $1 million to redo the area footprint. So, in addition to the launching of our pilot project, we did a group tech matrix on the heat treat area.

It took 3 weeks with two of us gathering data to determine the root cause and solution. We used a group tech matrix to help us identify families of parts for the heat treat area. We were able to sort the parts based on their material type and heat treat profile into three families. The result was the capacity for each profile could be more than satisfied by dedicating one of the ovens to each profile. The side benefit by standardizing on the profile was we eliminated the changeovers on each oven, thus we needed only three of the four ovens. We did not need to purchase another oven and freed up an oven that could be utilized while another was shut down for PM. What were the savings?

- The cost of the oven we didn't purchase
- The wear and tear being borne by the existing ovens would be eliminated
- The scheduling bottlenecks and impact on their customers due to ongoing late deliveries (and this was in the automotive industry)
- Reduction of work-in-process inventory
- The cost to purchase the item by procurement

- The cost that would have been spent by their maintenance folks to manage, support, and prep the installation
- The cost of additional electric and facility's needs
- The space savings gained by not having to install another oven
- The costs of maintaining the new oven
- Ability to schedule regular PM items
- Increased production capacity due to elimination of setups for product changes
- Improved quality performance

When the project was over, we asked finance to calculate the savings for us in order to justify to the president the 3 weeks of labor time for one consultant and one dedicated company employee. The answer came back that there was no savings since the company didn't actually purchase the new oven. As amazing as it sounds, this happens all the time. In the finance team, since we didn't lay anyone off, there was no savings.

We could fill another book with these types of stories. The millions saved through cost avoidance and soft savings versus the savings finance is willing to recognize. The existing company president took us to dinner one evening and said we had saved the company from bankruptcy through our Lean efforts not knowing he was soon retiring. The end of this story was interesting. The first move of the new president was to eliminate the dedicated Lean team as those were costs he could cut and not impact any area. This is the difference between traditional cost cutting versus the Lean principle of cost reduction.

Lesson Learned: Follow the data as it will provide the answers. Implementing Lean should not be based on labor savings but on continuous improvement. Focus on the process, eliminate waste, and the opportunity for defects, and the savings will come over time.

## Hidden Costs: The Sixth Level of Waste

This section is dedicated to what we call the sixth level of waste. This level is the waste that hides behind the obvious wastes and is difficult to see. It doesn't show up in financial reports. Dr. Shigeo Shingo was quoted as saying

> The real problem is when people do not recognize waste when they see it... The most dangerous kind of waste is the waste we do not recognize.[6]

Examples of hidden waste costs are as follows:

- Cost of management—inefficient meetings and firefighting
- Cost of setup times
- Cost of not developing our people
- Cost of hiring a warm body versus a qualified body
- Cost of idle time and unnecessary searching
- Cost of expediting at the highest levels
- Cost of sales lost due to our existing policies and systems
- Cost of poor customer service
- Cost of rework everywhere (first pass yield)
- Costs associated with lack of flow and throughput time
- Cost of layoffs and fractional labor in the office and plant

These are just a few examples of hidden costs. We could sight hundreds of hidden costs that occur each and every day that contribute to lost profitability. If seriously pursued, eliminating the hidden wastes can positively impact the organization's ability to grow today and in the future. Why are these costs hidden? The answer is because we don't track them and have no system (financial or otherwise) in place to expose them. Most organizations are accustomed to the day-to-day work-arounds (boiled frog waste) and do not view this activity as costly. The result would be a better product or service with less rework, fewer defects, and higher quality with less associated costs if many of these wastes were eliminated. In most cases, however, when any financial challenges occur, the first cost-cutting measure most organizations take is in the form of labor reductions. The wastes that contribute to hidden costs are like leeches sucking the life blood out of the organization. Like leeches, we don't always notice them right away, and they are difficult to remove.

Why don't we track them? Because in many cases, we don't have accurate data, the information may be difficult to quantify, there are no resources available for manual collection, or we just don't consider them that important. What data do we track? Budget, material variance, standards (if they exist), and number of people. Why? Because people are easy to track and visible. Historically, it is what has always been tracked, it is acceptable within the industry, and it is what the auditors are looking for. We focus on what we call results-focused management with the results defined by finance. How many finance team members have worked on the floor? How many finance people have run a product line or interfaced with customers?

Organizations need revenue and need to meet a budget to remain viable, thus it is the finance department's responsibility to monitor and report on the organization's financial health. Finance plays an integral role in running most of our companies and corporations around the world, but in many cases, they have little to no domain knowledge.[7] This is a key ingredient of big company disease. In the end, if we don't fix our processes, we are forced to cut people to meet finance's targets. Who is to blame? The blame belongs to our system, our culture, pressure from financial markets and shareholders, and our higher education business and finance programs. We need finance to learn and embrace the Lean principles and take a leadership role as we are implementing Lean. We recommend that finance provides a full-time person on our teams to learn the tools and to help sell Lean to the organization. When finance has provided a person, they learn that Lean is not about cost cutting but is about eliminating waste and streamlining processes. They also help with return on investment (ROI) calculations when required, creating systems to capture metrics and creating dashboards for senior executives.

## Creating a Blameless Culture

Creating a blameless culture is critical for Lean to work. Lean is about surfacing problems and acting to fix the problems to ensure they never come back. If one is afraid to admit a mistake, we will never know a problem existed or, worst case scenario, the problem manifests itself into a more significant problem. If we blame people, we won't solve the problems. Who ultimately creates the culture? The leadership team does, which, in turn, creates our systems. Only the CEO and senior leadership team can change the focus from cutting people to a process improvement-driven culture. In general, management cost cutting is a very shortsighted fix for short-term financial health, and the person coming in behind them bears the brunt of it. However, if you focus on fixing the processes, the results will come. Finance plays a pivotal role in most organizations as they attempt to control costs through trying to improve productivity by forcing labor reductions each year as they go through the budget cycle. Leadership is under constant pressure to cut labor and material costs each month. We are not discounting the merit of managing labor and materials and sticking to a budget, but it is not the only way to reduce costs.

What behaviors does this type of results-focus drive? Managers have not altered the way they do business; thus, they must then go through a process to identify services they can reduce or eliminate, or find a way to transfer their costs to another area's cost center's budget to achieve the expected results. Although this method can result in labor reductions and attaining their budget, it does not normally result in any real improvement of productivity and can potentially impact the quality and safety of activities and services provided. Normally, these problems go undetected until a major issue arises, when it is determined something fell through the cracks after a position was eliminated.

> In Company X, the maintenance director was asked to cut overtime to zero. In reviewing the activities, they found the supervisor had been doing preventative maintenance (PM) to several machines, not on the official PM list, and this task had been done this way for many years, but they received no credit in their budget. The director unilaterally determined that he would eliminate these tasks without notifying anyone. After a while, production was impacted because of the unplanned downtime which suddenly appeared in this work center. The work center supervisor was terminated because for years there was never a problem, but it was now obvious the supervisor didn't have what it took to manage his work center.

Lesson Learned: Invoking budgetary reductions without a plan to identify and eliminate wastes and understand hidden costs can impact quality, service, and operator safety. It can overburden employees who are now required to perform the same tasks in the environment ridden with wastes with less staff or perform fewer services that may impact customer satisfaction.

## Cool Whip Free®8

A friend of mine loves Cool Whip Free. When shopping at a well-known store, he always took it as a challenge to look for it but at the particular store he frequented, he found many times that they did not have it on the shelf. Instead, he found they typically stocked the incorrect product in the Cool Whip Free slot. When he would ask if they had any Cool Whip Free, the employee would go back into the refrigerated stockroom and normally come out with some. One day, he noticed that the item wasn't restocked, because the employee walking around with the reorder scanner saw a stocked shelf and just assumed it was stocked with the correct item. Since they never restocked the shelf with the correct item, people obviously didn't buy it. When he asked the store manager why they dropped the item, the manager stated it was because the item wasn't selling.

## Gift Wrap

The Mother's Club of a local high school had a very successful gift wrap program for many years, which brought almost $25,000 per year. This was 30% of their overall budget revenue, which was donated to the school at the end of each year to cover non budgeted items. One year, for instance, the Mother's Club was able to provide all new lab equipment to the school. The gift wrap was high quality at a very affordable price and easy to sell. The program also gave the boys prizes based on how much they sold and pizza parties for the classes that had 100% participation. The school then hired a new president who felt he didn't want the boys to have to sell the wrapping paper and that it was such a small amount of revenue (compared to the school he came from) that he could just get a donation to cover it. The Mother's Club still conducted the gift wrap that year. However, at the end of that year, the new president came to the Mother's Club to ask for $15,000 explaining that he couldn't get the expected donations to cover it. Amazingly, the next year the president canceled the gift wrap incentives for the boys, and the sales dropped to $9,000 significantly reducing the Mother's Club revenue. The next year the president insisted they sell the wrapping paper online. The revenue further declined to less than $6,000 and the next year to less than $4,000. It had now been 3 years since the new president's arrival and the Mother's Club had only 10% of the members still on the committee who remembered when they used to make $25,000 a year from the gift wrap. One of the new members suggested they just get rid of the wrapping paper because the money they were now bringing in was not worth their time. The group voted and decided to continue to sell it online.

Here was a program that was previously very successful but was now on the chopping block because so much time had passed, members changed and the recipe for success was lost resulting in a complete loss of their largest revenue stream.

Lesson Learned: We see the Cool Whip and the gift wrap story happen over and over again in companies. Carefully review a program that used to be successful before canceling it. Very successful projects can be discontinued because the recipe, know-how, or tooling was lost. The reason Toyota has been able to sustain for so long is because they had standard work. Standard work ensures that the recipe is never lost.

## Lean Answer

These situations are found in manufacturing, service, and government. Lean offers an escape from this gift wrap trap by analyzing the process and collecting data on which to make sound data-driven budgeting and staffing decisions, thus managing by fact.

When the Lean team first arrives and visits the lines or office areas, we hear from staff phrases such as, "We don't have enough space, we don't have enough equipment and we need more people!" When asked what managers use to construct or adjust their budgets, in many cases they say, "Well, I ask my people in the area what they need or I just know from experience... just look out there it's obvious." Therefore, most budgets tend to be based on perceptions, past experiences, assumptions, and ultimately what finance dictates. In most cases, there is little or no data available, so the requests for more people and space continue. It is no wonder finance is always focused on cutting labor and materials. Does adding space and people really fix the problems? We find it works for a while, but it really just hides the underlying problems.

Waste hides waste for a time, but then the problems come back worse than before because the root causes of the problems were never identified and fixed. The organization (including finance) has no process to keep track of these hidden costs and normally has weak standards or standards based on purchased standards databases or benchmarked consultant reports. Finance does what they do best during the budgeting process to keep the organization financially viable; they spend their time pushing back and insisting on cuts in labor and supplies, hoping managers will adjust and meet these seemingly impossible goals. Many of the perceived impossible goals could be achieved or surpassed if managers were taught Lean and how to identify and eliminate wastes and streamline their processes. Educated managers need to work together with finance to develop the goals and outline the improvement plan (which needs to be a multiyear Lean journey) to achieve the goals.

> Since Company X needed to reduce costs, each department was required to contribute by reducing labor. The maintenance department decided to let one of its technicians go, and everyone was happy because they saved one person. But what did it cost? In the long run, they could no longer support all the equipment in the shop, so over time, they ended up cutting the production schedule by 40%. Due to the downtime, they no longer had the hours of required capacity. Even though the product line generated significant revenue, no one ever looked back to the budgeting concessions or recognized the revenue they were losing due to the lost maintenance person.

Lesson Learned: Cutting labor to meet budget without understanding or confronting the reality of the impact is a shortsighted approach to any type of improvement. Indirect labor is the easiest target, but this practice can be a symptom of uninformed management. Millions of dollars are lost each year due to these hidden wastes. Financial reduction targets should require a cost reduction strategy with detailed month-by-month process improvement and waste elimination plans outlining how the goals will be achieved.

## Hidden Cost within the Concept of Critical Mass

Most companies' processes (due to layouts and skill sets) need a critical mass or minimum number of personnel to operate. This critical mass is defined as the number of people required to support the area if only one of each product line was ordered/produced at any time. In an emergency room, critical mass is how many full-time equivalents (FTEs) and what skill sets are required and what operating expenses are incurred if only one person walks in the door. We find that this phenomenon particularly pertains when a small business is acquired by a large corporation. The small business doesn't have the staff to process all the paperwork, reporting, operational and corporate staff video conferences, planning and budgeting requirements, and corporate staff committee inputs required for their reporting as there can be critical resources allocated to meet the corporate requirements.

When an organization's staff is at or falls below critical mass, they may meet the labor goal, but normally give up something in return. They may knowingly or inadvertently compromise product quality, customer satisfaction, or throughput time. Remember, one bad customer experience will most probably be communicated to at least ten people. For example, if we staff below our critical mass and miss our delivery dates (fill rate), where do customers go next time? How will it impact our sales and profitability? Do we measure it? Many companies don't track their hit rate or percent of jobs won out of those quoted or those that could have been quoted. Ultimately, customers will go to places easy to do business with unless they have no other choice. If they have a bad service experience with your company, will they come back? Another common strategy is chasing the lowest labor rate around the world. We feel this is a short-sighted approach and is now promulgated by our business schools and overall pursuit of short-term quarterly earnings which is the result of our stock market financial system.

So, in the words of my Lean sensei, Mark Jamrog, "We make the numbers, but at what cost?"

The other problem we find is when we discover we can take market share from our competitors, but it requires adding staff. Why not staff accordingly and grow the business? Departments need to be allowed to staff for growth as long as they are continuously pursuing opportunities to eliminate waste. We have found that this is a difficult concept and practice for organizations to adopt. How much growth is lost at the expense of cutting labor to meet the budget?

## *Hidden Costs in Our Budgeting Processes*

As we have discussed, we have watched budgeting processes at various companies with some amazement. The financial arm of the organization determines the global cost cutting required, pads it, then breaks it down, and sends it out to each department as their budgets for the upcoming year. The budgets include the expected labor reductions needed for the organization to remain fiscally sound. Managers spend at least a month and, in many cases, several months in preparation determining what their real needs are for the upcoming year and what they are going to cut, in most cases in labor, travel, services, and supplies, to meet the budget. Of course, each department pads their budget as well. Negotiation occurs between departments to offload labor and services to meet the reductions. We have witnessed the budgeting process go on for literally 6 months or more at some companies. What does this cost? We will never know because it is not tracked. How many real issues were put on hold just to get the budget in place?

Organizations spend a tremendous amount of hidden untracked costs preparing and negotiating during the budget season while everything else literally is put on hold. Managers and directors cannot be accessed because they are too busy either getting ready for a budget meeting or attending one. In many cases, any preparations to justify increases turn out to be a waste of time as they are told, "It's not enough 'take out'; we need you to come up with more cuts." In the end, finance still dictates the final budget that can only beg the question, "Why don't we just cut the months of budgeting work out of the process and tell the departments what is going to be mandated in the end anyway?" Often, the budget numbers are reduced so low that there must be some actual giveback at the end. It often feels like the budgeting process isn't complete until a certain pain threshold is reached.

> At Company X, the value stream manager told finance that they were going to increase market share and sell 1,000 more units to meet their budget. Adding sales was the only way they could justify the budget put in place. No one validated that obtaining an additional 1000 units was even possible in the current marketplace. There was no market share analysis performed or marketing plan developed to ensure selling the additional units. In addition, the current processes could not even produce 1,000 more units a year. So, they spent; then downsized their forecast each month; but, continued spending at the 1.000 more units a year level.

Once the budget is in place, to what extent are people measured against it? How realistic are the assumptions? How good is the data behind the assumptions? How much padding and positioning occurs throughout the year wasting time that could be used on making improvements and cutting waste? We are not saying finance should not ask the tough questions and expect good financial performance; however, process improvement and increasing productivity are other methods that can be leveraged to achieve the same or even stretch goals.

## *Hidden Costs in Materials Replenishment*

Hidden costs in materials can be found throughout most companies. How often are materials not stored where they are needed? What is the impact and how does finance reflect the cost of material stock-outs? What does it cost to make a subassembly and then stock it and then pull it out again and then assemble it some more and restock it again under yet a different part number and then pull it out again?

We are told we have to do this because that is what the material requirement planning (MRP) system and our ISO procedures say … right? How much does excess stock cost us in cash flow, space, additional shelving, carousels, restocking, etc.? What additional labor does this add to the organization, and how does this balance against the cost of having the stock in the right place at the right time when it is needed? In general, these costs are not captured anywhere in financial systems or scorecards. It is not unusual on inventory projects to find tens of thousands of dollars in obsolete or expired inventory.

## The Plug Number

Company X didn't utilize a formal materials department. Most of their materials were subcontracted to a distributor who was supposed to manage the inventory. The roles of the company and its partnering distributor were not well defined, which caused blame and waste in all the handoffs inherent in the existing process. Every year, a physical inventory was performed; yet finance still "calculated" the "plug" number that was needed each year to make sure the company hit its profitability goal.

## Negative Inventory

During my time at Bendix Communications (which became AlliedSignal and is now part of Raytheon) as the materials manager, I was assigned the challenge of forecasting inventory each month. I had control over the input number because I could dictate what and when the suppliers shipped but had no control over the other component, "relief," which consisted of sales and manufacturing capacity. Each month, marketing would provide their forecasted sales but would never meet their target. In the end, I worked very closely with the master scheduler to "guard band[9]" the forecast by guessing what percentage of the sales forecast would be met. Over time, we became pretty good at it. Coincidentally, we started receiving the financial inventory reports and noticed something strange. Some of the product lines actually had negative inventory. How can that be? We sarcastically asked the finance person: "If he wanted us to go out and count all the inventory, we didn't have to make sure it all wasn't there." When questioned, finance said that they had to come up with a "plug" number to meet the profitability goals. So, in the end, all the inventory management was for naught because it was "plugged" anyway.

## Hidden Cost of Software That Will Solve All Our Problems

At a machining and assembly company in Europe, a Lean initiative was planned for a product line but was delayed due to the new MRP production tracking and inventory module being installed. The Lean team suggested that they abandon the shop floor tracking system until they had time to work with the line and install the new Lean processes. They also stated that a tracking system may not be necessary once the new line was implemented. They already had the $750K approved in the budget, and didn't want to take a chance on losing the capital at year's end, and since they couldn't carry the money over to the next year, or they would lose it, they thus purchased the system anyway. Since they went ahead with the software system, the Lean initiative was put on hold indefinitely. When we asked how the tracking system was going a couple of years later, we were told they took it out because they didn't have the manpower to keep it running and the supervisor who oversaw the implementation was transferred to another department.

Lesson Learned: Someone in the organization pushes a pet project through, piece of capital equipment, or new non-Lean layout in place at great expense only to leave or get promoted and then the person coming in behind them gets stuck with it.

# Hidden Costs in the Software Solution

## *Process Improvement in the Dentist's Office*

My dentist office was installing a new software system. Everyone was told how great it was and that it would solve all their problems. It would link all their offices and finally allow the X-rays to be seen on the screen as part of the patient record. However, the owners decided to rush the installation process and skip the training. Everyone in the office was left to fend for themselves with constant problems resulting in lost billing, missed appointments, frustrated staff, and upset patients. The staff started complaining to the doctors and the patients. Yet the owners, who didn't have to use the system every day, couldn't understand the problems. Six months later, most of the problems were ironed out, but they found they could not port over the X-rays from the old system. The office ended up transferring the data manually patient by patient running two systems for several years. No one tracked or seemed to care about the cost but at least they saved all those training dollars.

Lesson Learned: Automation and the introduction of new software do not always solve the problems. Automation does not always free up staff and, in some cases, results in more staff required. If you purchase a machine, or software, it should free up a person's time. If you purchase a new software system, it should make everyone's job easier. The trick is to streamline the waste out of your systems first and then find software to match the new system not the other way around. Companies consistently violate this rule.

Being assigned leader of the next enterprise resource planning (ERP) system implementation used to be a death slot. We are all told that this new system is going to solve all our problems. Often, a good job is performed investigating the system costs, but no one investigates the cost to keep the system fed (operational labor), including the number of staff required to input the data required to maintain the integrity of a "class A" system. Once the system is purchased, it is not unusual to work to cut the cost of implementation. The organization may allocate funds for the initial training and implementation, but instead of sending their best people to training, they send their available people. This results in poor rollouts, and many times the system is set up incorrectly.

We see this in government as well. A new program is passed but then Congress refuses to fund it, stopping it dead in its tracks. Most IT vendors sell the ROI based on using all the features and functions of the system. The organization expects that ROI ultimately falls short of achieving it as the full appropriation is not allocated due to budget cuts so they are not able to install all the modules intended. Even though enough resources might be allocated to perform the initial implementation, they fail to recognize the end users' learning curve, and resources needed to guarantee future users are trained appropriately to ensure continued data integrity. Refresher courses needed to reinforce learning are not put in place or are cut. The type of system being rolled out can significantly impact production for many years.

Lesson Learned: Companies literally become victims of their systems.

At a hospital in Ohio, the IT department purchased a new software program but didn't have the end users participate in the software selection process. On investigation, we couldn't determine what criteria were utilized to justify the purchase, but it certainly wasn't cycle time. When we performed a comparative time study of both systems, the data revealed that it took end users three times longer to enter the information in the new system because of the need to navigate through the addition of several more screens to achieve the previous result. System performance and response time had degraded as well. The next problem encountered was that IT assigned centralized printers to the workstations which then could not be changed without a formal request to IT.

When we videoed and time studied the new process (well beyond the learning curve of the new software), it was so slow that we were missing promised customer delivery dates. By showing the video to the IT director, we were able to prove entering the data manually was three to four times faster and we were able to get a temporary injunction to go back to the manual system.

Lesson Learned: When implementing new IT systems, it is important to understand current state versus future state impacts of deployment. Do not assume that implementing a new system will improve productivity, efficiency, quality, and safety. Videoing and/or simulating activities being impacted can be very useful to identify enhancements needed to streamline the process, help obtain approvals from leadership to change the process, or, in some cases, go back to the old manual processes, when appropriate. The key is not to put the new software system in place until after you have leaned and streamlined the process. The software should support the process in place, not dictate it.

## Hidden Cost in Inventory Management

When we worked with a hospital in New Mexico, we inquired about their inventory accuracy. They weren't sure but estimated it at around 95%. When we watched the stock pickers on video, we noticed that the first step was to pull up the pick list and manually go through the list of parts. Prior to picking the parts, they counted all the major parts on the list, which they knew typically had problematic counts. Sometimes several hundred parts per day. Once the parts were counted, they went into the system and adjusted the inventory numbers based on their hand counts. While observing the operator or staff member adjust the counts, we saw that several of the counts were entered incorrectly and had to be readjusted. We determined that the accuracy rate was really about 40% at this stage. Once all the counts were adjusted in the system, they reprinted the pick ticket and proceeded to pick the supplies for the work order. At the end of the day, they performed their cycle counting process which is where a random set of parts is manually counted and then adjusted. Once we started measuring, the cycle counting turned out to be only 80% accurate after all the daily adjustments.

Lesson Learned: It's amazing what is identified by observing or videoing a process; it is not until you actually see and measure it that you know the true state. How much money was lost in the expensive rework procedures being done by the material handlers, by the materials not being there when needed, or all the phone calls made to notify affected department heads? The wastes may not be exactly the same, but they are out there, ever lurking and hidden from view.

## Hidden Costs and Lack of Standardization at a System Level

At a US Company, we found the order entry department spends 7 minutes entering data into the first system and then spends an additional 7 minutes reentering the same data into a second system. Why? Because the two systems don't talk to each other. When we inquired, we discovered that the interface required was not purchased because they had to reduce the capital cost of the project to meet the 2 year payback (ROI) required.

## Standardizing on Equipment

At Company X, they purchased several machines for their operations over the years but never from the same manufacturer. Over time, they had numerous problems from having to maintain different spare parts for each machine, different training for each type of machine, and downtime waiting for parts or supplies.

In Lean, our goal would be to standardize equipment wherever possible to the extent that it makes sense. There is a significant amount of money to be saved by standardizing equipment and supplies across the board, and one could argue that there is probably a safety component as well since staff would not have to be trained on multiple types of equipment that does the same function. Southwest Airlines' original strategy was to standardize on their fleet, and reap the benefits. There was one set of spare parts, additional leverage gained in negotiation since they had large volumes with one partnering supplier and could standardize the training for all the mechanics.[10]

Lesson Learned: The costs of not standardizing can be staggering; however, these costs are not accounted for and are often hidden from the typical financial reporting systems.

## Lean Solutions and Lean Accounting

Lean and process driven improvements are the answer to attacking the hidden wastes mentioned above. Lean is about managing by fact, deploying concepts that will drive elimination of waste and leveraging tools and data-driven formulas. Once we implement Lean in an area, understanding what tasks are value added to the customer and what it takes (the work effort based on time) to get the process done becomes clearer. The data are based on hard evidence and backed up by video analysis.

It's amazing how often we visit an area and find out they are planning on adding more space or equipment, but when we study the process and do the calculations, we discover it not necessary. Once Lean is implemented, the supervisor has a standard package of data that will show the impact to the department or value stream whether it be additional demand, labor shortage, or sourcing issue. In the Lean environment, management should require that the Lean tools be applied prior to any requests for additional staff, space, or resources. As Lean is adopted throughout the organization, the budgeting process becomes easier and the role of finance in the organization should change. Financial analysts or cost accountants should be transferred to line jobs where they are responsible to make productivity improvements. The budget becomes straightforward as Lean calculations determine exactly how much capacity and labor are required for each product line or office process.

Some Lean organizations go beyond budgeting and provide forward-looking financial forecasts and metrics each month and free themselves from the annual budget process and past historical reviews to determine the future. Lean finds other operational savings by eliminating wastes and streamlining processes in the office environment. When the overall revenue stream is targeted for improvement, we find many opportunities to improve accounts payable (AP), receivable, and the capital allocation and budgeting process and order entry to the floor process. We also find improvements in the engineering design and document approval processes. It is sometimes difficult in the early stages of the Lean journey to obtain complete buy-in by finance leaders who may not see the Lean day-to-day operational and cultural changes as truly significant. We must involve finance in the teams up front otherwise we find that it takes a series of Lean initiatives over a year or two until the transformation of Lean thinking takes hold for finance to begin to buy in. The threat is that finance can shut the Lean efforts down during those 2 years. Unfortunately, it is sometimes difficult with GAAP accounting principles to see a direct financial performance link to some of the Lean initiatives in the short term.

Lesson Learned: Have finance leaders study Lean accounting prior to implementation. Send key financial team members to a Lean accounting seminar or to a Lean accounting expert consultant up front. Make sure that finance is involved in supporting the teams and has members on your teams up front. Lean is not a short-term solution or a quick fix. It is not unusual to take 2–3 years to see that truly sustained results start to impact the bottom line, even though one may see the results immediately in the areas you are improving. Remember, it took Toyota more than 60 years of applying Lean principles for continuous improvement to become the world's number one auto manufacturer.

## Lean: It's All about the Process, Not Labor or Full-Time Employee Reductions

We strive to improve the process, create flow, and make the customer experience the best it can be. We not only obtain productivity increase, but we also generally achieve improvements in customer satisfaction, quality (reductions in defects), safety (error reductions), space requirements, employee morale, etc. It is extremely important not to be focused solely on cutting costs but implementing cost reductions to embrace the full impact that applying Lean concepts and tools can bring with a Lean cultural transformation. When we initially create a pilot Lean process in an area with the goal of making that "business as usual" in the future, it normally impacts a small part of a department's overall process and budget so we are going to initially impact only a small portion of the overall costs and ROI. Eventually, the organization achieves enough results to eliminate the need to prove changes based on some ROI formulas which seldom get reviewed anyway, and Lean is viewed as an ongoing continuous improvement goal and is justified because it is the right thing to do.

## Lean Accounting Approach

Lean accounting eliminates traditional cost accounting standard reports and the concept of earned hours. As discussed earlier, the cost accounting staff is moved into the line organization to work on process improvements and support the value stream managers with information and analysis. This often causes much concern and uneasiness for the financially focused individuals. We find that it generally takes about 2–3 years to get financial teams on board with the notion of standards and Lean accounting. The best use of cost accountants I ever saw was several years ago when Rubbermaid converted its cost accountants to Lean project leaders or Lean team members. The next several pages discuss problems with the traditional cost accounting systems.

Lesson Learned: Lean accounting is an important part of the Lean Enterprise, requires the transformation of the traditional cost accounting system, and often takes several years for the system to take hold.

## Problem with Work Centers

A work center is an accounting designation given to a functional group of equipment (see Figure 7.1 (026x001.tif)). Operators are given a job card to record their labor against each work center in the factory and accounting costs the labor for each work center and compares it to the standards. Once we set up a Lean cell, this creates problems as we take equipment from each of these work

**Figure 7.1  Example of a functional gear manufacturing layout in early 1960s. All like machines, that is, gear cutters are grouped together into work centers. (Courtesy of Joe and Ed Markiewicz, Ancon Gear, www.ancongear.com.)**

centers to create a cell. Therefore, we often end up with five or six work centers to create just one cell, causing an immediate problem with accounting and the operators as to what work center they should charge their labor.

## Hidden Costs of Cost Accounting Standards

At a company in Ohio, the past owner was a CPA. He had total financial control over the business and held everyone accountable to the traditional cost accounting standards. However, after some questioning, we found that the standards had not been updated in years. The company was set up with work centers with all the same equipment together (functional layout). Materials had a router that showed the order of work centers the products had to follow.

The parts went to the "kerosene wash" work center after each operation for a total of seven hand wash cycles. Material was run in lots of 50–250 pieces and was stacked up in large steel baskets all outside the washroom and in each work center. To manage this schedule, the supervisor had to track every lot and meet with all the work center managers every day to get any product out the door. The first operation was saw cutting, which was performed in a different building 3 miles away.

After our initial Lean training, we picked a pilot line and selected a team composed of the supervisor and someone from each work center. After doing the process flow analysis (PFA) and questioning all the work center managers, no one could determine why the parts went to the washroom after every operation. It had always been done that way. After studying the process, we all agreed we could eliminate all but the last wash operation. The next step was to set up a cell with a machine from each work center, and we added packing the box to the end of the cell. We went through all the steps, PFA, a lengthy group tech matrix for every part, Workflow analysis (WFA), setup reduction, and block diagrams to develop families and new layouts.

The first problem we ran into was finance. They asked what we planned to do with the router now that we had created cells with a machine from each work center. Finance wanted to know how we were going to fill out the router and what we should do with the standard costs? Finance wanted us to do a routing for every part so that they could track the costs. Of course, they couldn't really track the costs before, but thought they could. We agreed on just filling in the last operation on the router, which was pack and ship, and noted the start and end times on the router, which in the end no one even reviewed. The next problem we ran into was an idle machine in the cell. The cell contained eight machines/operations and we were running mixed model production with two of their main machines in the cell. However, product A used only one of the main machines, thus the second main machine was idle. We asked the production manager if there was anything in the backlog that just used the second main machine and then was packed.

Upon review, we found an open work order for part B which only needed the second machine and could then be packed. When we timed the process and found that the team member could run both parts (A and B) in the cell at the same time. The team member asked how he should enter his labor in the system and what job he should charge it to. These simple questions created two problems. The first was how do we account for the second part in their shop floor computer system. Their software could accommodate only one part on the router between the beginning and ending run time. We told the team member for now just to enter part A in the labor collection system and we would deal with part B later.

This created the second problem as the team member refused to run part B. In his mind, he couldn't enter part B in the system, which meant we (management) were getting his labor for part B for free. We explained he was not paid by the piece but by the hour and so it did not matter how many parts he ran in the cell at one time. However, the operator was sharp and correct in which we really were getting that part for free because in the past someone would have stood idle and watched that machine the whole time until the part A work order was complete.

The company had to change how they looked at traditional cost accounting standards and develop a cost system based on the Lean cells versus work centers. Each cell was now considered a profit center. The equipment in the cell represented their investment (on which they needed a return), and they restructured sales to start pursuing jobs that could be completed within the cells. In the end, they instituted a bonus program, which all the employees shared.

Update: We recently emailed one of the owners of this company. I asked if he remembered this story. After reading it over, he responded: LMAO! One literally could not walk through this company as there was so much inventory everywhere; just baskets and baskets full of inventory. This company, after implementing Lean, completely revised their master layout, moved every piece of equipment to set up cells, and freed up an entire building 3 miles away. All those baskets were now empty and stacked up outside and eventually sold or scrapped. Now they are the market share leaders in their industry. It is a build-to-order, low-volume/very high-mix-type market. We told them to give their baskets away to their competition of which they have put several out of business!

Lesson Learned: Traditional cost accounting systems always get in the way of Lean projects and normally are the first barrier we run into. The sooner you can get the CFO on board with Lean, the more chances of success the effort will enjoy. As a Lean practitioner, those few times when you are lucky to get to work with the owners or the CEO directly, it is amazing how fast you can accomplish Lean with spectacular results.

## Earned Hours versus Lean Accounting

The following discussion is purposefully lengthy. The reason for this section is that this is the one of the major areas that creates conflict with Lean. Our initial discussions with CFOs focus on cost accounting standards and how Lean treats them. It should be pointed out, if companies do not utilize labor standards, the labor tends to be set on experience "demonstrated capacity" and day-to-day demands.

## Earned Hours

This system is so ingrained that there are several companies whose sole existence is based on the selling of operational analysis (i.e., labor management reporting) reporting systems. In this environment, the labor budget is set to labor standards typically based on a collection of companies in similar industries with similar processes. These are assigned for variable staffing, which is normally earned and directly tied to product volumes. The formulas include a variety of drivers, including output per person per square foot or other methods created for an area to earn hours for work performed. The formulas are derived to achieve the same goal: to determine labor hours needed so that earned labor or allocated labor dollars fluctuate with volume.

As the volume increases, more labor hours are earned. If volume falls, then managers must adjust the staffing accordingly such as proactively sending staff home early, transferring staff to another department, or reducing staff so as not to go over budget. There is also a fixed staffing component for labor that will not be directly related to changes in volume. This can be both a blessing and a curse. If labor standards are generous and volume increases, then the line will have, in some cases, a budgetary allowance that exceeds what is truly needed. This can cause managers to manage more loosely because they know they will meet their budget. If the labor standard is inaccurate to the downside, however, the line will forever find itself justifying to management why it is over budget. The decrease in labor causes the line to feel that they are continually fighting a battle to obtain adequate resources to provide the required service.

It used to be that standards were set by a time and motion study engineer. Most of these engineers have all but vanished, so standards in most companies are generally set by utilizing some sort of benchmark data. There is always a concern with benchmark data because definitions can be interpreted differently across companies, and there may not be full transparency as to how the labor standard was created thus the labor standard may not reflect that organization's reality. To determine how one product line's standards were set, we sat with the sales representative from a major standards operations analysis company that provides productivity and standards data. The standards were set on a combination of observations (quantitative) and employee interviews (qualitative) and were then compared with similar companies. However, some of the standards were set incorrectly. For example, the standard for one line that included costs for their department was not included by other companies providing similar data. So, the comparison data was ultimately misleading.

Lesson Learned: Is comparing your output per hour to a similar company really the right way to approach productivity increases?

## Standards and Variance Reporting

The typical variance report is generally distributed late and contains historical and unsanctioned information. Yet we spend hours or even days researching and trying to explain the variances to management. To what benefit? Since this information is generally not available in real time, operational managers must learn how their budget relates to actual staffing. When managers or supervisors get a report showing they are over budget, they work harder at sending staff home, and if they are on budget, they tend to be more lax with staffing. This can have little relation to what is actually occurring on the floor or in the office. In most instances, they do not, on an hourly or daily basis, manage staff to the demand in the process. Instead, they manage a budget partially based on subjective qualitative data. There is no push to improve if they are meeting or beating their budgeted labor allocation, which results in complacency.

Lesson Learned: Complacency is the most vicious enemy of Lean. One must move to real-time process-focused metrics and take immediate containment actions and then countermeasures to address the root cause to avoid complacency.

## Lean Accounting Approach

Lean accounting is different in that we put standards (i.e., standard work) in place based on data-based targets utilizing real-time metrics backed up by video analysis or floor observation. Standard work becomes the new standard! The goal is to continually reduce the standard over time with no negative impact to quality, safety, or customer satisfaction. There is no longer a need for variance reporting if Lean is implemented properly, since this is addressed in standardized work and visual controls. Lean accounting uses no traditional cost accounting standards at all. The need for earned hours disappears. Goals are set based on our future state map plans for improvement, which derive from our demand, operations, and financial planning, which is derived from our strategy deployment, which is derived from our strategic plan and flowed throughout the organization via Hoshin planning.

## Problem with Cost Accounting Standards

If the organization has determined they are using benchmarking data and implementing labor standards to drive budget and labor management, one needs to understand that once labor standards are introduced and adopted, they tend to remain fixed and can take an extreme amount of work to adjust. When managers or employees perform better than the standard, then they may want more money. If they have a generous labor standard, we have found that they do not readily volunteer to adjust the labor standard to reflect a tighter standard. How does any of this drive improvement?

At a company in Baltimore as we cleaned it up (5S), we found lounge chairs and magazines in the workers' areas (see Figure 7.2). The area was such a mess that no one even knew they were there. The workers would pick and choose what products they wanted to work on out of the batch of WIP units sitting there. They would always pick the units that had the "standards containing the most earned hours" so they could finish them early and then return to their lounge chairs and read their magazines. When the line beats the standard, the company might adjust it (raise it), but more often than not it never changes. This is probably rational and reasonable if one buys into the whole "standards" thing, because the mere act of raising it is a disincentive to the department. Why should anyone work to improve the standard when they figure out the standard is just going to be raised? What is in it for them?

This is what drives a behavior known as soldiering in Frederick Taylor's time. Soldiering is where an employee or employees as a group agree on how much work they are going to perform. Anyone who works harder gets harassed or gets their car keyed by fellow employees.[11]

Lesson Learned: Traditional cost accounting standards, contrary to popular belief, seldom drive improvement. Brian Maskell of BMA Associates said, "Think about it, if they did, every company today would be world class."[12] It needs to be everyone's job to drive improvement and working to raise the standards daily.

### Standard Costing Model

At a company in the Netherlands, we sat down during an assessment with their controller to discuss the impacts our new cell was having on the accounting system and discuss how to cost product A... Before Lean, they took the cycle time from the router, over the course of a year, along with

**Figure 7.2   Lounge chairs in the factory. This plant is now closed. (From BIG Archives.)**

the material cost and used that for the next year's standard cost. However, this did not consider rework or minimum buys of materials. The overheads are spread for lines by labor (FTEs) and the warehouse people are cost in the material burden, and the maintenance and utilities are allocated by square feet. Rework and all other inefficiencies are in the profit and loss (P&L) but not in the cost or price of the part. Sales are paid on revenue, but there is no margin component. We pointed out problems with this method to the controller listed as follows:

- There are some parts that require as much as 20% or more rework not counting the number of retests. None of this is priced into the part but is in the P&L by default.
- There is one area that is a clean room (HEPA filters) that is much more expensive to maintain and run than the other areas and has an outside contractor to manage it.
- Some lines use more electricity than other lines.
- The standards on the router are updated once a year, but no one knows exactly how. They don't do time studies.
- People are moved from line to line so there is no way to truly capture labor on each part or line.
- The labor on the router is based on part model, so it is more controlled than spreading the labor over all the parts.

- There is a danger the company could lose money on the P&L since none of the inefficiency is in the cost of the parts.
- We suggested they are probably shipping dollars out with some of the parts. We should know the rework involved in each part type and assess the impact to the cost.
- The costs of the minimum buys (i.e., having to purchase 500 when 10 are needed) are not factored into the pricing but are charged against the P&L. If the parts cost $500, then the order would be charged for $10 of parts. Reworked parts are not captured as part of the cost either. This means that they are discounting complex parts while increasing the price of simple parts.
- Because of how the overheads are spread, all of the lines are paying for the clean room.
- Time lost waiting for R&D is not included in the cost of the part.
- Time gained by batching (where there is a lot of variation) is lost due to extra handling of the parts and by lost time waiting at the machine for each work center.

## *Traditional Cost Accounting Question*

Cost accounting standards typically are calculated by the following equation:

$$Present\ Capacity = Realized\ Output + Waste$$

As stated earlier, cost accounting standards can be very misleading and, when utilized as metrics, can drive some crazy behaviors. There are several problems with these types of standards:

- Who sets the standards?
- How are they set?
- How often are they updated, and who is responsible to update them?
- What exactly are we trying to measure?
- When we use only direct labor in a standard, it can be misleading. How much indirect labor is necessary, and is it counted?
- How and when do you define output?
- What do we do with the data once we calculate it?
- Are people really measured on the standards? Do they lose their job if they don't meet them?

As discussed earlier, benchmarking companies utilize activities to help drive the assigned labor standard and other variables, and in many cases, managers are not even taught how the standards are calculated or how to manage them. Once that transfer of knowledge occurs, in most cases, if a manager is promoted or leaves, the subsequent manager is not trained and now is responsible for a number in a report without understanding the variables that contributed to its creation. We have repeatedly uncovered and found good managers, who have responsibility across multiple areas but do not understand whether the area is under a fixed labor model in which case there is no adjustment for volume changes, or if they are under a flexible labor model. We discovered areas where they were under fixed labor models, which should have had flexible labor standards.

In most cases, the financial department allows the manager no incremental increase and requires the standard assigned fit into the current budget. In many cases, this is not a true comparison to what it takes to perform actual tasks to the labor standard assigned. So, the dilemma continues. Even though there are significant challenges with labor standards, we have never found a standard we could not meet or significantly beat with Lean improvements. In the end, we abolish these types of earned standards.

Lesson Learned: The main caution and danger is people measured on labor standards work only to meet the standard, but they do not consistently work to improve on it.

### Labor Standard Report Said We Should Hire Three People: Lean Accounting Said No!

A hospital in New Mexico was using a well-known standard reporting company's benchmark data to set their standards. After we did our first Lean implementation in one of their departments, the previously set labor standard remained the same. Owing to our productivity improvements, we had days where we were performing at a rate of 175% of the current standard. Based on the strict definition of the standard and actions dictated by the standard, we were considered by everyone who saw the report to be way understaffed, and for several weeks, the manager was asked to add three people to the department. Meanwhile we were working on reducing the head count by another person through attrition.

Lesson Learned: Standards data can be very misleading and drive the wrong behaviors which can be very costly to the company and their customers.

### Lean Accounting Approach

Not all standards are bad. Lean has standards based on hard data, and we use these data to guide our decisions. Setting standards is different from standardization. As we move from functional departments to value streams, what do we do? What are the implications for organizational structure? One can argue that Lean has standards, which we would agree—but not in the sense of traditional cost accounting systems. It is a different type of system. In Lean, we don't need a published finance labor standard report a month later. Once we implement Lean, we know the total labor time and takt time or required cycle time, and we can determine the proper staffing level in real time. We then put visual controls in place such as day by hour charts to make it immediately obvious.

Lesson Learned: Lean is about reducing waste and exposing hidden costs. Lean tools make waste obvious and easy to quantify, but only to the extent to which the Lean project will impact the area.

#### Inventory Impacts to Traditional Accounting

When implementing Lean, another problem we run into with the accountants is profitability issues. As we reduce the inventory in the system, traditional accounting statements will show a loss in profitability. This is because we are reducing an asset account (inventory on hand), and it translates to an increase in the cost of goods sold, which is an expense on the income statement. So initially, when implementing Lean, it appears that our overheads are skyrocketing and we are losing money. Non-Lean-trained accountants will quickly approach the CFO who will approach the CEO and tell them that this Lean stuff is killing the company's profitability!

### Allocating Overhead

If finance is spreading overhead by square foot (or some other method), we would postulate that we will never know the true costs of the product. In Table 7.2 we show the difference the Lean

**Table 7.2    Batch versus Lean Cost Analysis for 1 Unit and Then Annualized with 100 Unit Sales Increase**

| | | | | | | Variance | | |
|---|---|---|---|---|---|---|---|---|
| Product A | Percent | Batch Was | Percent | Lean Now | Percent | Dollars | Percent | Lean Can Be |
| *Product Cost—1 Unit (1/2 the People in 1/2 the Time)* | | | | | | | | |
| Selling price | 100 | $1,000.00 | 100 | $1,000.00 | | $— | 105 | $1,050.00 |
| Material | 33 | $333.00 | 33 | $333.00 | | $— | 30 | $315.00 |
| Material overhead | 7 | $23.31 | 7 | $23.31 | | $— | 7 | $22.05 |
| Labor | 10 | $100.00 | 2.5 | $25.00 | −7.5 | $(75.00) | 2 | $21.00 |
| Factory overhead | 200 | $200.00 | 800 | $200.00 | 0 | $— | 650 | $136.50 |
| Gross profit | 34 | $343.69 | 42 | $418.69 | 8 | $75.00 | 53 | $555.45 |
| | 15 | $150.00 | 15 | $150.00 | 0 | $— | 15 | $157.50 |
| G&A expense | 12 | $120.00 | 12 | $120.00 | 0 | $— | 10 | $105.00 |
| EBIT | 7 | $73.69 | 15 | $148.69 | 8 | $75.00 | 28 | $292.95 |
| Interest expense | 0.75 | $4.92 | 0.75 | $4.36 | | $(0.56) | 0.75 | $3.71 |
| Taxes | 46 | $31.63 | 46 | $66.39 | 3 | $34.76 | 46 | $133.05 |
| Net profit | 4 | $37.13 | 8 | $77.94 | 4 | $40.80 | 15 | $156.19 |
| *Annualized with Double Output* | | | | | | | | |
| Units sold annually | | 1,100 | | 1,100 | | | | 2,200 |
| Selling price | 100 | $1,100,000.00 | 100 | $1,100,000.00 | | $— | 105 | $2,425,500.00 |
| Material | 33 | $366,300.00 | 33 | $366,300.00 | | $— | 30 | $727,650.00 |
| Material overhead | 7 | $25,641.00 | 7 | $25,641.00 | | $— | 7 | $50,935.50 |
| Labor | 10 | $110,000.00 | 2.5 | $27,500.00 | −8 | $(82,500.00) | 2 | $48,510.00 |
| Factory overhead | 200 | $220,000.00 | 800 | $220,000.00 | 0 | $— | 600 | $291,060.00 |
| Gross profit | 34 | $378,059.00 | 42 | $460,559.00 | 8 | $82,500.00 | 54 | $1,307,344.50 |
| Selling expense | 15 | $165,000.00 | 15 | $165,000.00 | 0 | $— | 15 | $363,825.00 |
| G&A expense | 12 | $132,000.00 | 12 | $132,000.00 | 0 | $— | 10 | $242,550.00 |
| EBIT | 7 | $81,059.00 | 15 | $163,559.00 | 8 | $82,500.00 | 29 | $700,969.50 |
| Interest expense | 0.75 | $5,414.56 | 0.75 | $4,795.81 | | $(618.75) | 0.75 | $8,386.17 |
| Taxes | 46 | $34,796.44 | 46 | $73,031.07 | 3 | $38,234.63 | 46 | $318,588.33 |
| Net profit | 4 | $40,848.00 | 8 | $85,732.12 | 4 | $44,884.13 | 15 | $373,995.00 |

*Source:* BIG Archives.

implementation made to the bottom line going from a 4% net profit to a 15% net profit for both one unit (top) and annualized with a 100-unit increase in sales. However, look at what it does to the overhead, which goes from 200% to 800%! Another thing to consider: does it make sense for sales to discount items in the Lean environment? We feel that in the long run, all you are doing is creating artificial demand or moving the demand and then discounting it. Meanwhile, it costs us more labor (i.e., in overtime) to get it out the door.

At AlliedSignal, we had a product line which had much less square footage than product line 2. Which one has higher profitability? Because finance spread overhead costs across all the product lines based on square footage, it was obvious that product line 2 was more costly. So, the plant manager eliminated product line 2! However, when we went back and looked at why the division started losing money each quarter, we found product line 1 was much more capital equipment intensive and had a very costly clean room environment from an energy point of view. Also, the labor was specialized, highly trained, and more expensive. Product line 2 was mostly assembly and test labor in a non-clean room. Since much of product line 1's overhead was applied to product line 2 as it had more square footage, it appeared more expensive on paper. Thus, with this cost accounting methodology, we ended up selling our most profitable line while keeping our least profitable line.

Again, at our AlliedSignal plant in Maryland, we were mandated to outsource 20% of our purchased materials. This thinking came from Jack Welch at GE. We eventually ran out of things we could outsource due to our buy America clauses, so the leadership chose to outsource our internal model shop to hit the 20% target. Can you imagine the problems this caused? In the past, we could take a napkin drawing to the model shop in the morning and have their tooling or fixture in the afternoon. Now it took a formal drawing request, quote, discussions with one of three suppliers and constant back and forth iterations with the parts prior to getting the request approved. On average, it now took a minimum of 2 weeks to get their tool or fixture. Over time, the outsourcing mandates took their toll. Because each time an operation was outsourced, it reduced the labor and square feet available to absorb the overhead. Therefore, our parts were continually (on paper) getting more expensive over time. As overheads increased, the pressure increased to outsource more and the downward spiral continued. Eventually, the plant was sold and all the equipment combined with another plant in Florida.

## Part 2: Lean and Collecting Costs

With Lean, we collect the costs by cell, product family, or value stream. We don't differentiate if it is direct, indirect, or overhead. We eliminate the need for earned hours and the need for absorption accounting. Prior to implementing Lean accounting, we utilized contribution margin, when possible, to understand what can be gained from improvements. We consider labor cost to be fixed, and when we use contribution margin, we take only truly variable costs. We recommend the organization understand the true overhead costs of each area.

### *Contribution Margin*

We also like to modify the contribution margin approach to look at all labors versus separating out direct and indirect employees. This includes centralized and supervisory personnel. This way, one gets a look at the total costs versus slices of direct or indirect costs. When making decisions, we look at the true impact on the value stream costs and profitability. This includes everybody and everything that is in the value stream; however, monuments—like wave solder, or large machining or plating/processing equipment, etc.—create a problem, and we have to allocate them in a simpler way. Another good measure is earned value analysis.[13] This metric focuses on return on capital or return on net assets.

## Machine Utilization

When implementing Lean, machine utilization is no longer as important as it was in the good old days of batching. Depending on the cell configuration, some machines will not have to run all the time or, in mixed models, may not run at all while certain models are produced. The machine, which is the bottleneck, should be running all the time but not producing more than what we need (i.e., # waste of overproduction). Remember, people get more expensive over time whereas machines get less expensive over time.

## Why Do We? Why Can't We?

Why do we need to track every supply in the factory? What is the labor cost to accomplish this? What is the value added? Why can't we expense the cost for category C, and in some cases even B items, and manage and account for category A items? Why is there this relentlessness needed by finance to have to control every part in the factory or office? At one company we worked with, everyone had to literally furnish their own pens!

## Should You Always Benchmark Other Companies?

Benchmarking is a process where we compare our company's processes to similar companies. True benchmarking, however, involves selecting a process and benchmarking it against not only similar companies but also non similar companies that have similar processes and then implementing those improvements. For instance, if you wanted to benchmark how to process orders, you may go to an Internet company that is good at that process. The problem with just looking at benchmark data is that many times what is reported to the benchmarking firm is not necessarily aligned with how it may be measured at your company. Organizations need to fully understand the reference to which they are benchmarking themselves to ensure validity.

## Lean and Marketing

While reducing costs, it is important to begin to grow the business. In many instances, the true impact of Lean initiatives will not be realized if marketing and sales are not engaged early on in the process (see Figure 7.3). As waste is eliminated, the organization will find that its throughput time is reduced and they are able to attain more output with the same or less staff and in the same amount or even in less time. Lean is an enabler for growth but does not guarantee growth or even business survival.

Marketing needs to proactively develop plans to generate more business to fill available new capacity. Most companies we have encountered do not have strong marketing departments. While some may have qualified marketing personnel, they tend to lack clarity in the alignment between organizational strategy, operational infrastructure, and marketing. Some marketing departments have plans and great ideas, but in many cases, they do not have good data to support their projections. One company targeted growth and created a new business plan and strategy that seemed

**Figure 7.3 Customer First? (From BIG Archives.)**

sound, yet it was lacking hard data projections. The forecasts provided were "soft," in other words, what people hoped would happen. They determined that there was market share to gain, but there was no clear plan to align the operational infrastructure to the growth plans. While all this seems to be common sense, it is often difficult for organizations to understand clearly the financial benefits of Lean in the current cost accounting environment. Results may take 6 months to a couple of years to be fully recognized because the value stream crosses the entire continuum, and several initiatives may have to be performed sequentially, extending over a period of years, to make a significant impact.

## *Lessons from an AP Kaizen*

During an AP kaizen at a plant in upstate New York, we learned how accounting departments can have a lot of waste built into their processes. Over time, one learns that the sins of other processes like sales and purchasing come to roost in accounting. Any errors on the front end, like receiving quantity errors, purchase order line item pricing errors, inspection decisions including MRB, Use As Is, or rework in-house all, impact AP. We found that it made sense to relocate the AP person (used to be three people) to the purchasing department. This way as problems were found, the AP person could now immediately inform the buyer. It is important that the accountability for all these AP issues rest with the purchasing person.

We found similar results for accounts receivables. Accountability for any customer issues, like pricing discrepancies, quantity discrepancies, returns, etc., should lay with the sales side, and we relocated the accounts receivables person to sales. However, sales and accounts receivables have competing metrics. If there is a return, there will be a reluctance to write off the sale due to the sales revenue goal. So, in some instances, we will continue to ship to a supplier that doesn't pay us on time or issue a credit memo to record the sales revenue.

## Traditional Metrics Discussion

What's wrong with traditional metrics? Well, let me ask you a few questions:

- What is your root cause analysis success rate?
- What is your percentage of overprocessing by product type?
- What percent of the time do your people have to leave their workstation in order to get their own materials?
- How much time is spent on unwrapping parts prior to use?
- What percent of the time does the operator pick up a part or tool and use it immediately versus setting it down and then using it?
- What percent of the time is spent on reworking parts? Do you need the ultimate oxymoron...? The Lean rework line? I actually had a company ask me for that recently!
- How much in-process inventory is waiting on long epoxy cure times?
- How much ownership does engineering have in the production line or floor?
- How many improvements are you implementing per day?
- What percent of your overhead staff's time is value added? The answer has to be none!
- How much time does your overhead staff actually spend making the operator's job easy?
- What percent of the time does the operator have the right tools and parts to do the job?
- What is the operator's job easiness index?
- What percent of the time does the operator have to go to the stockroom to get a part or has to wait idle until a part is available?
- How much time a day does your machine sit idle, unplanned downtime?
- What percent of the time does your machine operator sit idle?
- How many machines per operator?
- What is your mistake proofing index?
- What is true north and how are you performing against it?
- What is your people development scale?
- What does your succession plan look like?

How much time do you spend on the following?

- Inspection.
- Expedited freight.
- Customer expediting.
- Supplier expediting.
- MRP input time.
- Waiting at the Xerox machine.
- Waiting for a centralized printer.
- Waiting for a help request from IT.
- Logging in time every 15 minutes.
- Time spent on bills of material (BOM) and drawing errors.
- Time spent requesting and then waiting for engineering change.
- Improvements not made due to length of time spent on engineering change.
- Knowledge base lost when an employee leaves or retires.
- Excess space tied up due to inventory.
- Time and money lost failing good parts (and passing bad ones).

- Time lost due to lack of cross-training.
- Time lost due to employees sitting or station balancing.
- Time managers up to the president spend expediting.
- Time lost due to the employee who doesn't want to work, and time lost because HR won't back the supervisors with problem employees.
- Time lost going to useless meetings.
- Time lost due to lack of company loyalty.
- Time lost due to poor supervision—they don't make one person work so everyone else slows down.
- Time lost to not improving every day? Wouldn't you have it just about right by now?
- Time lost due to getting bad information from someone.
- Time lost due to inflexible utilities. At one plant, we couldn't even raise the stations to stand up height because hard conduit piping was tied to the workbench.
- What is your employee attrition rate? Cost of retraining?
- What is the cost of losing the recipe?
- What is the cost of waiting for approvals?
- Time lost watching a coworker (not for training purposes).
- Interruptions to floor operator by engineering, stockroom, supervisor, etc.
- Money was lost because the website link didn't work.
- Money was lost because picking up calls took too long. Money lost waiting to leave a message on someone's voicemail? Money lost getting messages off of voice mail?
- Capturing data you don't need? Holding on to that data?
- Making copies you don't need? Holding on to those copies.
- Machine that never seems to run right, doesn't run right, or is making defective parts.
- Trial-and-error building of parts because sales or engineering promise specs that can't be met.
- Selling parts for cheaper than they cost to build.
- Time lost trying to release an order to the floor.
- Money lost because we didn't have it when the customer wanted it. But since we don't track it, we think that there is no demand. Like Obama saying the arrest rate is lower at the border because fewer people are trying to cross it. Maybe, it is because we don't have the manpower we used to have or they are tied up doing so much paperwork that they don't have time to patrol or maybe they have figured out another way in and we are missing them entirely.
- Money lost because marketing, sales, and customer service don't communicate with production.
- Money lost trying to manufacture the engineering prototype that can't be duplicated.
- Money lost because there are no manufacturing engineers or they are catalog engineers.
- Building to a print that is wrong and not questioning the obvious.
- No way to signal anyone when there is a problem and having to wait.
- Waiting for a test program to complete so you can hit a button to keep it going.
- Parts that take more than a 1/4 turn of the wrist.
- Using manual versus power tools.
- Cost of people watching the robot to make sure it doesn't crash. Weren't we supposed to free up those people? Cost due to rework of the work the robot really doesn't do well or correctly.
- Time lost due to MRP signaling the machine shop versus Kanbans.
- Problems experienced with bad or mixed parts.
- Time lost by trying to return good parts the incoming inspection said was bad.

- Time spent building and stocking machined parts or subassemblies just to reissue them later.
- Time and money lost because of your mfg. The process was built to follow the MRP process.
- Time lost because you couldn't make what a customer needed right away because you were working on parts you didn't need.
- Time lost due to returning late from breaks, starting late in the morning, and quitting early to get to the time clock.
- How much time wasted reporting out all the good things we are doing when we could be working on the problems.
- Time lost preparing for the corporate executive's visit! Parade route, cut the grass, etc.
- Time lost preparing the PowerPoint™ for the new president. At Company X, "PPTs" will take weeks to prepare with every word on each slide carefully discussed, deliberated, and debated.
- Time lost because only one person can do the job.
- Money lost because there is no quality standard.
- We track on-time delivery but normally to scheduled or promised date, not requested date.
- Lost time due to machines not operating at the right speed.
- Time spent reworking parts.
- Cost of customer returns. Cost of goods sold will be lost.

Isn't it amazing that we get any product out at all? But we don't measure any of this stuff. We are not suggesting that every company measure every one of these items. We are just trying to make you think! One could argue that it all comes out in the wash, cost of quality, scrap, etc., but most companies don't measure that either. Most companies can't tell me the hours or minutes per unit they have in their parts, daily output of parts, etc. How can we be in the twenty-first century and yet in many cases still in the dark ages? What are you going to measure?

At a casting company in Illinois, they were working on finishing parts destined for a Russian company. Each Russian inspector had a different standard for what was visually acceptable, and there were no formal finishing standards. The operators were very frustrated because since each customer inspector had a different standard, each of the company's inspector had a different standard as well, depending on the Russian inspector he worked with. Each Russian inspector felt that they had to find something wrong with each part to justify their job and travel expenses. This made it impossible to meet schedule dates and to eliminate rework of the parts. A separate line was set up for the inspector just to do their rework. Words cannot even begin to share the frustration and morale issues caused by this system. The company was afraid to go back to the customer as the Russian inspectors might lose face and would then delay the parts even longer. In the end, we brought all the Russian and company inspectors together in a room to agree on a finishing standard. Despite the agreement, the inspectors would still occasionally change their mind on what passed their visual inspection criteria.

What we really need is a cost of waste metric because all of these are a hidden waste in our systems that virtually none of us see, or if we do, we are too busy fighting the day-to-day problems to do anything about it. When we watch the video, the participants are amazed at what they see and we are amazed at what they still don't see. Video is a great equalizer. We have to train ourselves to see all the waste out there. I can't tell you how many times we bring up waste to operators, supervisors, managers, and engineers, and they argue that it is not waste. "You don't understand" they say, "we have to do it that way. We have always done it that way."

Lesson Learned: You can actually tell where people are in their Lean journey by the questions they ask or the tasks they want their consultants to work on while they are there.

## We Should Have Part of Our Accounting Report Entitled; Discover the Opportunities …

> Company X asked us… Can you work on these two machines for two weeks because they are getting low output? They stated, We started measuring our downtime, and these two are the worst machines but we don't know why. We know the operator will let them sit while they do a setup, but other than that we are not quite sure ….

Sure, if you want me to spend our time filming two machines and work with a team of six people to figure out why the machines don't have more uptime, we can do that. But why don't you stop and take a minute to go to the floor and look at the overall department? What you will see is virtually every operator standing there watching a machine. But isn't that what machinists do? The accountants measure machine downtime like it is a god, yet they don't take into account the highly paid machinists standing there watching it with 70% or more of their time being idle. After all, it's normal. The machine might crash, and we don't want that!

The accountants want to track every nut and bolt yet don't track the parts swept up from the floor each day? The reason to keep lowering inventory (to hours' worth) is to continually flush out more problems. The accountants want to track efficiency, yet the measures are sometimes so complicated that no one can figure it out. We have another good one… how about minutes per unit? Accountants want to measure overhead yet, ironically, they are overhead? I actually heard we needed to hire more accountants because they couldn't keep up with all the reports they were generating. We want to measure production and then tie up all our production people in meetings and wonder why they can't get the product out. Listed below are some additional questions designed to provoke thought:

- Electronic Kanbans have their place maybe with suppliers. But do they internally?
- Should we be putting day-by-hour charts on the computer?
- Do we want to live by the system? If so, are you prepared to die by it?
- We measure quality but? Do we measure… cost of incoming inspection? Cost of in-process inspectors? Cost of adding inspection operations to meet corrective actions and then never removing them?
- We might measure productivity, but do we measure what it could be? Do we measure value added? Do we measure unnecessary work?
- We measure efficiency, but do we measure the cost of putting a new untrained person on the line? Do we measure the cost of putting a new manager in place? What about the overhead person that doesn't have enough to do so they created a bunch of work for the people already busy all day?
- What about the person that only works 8–5?
- We measure past due dollars, but what is the cost of moving ahead a job the president has promised another customer? or we move it in to make the numbers?
- What is the cost when they don't allow you to hire that extra person(s) required to meet demand?

Don't you hate it when you know you are being told to do something that is going to come back in a couple of months and you're going to catch holy hell for it? I would be told to order a part from a new untested supplier that engineering wanted and then chastised when it was wrong when it came in. Or when you are told to buy something which is already within lead time? And then chastised for getting the part in late!

## Summary

Our goal is not to pick on the accountants or finance people or suggest that all accountants fit the generalizations listed above. Our goal is to highlight the paradigms we encounter from traditional finance organizations. These paradigms must change if the organization is to make a successful Lean culture transition. There are many books and classes available for those seeking more information on Lean accounting. We have listed some at the end of this chapter. We have lots of hidden wastes in our organizations. We must learn to see this invisible waste, expose it, and eliminate it. This is a very difficult task. Hopefully some of the stories we shared you can identify with and will help you to see your hidden wastes. The bottom line is that we need a new system for accounting. This will be described in Part 3 of this chapter.

Exercise: Look for hidden waste in your organization and list them. How much can you find? Do you have any activities that fit under the "How Stupid Is This Category?"

## Part 3: Lean Accounting by Jerold Solomon[14]

Note: The entire content of Part 3 of this chapter entitled Lean Accounting was contributed by Jerrold Solomon, Accounting for World Class Operation (Fort Wayne, IN: WCM Associates) 2007, Who's Counting (Fort Wayne, IN: WCM Associates) 2003. Both books won the Shingo Prize.

It has become common practice to use the terms Lean accounting and Accounting for Lean interchangeably even though there is a significant difference between the two concepts. Lean accounting is no different from Lean manufacturing in that Lean tools are utilized to eliminate waste in the accounting function; whereas accounting for Lean represents an accounting system that captures the benefits of a Lean implementation as well as motivates Lean behavior.

Lean Accounting is defined as:

- An accounting system that utilizes the Lean tool kit to minimize the consumption of resources that add no value to a product or service in the eyes of the customer.
- A discipline focused on providing actionable information to users and eliminating transactions, reports, and historical data collection.
- A department of financial advisors to a series of focused factories, along with associates who are involved in the day-to-day activities of all areas of the company, and are willing to work in the plant and participate in kaizens.
- An accounting department whose Lean efforts are fully compliant with GAAP and all internal and external reporting requirements.

This definition of Lean accounting includes the elimination of waste by utilizing the Lean tool kit and adds a number of other dimensions as well. Accounting departments have mainly focused their efforts on presenting historical information. A Lean accounting organization provides value-added analysis to its customers in a very simple manner so that improvement actions can be taken immediately. Furthermore, accountants actively participating in these improvement activities have a much greater understanding of the underlying processes. This new perspective promotes accountants from strictly historical reporters and clerical bookkeepers to navigators, or mini CFOs for their organization's various value streams.

## Value Streams

A value stream contains all of the actions (both value-added and non-value-added) currently required to bring a product through the main flows essential to every product: (1) the production flow from raw material into the arms of the customer, and (2) the design flow from concept to launch. Value streams can encompass an individual product family, entire business units, or subsets of a larger value stream.

**Lesson Learned:** It is highly recommended the process improvements associated with Lean accounting begin very early in the Lean journey so that everyone becomes familiar in the use and application of Lean tools throughout the company.

## Accounting for Lean

As an organization transitions from traditional manufacturing encompassing batch processing to Lean manufacturing where pull and flow are the norm, traditional cost accounting methods developed in the early twentieth century become irrelevant; the old batch and queue environment with large lot sizes, long set-ups, massive inventories, and a push production system required extensive control points, detailed job tracking, and sophisticated cost allocation routines, which unfortunately were usually incorrect, outdated, and undecipherable for most of the organization.

In a Lean manufacturing environment, product is quickly pulled through the plant via one-piece flow, inventory levels are minimized as well as standardized, skilled labor operates multiple machines simultaneously, water spiders rotate into skilled positions as needed, and generic materials are used to provide greater flexibility and standardization. The overall speed of the operation is many orders of magnitude greater than a batch operation. In this environment, the traditional standard cost system and absorption accounting are not only ineffective but may also become a significant barrier to a successful Lean conversion.

Accounting for Lean is defined as follows:

- An accounting system that provides accurate, timely, and understandable information to motivate the Lean transformation throughout the organization and improve decision-making, which leads to increased customer value, growth, profitability, and cash flow.
- An accounting system that supports the Lean transformation by providing relevant and actionable information that enables continuous improvement at every level of the organization.
- An accounting system that utilizes value stream costing, "Plain English" profit-and-loss statements, box scores, and other straightforward means to convey performance activity.
- An accounting system that meets the needs of all of its customers, including tax authorities, the Board of Directors, creditors, internal and external auditors, and internal customers such as manufacturing.

As both the definitions of Lean accounting and accounting for Lean demonstrate, under no circumstance will adherence to reporting requirements by regulatory agencies such as the SEC, IRS, and GAAP be compromised.

Accounting for Lean is twenty-first century cost management in support of world-class operations. The accounting department is in the unique position of having to do two things during the Lean conversion process: (1) apply Lean tools to eliminate waste in the accounting department;

and more importantly, (2) change the overall method of keeping score for the internal operations of the business. The latter task is daunting, but nevertheless, one that has to be completed for a successful Lean conversion. Given this challenge, it is easy to see why accounting department resources will be stretched during a Lean conversion. The ideal Lean accounting progression should begin very early in the Lean journey with the accounting staff participating in the events taking place on the manufacturing floor. Enlightened accounting leadership should then immediately deploy the same tools in the accounting department to eliminate waste and all of the non-value-added clerical work that is too often all consuming. By following this path, when the time comes to implement accounting for Lean, accountants will not only understand what has taken place in production, but they will also have the knowledge, time, and resources necessary to devote to the change process.

Unfortunately, the accounting department typically is not brought into the Lean conversion process until well into the journey, when significant changes have been made in manufacturing processes and traditional reporting conventions are providing management with confusing signals that contradict the physical gains made to date on the shop floor. At this point, accounting has a very long learning curve, which either slows down the Lean journey or derails it completely. The accounting profession regrettably is at least a decade behind the Lean manufacturing movement in North America and faces a rather steep hill to climb. Accountants must decide whether they will be an ally or an obstacle in a company's efforts to successfully navigate the formidable Lean journey.

## Why a Traditional Standard Cost System Is Incompatible with Lean

### Historical Cost Structures, Direct and Indirect Labor

Without going into an in-depth study of the origins of cost accounting, we should all be aware that standard cost systems were originally developed for a totally different type of operating environment. There have been numerous works critical of traditional accounting methods, such as Relevance Lost, The Rise and Fall of Management Accounting by H. Thomas Johnson and Robert S. Kaplan[1]; Real Numbers: Management Accounting in a Lean Organization by Jean Cunningham and Orest Fiume[2]; and Practical Lean Accounting by Brian Maskell and Bruce Baggaley.[3] But perhaps the best depiction of the current state of management accounting can be captured with the two quotes:

> All of the essentials of modern management accounting were established by 1930 without any significant changes since then.[4]

> **Brian Maskell**

> Accounting is 100% the enemy of productivity.[5]

> **Eliyahu Goldratt Author of The Goal**

Despite the fact the world has changed significantly, and that the cost structures of the typical organization today bear little resemblance to the labor-intensive organizations of 70 plus years ago, we continue to use the same cost management systems. As shown in Figure 7.4, in the first half of the twentieth century, "labor" was the most significant cost component for manufacturing companies. Labor is labeled "labor" rather than "direct labor," because as you will come to understand

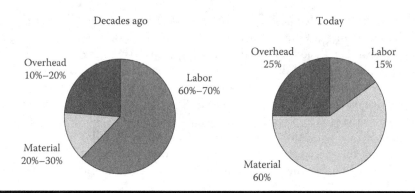

**Figure 7.4   A depiction of cost structure changes over time. (Courtesy of Jerrold Solomon and WCM Associates LLC.)**

during the Lean journey, very little of what we have traditionally called "direct labor" has anything to do with changing the form, fit, or function of the product, i.e., value-adding activities.

Over time, companies migrated to lower cost labor markets and focused more heavily on substituting capital for labor. As the use of computers became commonplace, labor expenditures shifted from direct labor to overhead, as a greater emphasis was placed on sophisticated MRP and ERP systems to manage more complex internal operations as well as national and global operations.

Use of a traditional standard cost system, where overhead expenses are determined as a multiplier of direct labor costs, was appropriate when overhead was the smallest piece of the cost pie, direct labor was the largest piece, and a batch and queue philosophy was universally accepted. Overhead rates of 10%, 20%, or 30% of direct labor were not that and did not distort costs a great deal. However, in today's typical cost system, where direct labor has continually declined and overhead has increased dramatically, we typically have overhead rates of 300%–600% of direct labor. The practice of allocating overhead via a multiple of direct labor or having overhead "ride the backs of direct labor" becomes more and more meaningless as the numerator of the ratio grows (or at least remains constant) and the denominator declines. The combination of a diminishing role for direct labor and the transformation from batch-and-queue production to one-piece flow renders the standard cost approach inappropriate or even detrimental in a world-class operation.

An interesting offshoot of this discussion is an analysis of the current reports emanating from the accounting department and the intense focus on labor analysis. When labor constituted the lion's share of an organization's cost of goods sold, it made sense to track it very carefully. The problem is in today's environment, we still have the same intense focus on many direct labor reports, despite the fact that direct labor is usually the smallest component of a firm's production costs. Similarly, firms often try to improve product line margins in response to competitive market pressures with an intense focus on cost reduction, and in particular, direct labor cost reductions. Yet, this is absolutely the wrong time for this strategy. A Lean company develops products with target costs in mind and establishes competitive direct labor and total cost targets. Focusing on labor reductions after a product has been conceived, developed, and released into the marketplace is not only wasteful; it is usually ineffective and extremely costly. Organizations must establish rigorous cost targets during the initial design of products for manufacture and assembly.

We will conclude this topic by examining what we currently call direct labor in the typical standard cost system. If you have participated in a kaizen event for an assembly operation or a set-up reduction event in a machining environment, you most likely observed that about 75% of the direct labor effort is waste. Some common activities that require wasted time and effort include searching for the right material, parts, tools, and fixtures; performing a setup; moving parts within a work cell with pallet jacks, cranes, or other means; transporting the material or completed part from workstation to workstation; and interpreting work instructions. As we transition to a Lean workplace and eliminate these wastes, the portion of expense we traditionally call direct labor will decline dramatically while the effort devoted to the in-house logistics system will likely increase.

The in-house logistics system will require an increased emphasis on delivering materials in small quantities directly to the point of use throughout the day, as well as kitting materials to both error-proof and eliminating searching for parts. These new activities require tremendous focus and standardization and are critical to a smooth running Lean operation. In a traditional manufacturing environment, the functions of the in-house logistical system are performed by material handlers, who are classified as indirect labor since they do not alter the form, fit, or function of the parts. Traditional manufacturers typically view material handlers as unnecessary overhead and strive to increase the ratio of direct to indirect labor. During a Lean transformation, the exact opposite will occur, as direct labor will decline per unit of output and indirect labor will likely increase until an efficient material handling system has been implemented. The ratio of indirect labor to direct labor will increase from historical norms (in some cases quite dramatically), and Lean cost management techniques will be required to motivate proper behavior.

## Specific Example of Mixed Signals Provided by a Standard Cost System

To better understand the mixed signals provided by a standard cost system, we are going to walk through the steps of a Lean simulation, including the typical metrics involved. This simulation, which consists of a four stage production process, has been performed across the globe, by thousands of people from all functional areas, with virtually the same outcome every time. The simulation guides a group of people through the assembly of a two-piece Styrofoam box. Step 1 is to affix two adhesive dots to one end of the top of the box. Step 2 is to then place two push pins into the other end of the same side of the box. Step 3 is to tape the two halves of the Styrofoam box together with masking tape. The last step, Step 4, is to insert the completed Styrofoam box into an outer cardboard packing box. The first round of the simulation is laid out as depicted in Figure 7.5

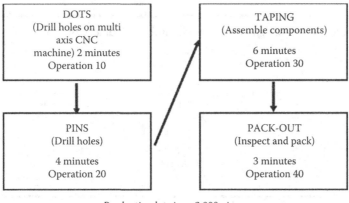

Production lot size = 3,000 pieces

**Figure 7.5    Simulation layout of traditional production process. (Courtesy of Jerrold Solomon and WCM Associates LLC.)**

and replicates the traditional manufacturing environment, with poor workflow, workstations haphazardly spread around the plant floor, large inventories, and totally unbalanced production.

At the end of this exercise, the group is asked to calculate the cost to produce one complete foam box using typical cost accounting methods and the data given in Figure 7.6 in conjunction with the process data shown in Figure 7.5.

(For this exercise, all references to hourly labor rates mean direct labor rates.) During these simulations, it is made clear that there are no tricks involved in calculating the cost per completed box. The operating metrics are provided as additional information to be used after the game and have no bearing on the cost calculations. Surprisingly, the author's experience shows that regardless of the audience's work experience, whether it is a room full of accountants or operations managers, the percentage of correct responses is always about 50%, with a very wide range of individual answers from pennies to thousands of dollars.

Test yourself before looking at the correct calculation shown in Figure 7.7.

The product cost is calculated by adding up the number of minutes required to make one Styrofoam box, which is 15 minutes, or one-fourth of an hour. Since the direct hourly labor rate is $30, then the cost of direct labor per unit produced is one-fourth of $30, or $7.50. Overhead is three times direct labor, which equals $22.50. Finally, we have to add the $10 for material to arrive at the total cost of a completed foam box, which is $40. This represents exactly what is happening in the typical standard cost system. The cost accounting program simply adds up all of the time worked at each operation and multiplies the result by the standard labor rate, then applies the predetermined overhead multiplier, which could be the same across a plant or different for every work center. Finally, material is added, and a standard cost is established for the product. This is done over and over for every stock-keeping unit in the business.

During the second round of the simulation, the group performs a kaizen event and forms a U-shaped cell, co-locates the processes, rearranges the sequence into a logical flow, begins to right

| Cost data | Product cost | Operating metrics |
|---|---|---|
| Direct labor hourly rate = $30 | | Average inventory 5,000 |
| Overhead multiplier = 3× | | Lead-time 8 weeks |
| Material cost per unit = $10 | | On-time-performance 75% |

**Figure 7.6 Data to use in cost calculations—Round 1. (Courtesy of Jerrold Solomon and WCM Associates LLC.)**

| Cost data | Product cost | Operating metrics |
|---|---|---|
| Direct labor hourly rate = $30 | Direct labor $7.50 | Average inventory 5,000 |
| | Overhead $22.50 | |
| Overhead multiplier = 3× | | Lead-time 8 weeks |
| | Material $10.00 | |
| Material cost per unit = $10 | Total $40.00 | On-time-performance 75% |

**Figure 7.7 Calculation of product cost—Round 1. (Courtesy of Jerrold Solomon and WCM Associates LLC.)**

size the equipment, and utilizes Kanbans to trigger production. These changes significantly reduce the lot size.

The group is once again asked to calculate the cost to produce one complete foam box using the data in Figures 7.8 and 7.9. Again, experience shows that despite previous instructions on the nature of cost calculations, the number of correct answers does not increase nearly as much as one would expect for an audience that is largely responsible for using the cost system to make decisions.

The correct cost per unit is $46 as shown in Figure 7.10.

The labor component of the product cost is derived by once again adding up the total time required to make the product, which in this case is 18 minutes, or 30% of an hour. With a labor rate of $30 per hour, 18 minutes costs $9 per unit. Using the same multiplier for overhead and adding $10 for material

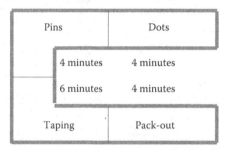

| Pins | Dots |
|---|---|
| 4 minutes | 4 minutes |
| 6 minutes | 4 minutes |
| Taping | Pack-out |

Production lot size = 300 pieces.

**Figure 7.8 Production cell after kaizen event. (Courtesy of Jerrold Solomon and WCM Associates LLC.)**

| Cost data | Product cost | Operating metrics |
|---|---|---|
| Direct labor hourly rate = $30 | | Average inventory 500 |
| Overhead multiplier = 3× | | Lead-time 2 weeks |
| Material cost per unit = $10 | | On-time-performance 5% |

**Figure 7.9 Data to use in cost calculations—Round 2. (Courtesy of Jerrold Solomon and WCM Associates LLC.)**

| Cost data | Product cost | Operating metrics |
|---|---|---|
| Direct labor hourly rate = $30 | Direct labor $9.00 | Average inventory 500 |
| | Overhead $27.00 | |
| Overhead multiplier = 3× | | Lead-time 2 weeks |
| | Material $10.00 | |
| Material cost per unit = $10 | Total $46.00 | On-time-performance 95% |

**Figure 7.10 Calculation of product cost—Round 2. (Courtesy of Jerrold Solomon and WCM Associates LLC.)**

**Table 7.3   Comparison of Performance before and after Lean Improvement**

| Metric | Before | After | % Improvement |
|---|---|---|---|
| Inventory | 5,000 | 500 | 90 |
| Lead time | 8 weeks | 2 weeks | 75 |
| OTP | 75% | 95% | 27 |
| Batch size | 3,000 | 300 | 90 |
| Sq. footage | 8,000 | 3,000 | 63 |
| Quality | 50 PPM | 15 PPM | 70 |
| # of transactions | Many | Few | Dramatic |
| Throughput | 10/hour | 10/hour | No change |
| Flexibility and teamwork | Poor | Improved | Dramatic |
| Unit cost per cost acctg. | $40 | $46 | (15%) |

*Source:* Courtesy of Jerrold Solomon and WCM Associates LLC.

yields a total cost of $46, as shown in Figure 7.10. Herein one of the problems of using a traditional cost system as a company progresses down the Lean conversion path. While shop-floor personnel are doing all the right things, such as improving lead times and on-time performance (OTP), and reducing production lot sizes, the cost system is reporting that costs have increased. See Table 7.3 for a summary comparison of Round 1 and Round 2 simulation results before and after the Lean improvements.

The production cell experienced tremendous improvements in all of the metrics that matter to the customer, such as quality, lead-time, and on-time performance. Internal performance has also improved, as the space utilized has significantly decreased, inventory (and therefore cash) has declined dramatically, and the workforce is more engaged. When one questions the simulation participants, they all mention their work has become less stressful, they can communicate better with their upstream and downstream teammates, and they are more inclined to offer suggestions to each other. The change in their work environment, along with reduced lot sizes, noticeably improves quality. However, Table 7.3 shows the internal cost reports will report the cost of this product increased by 15%. This demonstrates the problem with a traditional cost system, as everyone is focused on the departmental statement or area profit-and-loss statement, which incorrectly broadcasts to everyone that performance is deteriorating.

Another example will clarify the distortions of a traditional cost system. In Table 7.4, the throughput results of the two simulations are left unanswered. Yet, this is a critical measure for both the customer and the business. From a customer perspective, knowledge of capacity and throughput allows the company to accurately respond to the market and provide accurate lead times. From a business perspective, the only way to achieve sales is to ship products and invoice the customer, and that means all manufacturing operations have to be completed.

So how do we determine the before and after throughput numbers? Since the taping operation is the bottleneck constraint in both simulations, total output is limited by the ability of the taping operation, which is 6 minutes. Therefore, regardless of what happens at the three other operations, the maximum output of taping is 10 units per hour, which in turn limits the output of finished product to 10 units per hour. The process is not in balance, and this becomes much more visible when the operations are all located in one area.

**Table 7.4 Comparison of Performance before and after Lean Improvement**

| Metric | Before | After | % Improvement |
|---|---|---|---|
| Inventory | 5,000 | 500 | 90 |
| Lead time | 8 weeks | 2 weeks | 75 |
| On-time-performance | 75% | 95% | 27 |
| Batch size | 3,000 | 300 | 90 |
| Sq. footage | 8,000 | 3,000 | 63 |
| Quality | 50 PPM | 15 PPM | 70 |
| # of transactions | Many | Few | Dramatic |
| Flexibility and teamwork | Poor | Improved | Dramatic |
| Unit cost per cost acctg. | $40 | $46 | (15) |

*Source:* Courtesy of Jerrold Solomon and WCM Associates LLC.

The business would be better off by slowing down all operations completed in less than 6 minutes until the cell is "leaned" out by either eliminating waste in the 6 minutes operation and therefore reducing cycle time, combining operations, or redesigning the product. But slowing down an operation is totally at odds with everything we have learned in the past, because the cost system will indicate further erosion in unit costs. A traditional standard cost system encourages faster production in all operations in order to absorb more overhead and generate healthier month-end numbers. Because a traditional factory usually has its work centers spread throughout the plant according to functionality (e.g., all like equipment is located together such as drill presses and lathes), it is virtually impossible to "see" the flow until one relocates and right sizes the equipment into a cell that contains all of the necessary equipment to complete the process from start to finish.

## Added Benefits of Cellular Manufacturing as It Relates to Cost Management and Customer Service

From an accounting and financial perspective, there are some tremendous advantages of organizing in cells and value streams at the plant level. In traditional production environments, chaos is the order of the day. It becomes virtually impossible to predict when a product will be available to ship unless there is a huge finished goods warehouse from which to pull the product. Our sympathies are extended to the production managers and supervisors have to provide a completion date for those all-important special orders that have to snake their way through multiple operations in the plant, with each operation having different processing times, work-in-process inventory levels, and large batch sizes. Despite the proliferation of sophisticated computer systems, providing a reliable completion date is almost impossible.

## Pull System

A Pull System is characterized when the flow of parts, products, and information occurs as a result of the consumption of that item at the immediate downstream operation. A signal is provided to the upstream operation to replace what has been consumed.

On the other hand, if custom sales orders must be filled from production without the benefit of an inventory buffer, utilizing cells with balanced work flows allows for much more predictable results, which in turn leads to better forecasting of cash flows and avoidance of late-delivery penalties. This is the added benefit of pull systems. Another benefit resulting from the formation of cells is a much improved capital investment process. When operations are disconnected and spread haphazardly around a plant, then capital investment decisions are based on local optimization. If the first operation in Figure 7.8 could be improved by buying another piece of equipment that would process the dots in half the time, it is probable that such an investment would be approved. But in reality, not one more product would be produced each hour with the enhanced equipment, because the process is constrained by a downstream operation that may not be visible in a traditional operation. In fact, speeding up any process in front of a bottleneck is always a poor investment, as it will result in "feeding" the system with more inventories. Value streams, if measured correctly, will become the Finance Department's "best friends," because they allow for a huge magnifying glass to be held over the area. With this structure, one can fully understand and appreciate the system, and consequently work with the team to continuously improve it.

## Summary

As illustrated in the previous examples, it is imperative to change the cost management system in concert with the physical changes occurring in the plant; otherwise, traditional accounting practices will send misleading signals to management that just might derail the entire Lean effort. In the end, one must ask which cost system will allow for more accurate reporting of results, enhance the ability to analyze and improve operations, as well as provide proper incentive to continuously improve customer service, quality, overall cost, and inventory turns. The only answer is a Lean cost management system supporting a Lean operation. In summary, as you embark on your Lean journey, the Lean practitioner must understand, anticipate the challenges of the changing paradigms in Lean thinking that both management and workers will encounter and either embrace or contest. It is essential that there is a well thought out plan to bring all stakeholders along the journey to learn, grow and adjust their views and practices in order to remove or manage barriers and propel the lean successfully forward.

## Chapter Questions

1. Can the accounting process really be transitioned to Lean?
2. What is hidden waste?
3. How do you find hidden waste?
4. What are some problems with cost accounting standards?
5. Is the machine utilization still important in a Lean operation?
6. What is a pull system?
7. What happens to fixed overhead standards after Lean implementations?
8. What problems does one find in traditional budgeting processes?
9. How can finance and the CFO help the Lean transition?
10. What are some of the mixed signals provided by standard cost systems?

## Notes

1. https://www.brainyquote.com/authors/e-f-schumacher-quotes
2. Shingo Prize—winning author Jerrold Solomon provided the title for the chapter and contributed to part 3, where he explains the differences between Lean accounting and accounting for Lean. The entire content

of Chapter 26 Part 3 entitled Lean Accounting was contributed by Jerrold Solomon, Accounting for World Class Operation (Fort Wayne, IN: WCM Associates), 2007, Who's Counting (Fort Wayne, IN: WCM Associates), 2003. Both books won the Shingo Prize. Note 1-5 from part 3 are part of end note 2 and these end notes are included in that book.

3. Much of this material from Leveraging Lean in Healthcare.

4. Brian Maskell and Bruce Baggaley, Practical Lean Accounting (Portland, OR: Productivity Press), 2004; Brian Maskell and the BMA Team, Making the Numbers Count (Portland, OR: Productivity Press) 1996; Brian Maskell, The Lean Business Management System. Brian H. Maskell, Bruce Baggaley, Nick Kato, David Piano (Philadelphia, PA: BMA Press), 2007; these books are available from the BMA website, from Amazon.com, and other business book websites.

5. https://quoteinvestigator.com/2010/05/26/everything-counts-einstein/ Quote Investigator: QI suggests crediting William Bruce Cameron instead of Albert Einstein. Cameron's 1963 text "Informal Sociology: A Casual Introduction to Sociological Thinking" contained the following passage. Emphasis added to excerpts by QI:[1]

6. Shigeo Shingo, Non Stock Production: The Shingo System for Continuous Improvement (Portland, OR: Productivity Press), 1988.

7. Kenneth Hopper and William Hopper, The Puritan Gift: Reclaiming the American Dream amidst Global Financial Chaos (New York: I.B. Tauris), 2009; David Mann, Creating a Lean Culture (Portland, OR: Productivity Press), 2005.

8. Contributed by Sam Jaffa, Senior Manager, Strategic Sourcing for a leading telecommunications company.

9. Guard band is a term used in the electronics industry. Normally it means there is a narrow frequency range used to separate two wider frequency ranges to ensure that both can transmit simultaneously without interfering with each other. In this usage, the author is stating that more of a risk tolerance was assumed since the forecast was always wrong. This gave us some play in our inventory predictions so we would not be wrong when the final numbers came in.

10. Chapter 14. Nuts! Southwest Airlines' Crazy Recipe for Business and Personal Success [Paperback] Crown Business, First Edition (February 17, 1998), Kevin Freiberg, Jackie Freiberg.

11. Frederick Taylor, Principles of Scientific Management, Harper & Brothers, 1911.

12. Correspondence dated December 31, 2009, from Brian Maskell of BMA Associates, BMA website (www.maskell.com), who was highly influential in this section.

13. David Young and Stephen O'Byrne, EVA and Value Based Management (New York: McGraw Hill), 2001. EVA is equal to return on net assets weighted average cost of capital × invested capital [(RONA − WACC) × invested capital].

14. The entire content of Chapter 26 Part 3 entitled Lean Accounting was contributed by Jerrold Solomon, Accounting for World Class Operation (Fort Wayne, IN: WCM Associates), 2007, Who's Counting (Fort Wayne, IN: WCM Associates), 2003. Both books won the Shingo Prize.

# Additional Readings

Cimorelli, S. 2005. Kanban for the Supply Chain. New York: Productivity Press, p. 10.

Cunningham, J.E. and Fiume, O.J. 2003. Real Numbers: Management Accounting in a Lean Organization. Durham, NC: Managing Times Press.

Fiume, O.J. 2003. Real Numbers. Durham, UK: Managing Times Press.

Goldratt, E. (November, 1983). Cost Accounting: The Number One Enemy of Productivity. American and Inventory Control Society 26th Annual International Conference Proceedings, New Orleans, LA, pp. 433–435.

Helfert, E. 1997. Techniques of Financial Analysis. Homewood, IL: Irwin Publishing.

Johnson, H.T. and Kaplan, R.S. 1987. Relevance Lost: The Rise and Fall of Management Accounting. Boston, MA: Harvard Business School Press.

Maskell, B.H. 1991. Performance Measurement for World Class Manufacturing. Cambridge, MA: Productivity Press.

Maskell, B.H. 1994. New Performance Measures. Portland, OR: Productivity Press.

Maskell, B.H. 1996a. Making the Numbers Count. New York: Productivity Press, p. 16.

Maskell, B.H. 1996b. Making the Numbers Count. Portland, OR: Productivity Press.

Maskell, B.H. 2004. Practical Lean Accounting. New York: Productivity Press.

Maskell, B.H. and Baggaley, B. 2004. Practical Lean Accounting. New York: Productivity Press.

Monden, Y. 1989. Japanese Management Accounting. Cambridge, MA: Productivity Press.

Monden, Y. 1992. Cost Management in the New Manufacturing Age. Cambridge, MA: Productivity Press.

Monden, Y. 1995. Cost Reduction Systems. Portland, OR: Productivity Press.

Pryor, T. 2000. Using ABM for Continuous Improvement. Arlington, TX: ICMS.

Ross, R., Executive Director, Shingo Prize. Utah: Utah State University.

Rother, M. and Shook, J. 1999. Learning to See. Brookline, MA: Lean Enterprise Institute, p. 3.

Solomon, J. 2003. Who's Counting. Fort Wayne, IN: WCM Associates.

Solomon, J.M. 2007. Accounting for World Class Operations. Fort Wayne, IN: WCM Associates.

Stern, J.M. 2001. The EVA Challenge. New York: John Wiley & Sons.

TPS Throughput Solutions. (April, 2007). http://www.tpslean.com/glossary/tpmdef.htm.

Various Authors. 1991. Measuring Corporate Performance. Boston, MA: HBR Press.

Womack, J.P. and Jones, D.T. 1996. Lean Thinking. New York: Simon & Schuster.

Young, D.S. 2001. EVA & Value Based Management. New York: McGraw-Hill.

# Appendix A - Study Guide

## Chapter 1 Questions and Answers

1. What are three characteristics that display respect for humanity?
   There are various characteristics that display respect for humanity, to include:
   - Being respectful to employees
   - Employing active listening
   - Coaching employees to think of the answer for themselves
   - Making sure the employee can be successful in your environment prior to hiring them
   - Making sure we constantly solicit ideas from the employee on how to improve
   - Constantly challenge team members with new problems
   - Holding employees accountable to promises and deadlines
   - Creating development plans and paths for employees
   - Disciplining employees as needed
   - Allowing employees (team members) to fail and then coaching them on how to learn from the failure
   - Empowering employees to the proper level
   - Giving back to the community

2. What benefits are derived from embracing and implementing jidoka in a typical manufacturing factory producing automobiles?
   The goal is to always strive for 100% quality in products by producing zero defects; thus, systems must be designed to catch the error prior to it becoming a defect. Properly implemented jidoka will result in less cost of repair during the warranty period (resulting in lower costs to the manufacturer) and ultimately higher customer satisfaction (less time at the dealer and less costs after the warranty expires).

   The first goal of Lean is to never produce a bad part. In the worst-case scenario, if a defect is created, we must be able to detect the defective part before passing it to the next process. Machines in an automobile plant should check parts before they work on them, while they are working on them, and after they work on them. By incorporating jidoka, we design, modify, or customize machines to detect errors prior to producing a defect. The other goal of jidoka is to make sure the machines don't break down but if they do, make sure they stop before making a bad part or crashing.

3. Why is jidoka difficult to implement?
   One of the reasons jidoka is difficult to implement is that many of the Lean principles, thinking, and tools must be in place for it to work. In addition, most companies do not really understand Jidoka, thus compounding the issue that makes it very difficult to implement.

4. What are the two networks of operations described by Dr. Shingo?

5. Discuss similarities and differences between Herzberg and Maslow motivational theories.
6. What is the 5 Ws tool? When should we use it?

    Everyone should understand how to problem solve and you can't really solve a problem without knowing the problem. One of the basic techniques leveraged when problem-solving is the 5 whys. This familiar tool involves asking why up to five times to help get to the root cause of a problem. The hardest part of the 5 whys is getting people to use it. We should use the tool often during any problem-solving task, especially when working to find the root cause of the problem.

7. What are the 5 Ws and 2 Hs?

    The 5 Ws and 2 Hs is another tool to eliminate waste. The 5 Ws are composed of asking when, where, what, who, and why. The 2 Hs are how and how much. The following questions apply:

    — When is the best time to do it? Does it have to be done at a certain time?
    — Where is it being done? Does it have to be done here?
    — What is being done? Can we eliminate this work?
    — Who is doing it? Would it be better to have someone else do it? Why are we doing it?
    — Why is the work necessary? Clarify its purpose.
    — How is it being done? Is this the best way to do it? Are there any other ways to do it?
    — How much does it cost now?
    — How much will it cost to improve?

8. What are the two pillars of the Lean (Toyota) house?

    There are two pillars of the Lean (Toyota) house:

    — The first pillar—just in time (JIT)
    — The second pillar—jidoka

9. Explain JIT.

    The left side pillar of the Lean house is (just in time) JIT, which means using the minimum amount of inventory, equipment, time, labor, and space necessary to deliver our products JIT to the customer by creating flow using a pull system. The true purpose behind JIT is to reduce the inventory in the system in order to make problems more visible.[4] Excess inventory and idle time are always signs of waste and hide problems. A common misperception is JIT means zero inventories, which is not the case as all systems need inventory to function. JIT means there is a small amount of inventory available at point of use (POU) before it is noting operators have what they need on the line or at their desk so they don't have to search for their own materials; the material should be right where and when it is needed, which is defined as point of use ((POU) inventory.

10. Explain jidoka. Give an example.

    In the words of Taiichi Ohno, "At Toyota, the 'auto-activated machine' means a machine which is attached to an automatic stopping device." The first principle at work here is separating man from machine. Once a job is standardized, it becomes repetitive and should be semi- or fully automated. Machines should do repetitive and dangerous work. The next step is to create smart machines or machines that can automatically stop when a mistake is made or a problem occurs in the machine. This is a central principle of the TPS system, which is why jidoka is the right pillar of the Lean house. The true goal of jidoka is built-in quality, which integrates mistake proofing to prevent the error at the source to ensure a defect does not result. This ensures that quality is built in at each process and triggers an automatic response to an abnormality.

A simple example of jidoka can occur on automobile assembly lines. If an operator sees a mistake, the operator has the authority to stop the line and the supervisor and operator quickly review what the problem is to determine the course of action. There are two options; repair the part in line in one cycle or tag the part for offline repair later and continue to focus on and solve why the issue occurred. This example is easy to see and relies upon the skills of the people in the work area to function properly. The operator and supervisor must be trained properly to make the call to stop the line and help with the root cause analysis.

11. What is the difference between total quality and total company-wide quality?
12. Explain the difference between PDCA and PCDCA?
    The plan–do–check–act (PDCA) cycle is a four-step model for carrying out change.

    When researching the origins of this model, we discovered that act did not seem to be part of the original model or Dr. Shingo considered the act implied as part of check. The model Shingo started with was plan–do–check that was a spin-off of Shewhart's plan–do–study. However, Dr. Shingo added control after the plan; thus, we refer to this model as PCDCA:

    1. Plan
    2. Control
    3. Do
    4. Check
    5. Act

13. What is the importance of a standard problem-solving model?
    Every company should standardize on a problem-solving model with a priority to teach it to every employee. The standard problem-solving model provides employees with a common model, approach, and terminology when team members work by themselves or huddle to work in groups to fix problems. The standard problem-solving model is like standard work for problem-solving.

    Many companies have standardized on the Six Sigma define, measure, analyze, improve, control (DMAIC) model, Shewhart's/Deming's plan–do–study–act (PDSA), or the PDCA CCS model.

14. What is a quality circle?
    A quality circle is where the supervisor meets voluntarily with the group of workers to undertake various activities with the aim of solving quality problems relating to the circle members' work. Efforts are made to link these activities closely with the company's overall company-wide quality control (CWQC) program.

15. What is poka yoke? Give an example.
    Poka yoke is fixing the problem to ensure it does not occur or reoccur. Shingo was an early adopter and poka yoke involves implementing both warning and control in the process. A simple example is an electric sensor on an elevator door that prevents the door from shutting on passengers.

16. Does Lean implementation work in a union environment?
    We have found no real difference in implementing Lean in union versus nonunion environments. Union environments can be a bit more challenging; however, if you involve the union leadership from the start and make them part of the process, it works. Union leadership must be part of the development of changes and be brought into the process early.

17. What did you learn from this chapter?

## Chapter 2 Questions and Answers

1. What is sequencing? How is it accomplished?

   In manufacturing production, sequencing is utilized to level out the production of various or "mixed" models. This concept allows Toyota to run multiple car types down the same line one model after another.

2. What is demonstrated capacity? How do you know if the area is using it?

   "Demonstrated capacity" is when companies or departments use their actual daily or weekly demonstrated output totals as a measure of what they can produce versus scientific methods such as time and motion study.

3. Explain takt–flow–pull.

   In Lean, there is a saying which is takt … flow … pull, which is short for implementing a Lean system. Everything starts with the customer demand and we can calculate our takt time when we know available time. We can establish flow within the factory (or service company) from raw materials to finished goods/shipping in accordance with the beat of the takt time. Finally, we create a pull system with synchronized linkage to our customer and supply chain.

4. What is a build-to-order system?

   In a build-to-order system, the product is only made when an order is received.

5. What is a pull system?

   If a company triggers each order based on the shipment of a previous order where the shipment creates the trigger, this is considered a pull system.

6. Are all pull systems built to order systems?

7. Where should the heijunka box be located?

   The box is typically stored in the shipping area where the pull is started from finished goods.

8. What is peak demand? How does peak demand impact line setups and capacity planning?

   Peak demand is when the demand is highest, such as the electric demand on a generating plant in August when the outside temperature approaches 95 degrees mid-day. We generally look at peak demand either daily or hourly and determine the takt time and line constraints accordingly.

9. How would you schedule work in a process without using the MRP shop floor control system?

10. What is pitch, and how is pitch used in manufacturing planning?

    Pitch is the time required to supply a standard pattern of parts to a line. Pitch is calculated by multiplying the takt time (or cycle time) by the number of pieces in the pattern of parts needed for the line, which is normally a shipping box or container size.

11. What is a heijunka box?

    A heijunka or sequencing box is used as a visual control to know when or how we are doing according to the plan.

12. What is level loading? Why is it important? How is level loading accomplished? How is it linked to Kanbans and the Toyota House?

    Level loading is a technique for reducing the waste and is vital to the development of production efficiency in the Toyota Production System and Lean manufacturing. The general idea is to produce intermediate goods at a constant rate and to allow further processing to be carried out at a constant and predictable rate.

13. What did you learn from this chapter?

# Chapter 3 Questions and Answers

1. What is a Pareto chart and how is it used to support root cause analysis?
   A Pareto chart contains a bar graph and a line graph such that the individual values are shown in descending order by bars, and the cumulative total is shown by the line. The purpose of the Pareto chart is to highlight the most important factors and is used for root cause analysis to focus on the most common sources of defects or the highest occurring type of defect.

2. Are Six Sigma and Lean different? How do they relate to each other?
   Yes, Six Sigma and Lean are different. Six Sigma is related to quality, i.e., 3.4 defects per million, and Lean is an entire process related to total removal of waste from the value stream to include quality tools such as mistake proofing.

3. How are warning and control devices used?
   Warning devices alert the operator to a problem but don't prevent the error or the defect. Control devices shut down the operation or don't allow it to proceed until it is corrected.

4. Is self-check inspection permissible? What are the benefits, if any?
   Yes, self-inspection is permissible. The benefits are as follows:
   - 100% inspection occurs
   - Makes instant correction possible
   - Less psychological resistance to self-discovery than supervisor or even peer discovery

5. PDCA is often an acronym in Lean implementation. What is the relationship to Lean?
   PDCA is a system that is used widely throughout the Lean journey to plan, take action, check results, and to review any needed actions using root cause analysis.

6. What is poka yoke?
   Poka yoke is a Japanese term that means fail-safing or mistake proofing. A poka yoke is any mechanism in a Lean process that helps your team members avoid mistakes.

7. How do Deming and Dr. Shingo differ in approach to quality?
   Dr. Shingo approaches quality by reviewing processes and introducing process improvements to ensure zero defects using techniques such as poka yoke. Deming approached quality from a TQM perspective.

8. Can poka yoke be used outside of manufacturing systems? If so, provide two examples.
   Yes, poka yoke can be used outside of a manufacturing system. Two simple examples are gas pumps with an auto shutoff mechanism that prevent overfilling and moisture sensors on dryers that both save energy and prevent clothes from burning/melting.

9. Why is mistake proofing important?
   Mistake proofing, also known as poka yoke, is a critical component of Lean and provides a mechanism to eliminate the errors so defects won't occur.

10. What are some of the culture barriers to mistake proofing?

11. What is a waterfall chart?
    A waterfall chart is a chart that offers a high level of data visualization to support the understanding of the cumulative effect of sequentially introduced positive or negative values. Often in finance, it will be referred to as a bridge chart or a walk across chart.

12. What role do the 5 Whys play in mistake proofing?

13. What role do control charts play in mistake proofing?
    SPC should be used as a preventive tool to identify patterns before an out-of-control condition happens.

14. What is the mistake proofing goal with Lean? a. Six Sigma, b. 3.4 defects per million, c. zero defects, and d. none of these. The goal is to produce products defect free.

15. Are zero defects possible?

Yes. The only way to get to zero defects is to eliminate the error before it occurs.

16. Name some mistake proofing devices which we use every day but probably don't realize it.

17. What are the three types of defects?

Three types of defects are materials, processing, and design.

18. What is the difference between TQM and TCWQC?

19. What did you learn from this chapter?

## Chapter 4 Questions and Answers

1. What should the format for the daily huddle look like?

The 5- to 10-minute daily huddle, at the beginning of the day, is a great way to start the day, communicate any necessary information, and share performance against business critical metrics. The huddle should be very tightly scripted and not be allowed to turn into a long-winded meeting.

2. Where should the metrics for the +QDIP board come from?

Metric development should be evolutionary and focus on what the business needs and must be measurable when the metric is introduced. The metrics must ultimately be tied to customers, such as customer demand, quality, delivery, and affordability.

3. What are the advantages of a daily meeting?

The meeting is held daily to allow for a review of the metrics from the previous day as the metrics are purposefully broken down to the daily level to make the review meaningful and to allow the team to take corrective actions in their own areas when the previous day's metrics were not achieved. The huddle board should be designed to ensure the leader can quickly communicate the previous day's performance for each metric and should also be visual to show the performance trends for the month.

4. What is a learning minute?

The learning minute is an opportunity to hold a short daily training on a topic that is important to the business. The learning minute is a 1- or 2-minute training session to teach everyone more about the business. Usual topics for these mini-training sessions are finance terms, product applications, safety talks, Lean concepts, or customer information.

5. What is the linkage between the day-by-hour and QDIP board?

6. Why are gemba walks important?

Gemba walks ensure leaders are engaged with the business and employees. Leadership and cross-functional participation are needed for gemba walks to be effective with sales marketing, human resources (HR), and accounting to participate on occasion. Gemba walks should be point focused on data, root cause, and countermeasures.

7. Who should be involved in a QDIP meeting?

Cross-functional representation makes the huddle process more responsive and sustainable.

8. What is the advantage of having the QDIP information prominently displayed versus being in a computer?

Visual means it is on a board where everyone can see it, not in a computer. All employees need to see the information real time to ensure motivation stays high, employee engagement occurs, and corrective actions take place as soon as a metric fails to meet standards.

9. Should we worry about customer's seeing the QDIP board?

No. Customers who tour the facilities should be able to see the QDIP board and should be excited to see customer feedback information posted.

10. Who should run the QDIP meeting?

Manager should run the QDIP meeting.

11. What role does HR, sales, or engineering play in the huddles? Do they have huddle boards in their offices as well?

The huddle board covers a larger portion of the business such as an entire focus factory, department, or sometimes the entire business. Huddle boards are used as a communication tool to engage people and the office, including engineering, sales, and HR to show their performance against targeted metrics to guide behaviors toward improving the business metrics and to help employees think more like a business owner. Support staff, such as engineering, sales, and HR, are in attendance to provide needed support and feedback to ensure the operations run smoothly providing quality products and services to customers that are affordable. The employees from all of the different cells in a focus factory may all attend the same huddle in the morning, but they may each have their own +QDIP board for their individual cells.

12. What did you learn from this chapter?

## Chapter 5 Questions and Answers

1. What is a visual display?

Visual displays communicate important information but do not necessarily control what people or machines do. Visual displays such as signs and bulletin boards do not suggest or enforce any action. They only communicate the name of an area, machine, or some other type of information.

2. What is a visual control?

Visual controls communicate information in a way that helps everyone identify or prevent a problem and build in standards and make defects obvious.

3. What are the three components of a visual management system?

Visual management systems are made up of the following components:

- 5S
- Visual displays
- Visual controls

4. Does visual management apply to office environments?

Yes, visual management applies to office environments. The same principles in a factory environment can be used in the office. The key is to follow the same process, such as 5S, Kanbans (such as for office supplies), and TPM (equipment and facilities).

5. What are the benefits of a visual management system?

Visual management is a system where a device or devices are installed to detect or prevent defects or injury from occurring. The goal of a good visual management system is to make abnormal conditions immediately visible using 5S, visual displays, and visual controls, and taking the premise one step further by incorporating root cause, countermeasures, andon, risk mitigation, TPM, and mistake proofing. A good visual management system allows problems no place to hide and prevents defects from occurring in the first place. The goal of the system is to prevent or mitigate the defect.

6. What are the 5Ss?

- Seiri: Proper arrangement, sort, cleanup, clearing up, or organization.
- Seiton: Arrange, put in order and store, set in order, order, orderliness, organize logical order, or neatness.
- Seiso: Neat, tidy, sweep, shine, cleanliness, cleaning, or pick up.

   - Seiketsu: Cleanliness, standardize, neatness, or maintaining a spotless workplace.
   - Shitsuke: Discipline, sustain, conduct, changing work habits, or training.
7. Which S do you think is the most important?
   Sustain is the most difficult S of all. To sustain, the 5S program has to become part of the documented procedures of the company, monitored and audited.
8. Where do you see 5S being most useful for you?
9. How is 5S implemented in the office environment? Are there unique challenges?
10. What challenges do you see in using 5S?
11. What is management's responsibility with 5S?
    5S has to be led by every executive, manager, group leader, and team leader. Management must provide the training and resources to ensure 5S succeeds. If you walk by a piece of trash and don't pick it up or you see someone not put a tool back and don't say anything, you have just rewarded that person's behavior.
12. Why should management embrace a visual management system?
13. Who sets the standard?
14. How do you sustain 5S, visual controls, and visual management systems?
15. What are tangible benefits of a 5S factory?
    A cleaner workplace is a safer workplace.
    - Contributes to how we feel about and the pride we take in our product, process, our company, and ourselves.
    - Customers love it.
    - Product quality and especially contaminant levels will improve.
    - Cleaning typically reveals problems and areas that need repair.
    - Efficiency will increase.
    - Good program to get everyone in the organization involved.
16. What is a day-by-hour chart? How is it used?
    The day-by-hour chart displays the planned production for each hour, taking into account breaks, meetings or huddles, and exercise times. Each hour, the team lead or one of the operators enters the actual amount of product (or paperwork) produced. If there is a variance for the hour, the team lead or operator enters the variance and the explanation for the variance and whether any containment actions or countermeasures were required. The real value in the chart is twofold. First, it shows the team members how they are doing against the plan that originally comes from the workflow analysis and subsequent standard work. The second is to assess the reason for the variance. If the variance is negative, there should be some type of action taken by the team lead or supervisor to begin to root cause and take countermeasures to correct the variance. If the problem can be corrected right away, that is noted on the chart.
17. What did you learn from this chapter?

## Chapter 6 Questions and Answers

1. What does the acronym TPM stand for?
   TPM stands for total productive maintenance and is a combination of the following:
   - Preventative maintenance.
   - Predictive maintenance.
   - Participative management/employee involvement resulting in a productive maintenance program carried out by all employees.

2. Is TPM a cost reduction program? Please explain your position.
   TPM is not a cost reduction program. TPM helps to reduce equipment operating rates, improve costs, and minimize WIP inventory resulting in increased labor productivity and capacity.
3. Who has responsibility for TPM?
   TPM belongs with the senior leadership team or even better, the Board of Directors. It should be considered a company-wide initiative.
4. What are the factors used when calculating OEE?
   OEE is calculated by multiplying the three OEE factors: Availability, Performance, and Quality.
5. What are the goals of a TPM program?
   - Eliminate unplanned machine downtime
   - Increase machine capacity
   - Incur fewer defects (scrap or rework)
   - Reduce overall operating costs
   - Allow for minimum inventory
   - Increase operator safety
   - Create a better working environment
   - Improve environment and sustainability
   - Eliminate breakdowns
   - Reduce equipment start-up losses
   - Faster more dependable throughput
   - Improve quality
6. Why have some TPM programs failed?
7. What are some of the costs to consider when considering TPM at your plant?
8. What is the new Lean paradigm for maintenance?
   Maintenance is kept to reduce waste in the operation and improving quality. Maintenance should not be looked at as a cost center but as capacity generators.
9. How does your company handle maintenance issues and what do they do to prevent small issues from becoming large expensive repairs?
10. Should maintenance teams be centralized? What approach supports Lean best and why?
    The goal of centralizing maintenance is to ensure maintenance team members are not idle and to expand cross-training within the maintenance team. Decentralizing involves dedicating a maintenance team member to a product line, family, or value stream. The best model we have seen is to merge these two and have each maintenance team member dedicated to a product line as their first responsibility, and when their task is complete, they are available for the next centralized task in the queue.
11. What did you learn from this chapter?

## Chapter 7 Questions and Answers

1. Can the accounting process really be transitioned to Lean?
   Yes, Lean accounting is real and it starts with waste elimination. Lean accounting eliminates traditional cost accounting standard reports and the concept of earned hours. The cost accounting staff is moved into the line organization to work on process improvements and support the value stream managers with information and analysis.

2. What is hidden waste?

    Hidden waste that hides behind the obvious wastes and is difficult to see. It doesn't show up in financial reports. Examples are management meetings (inefficient) and not developing staff.

3. How do you find hidden waste?

    Finding hidden waste is very difficult. Videotaping (and analysis) is a useful tool that has been successfully deployed to find hidden wastes.

4. What are some problems with cost accounting standards?

    Traditional cost accounting standards, contrary to popular belief, seldom drive improvement. Cost accounting standards can be very misleading, and when utilized as metrics, can drive some crazy and unusual behaviors. There are several problems with these types of standards:

    – Who sets the standards?
    – How are they set?
    – How often are they updated, and who is responsible to update them?
    – What exactly are we trying to measure?
    – When we use only direct labor in a standard, it can be misleading. How much indirect labor is necessary, and is it counted?
    – How and when do you define output?
    – What do we do with the data once we calculate it?
    – Are people really measured on the standards? Do they lose their job if they don't meet them?

5. Is the machine utilization still important in a Lean operation?

    No, machine utilization is not important in a Lean system. When implementing Lean, machine utilization is no longer as important as it was in the days of batching. Depending on the cell configuration, some machines will not have to run all the time or, in mixed models, may not run at all while certain models are produced.

6. What is a pull system?

    A pull system is characterized when the flow of parts, products, and information occurs as a result of the consumption of that item at the immediate downstream operation. A signal is provided to the upstream operation to replace what has been consumed.

7. What happens to fixed overhead standards after Lean implementations?

    Overhead generally increases as the hours per unit decreases (less base absorption).

8. What problems does one find in traditional budgeting processes?

    There are multiple problems in traditional budget processes. As the budgets are developed, often each team adds extra (pads) budget before sending up for review and approval as the team knows the budget is usually cut. This is a very time-consuming and wasteful process. Invoking budgetary reductions without a plan to identify and eliminate wastes and understand hidden costs can impact quality, service, and operator safety.

9. How can finance and the CFO help the Lean transition?

    The finance team needs to embrace Lean, including the need to review accounting processes to align with Lean and not be in conflict. Otherwise, the results will show increased overhead with poor equipment utilization and the Lean process will stall.

10. What are some of the mixed signals provided by standard cost systems?

    The business would be better off by slowing down all operations completed until a cell is "leaned" out by eliminating waste in the operation and therefore reducing cycle time, combining operations, or redesigning the product. However, slowing down an operation is totally at odds with everything we have learned, because the cost system will indicate further erosion in unit costs. A traditional standard cost system encourages faster production in all operations to absorb more overhead and generate healthier month-end numbers. A traditional factory usually has its work centers spread throughout the plant according to functionality (e.g., all like equipment is located together such as drill presses and lathes); it is virtually impossible to "see" the flow until one relocates and right sizes the equipment into a cell that contains all of the necessary equipment to complete the process from start to finish.

# Appendix B - Acronyms

| | |
|---|---|
| **5Ws** | when, where, what, who, why |
| **5W2Hs** | when, where, what, who, why, how, how much |
| **5 whys** | asking why five times in a row in order to get to the root cause |
| **AGV** | automatic guided vehicle |
| **AI** | artificial intelligence |
| **AP** | accounts payable |
| **ASL** | approved supplier list |
| **AT** | actual time |
| **AT&T** | American Telephone and Telegraph |
| **BASICS®** | lean implementation model for converting batch to flow: baseline, analyze (assess), suggest solutions, implement, check, and sustain |
| **BFT** | business fundamental table |
| **BIG** | Business Improvement Group LLC based in Towson, MD |
| **BOM** | bill of material |
| **BPD** | business process development |
| **BRIEF** | Baseline Risk Identification of Ergonomic Factors |
| **BVA** | business value added |
| **C** | Cold |
| **CAD** | computer-aided design |
| **CAP** | change acceleration process |
| **CEO** | chief executive officer |
| **CM** | centimeters |
| **COGS** | cost of goods sold |
| **CQI** | continuous quality improvement |
| **CTP** | cost to produce |
| **CTQ** | critical to quality |
| **CV** | coefficient of variation |
| **CWQC** | company-wide quality control |
| **CYA** | cover your ass |
| **DBH** | day by hour |
| **DFA** | design for assembly |
| **DFM** | design for manufacturing |
| **DFMA®** | Design for Manufacturing and Assembly |
| **DIRFT** | do it right the first time |
| **DL** | direct labor |
| **DMAIC** | design, measure, analyze, improve, control |

| | |
|---|---|
| **DMEDI** | design, measure, explore, develop, implement |
| **DOE** | design of experiments |
| **DPMO** | defects per million opportunities |
| **EBIT** | earnings before interest and taxes |
| **EBITDA** | earnings before interest taxes depreciation, and amortization |
| **ECR** | engineering change request |
| **ED** | emergency department (emergency room) |
| **EDD** | earliest due date |
| **EDI** | electronic data interchange |
| **EHS** | environmental, health, and safety |
| **ERP** | enterprise resource (requirements) planning |
| **ERSC** | eliminate, rearrange, simplify, or combine |
| **EHS** | Environmental Health and Safety |
| **ETDBW** | easy to do business with |
| **EV** | earned value |
| **EVA** | economic value added |
| **FC** | full change |
| **FG** | finished goods |
| **FIFO** | first in, first out, replaced by EDD, earliest due date |
| **FISH** | first in still here |
| **FMEA** | failure modes and effects analysis |
| **FPY** | first pass yield |
| **FT** | feet |
| **FTT** | first time through (thru) |
| **FWA** | full work analysis |
| **GE** | General Electric |
| **GM** | general manager |
| **GMS** | global manufacturing system |
| **GPI** | global process improvement |
| **H** | hot |
| **H** | hour or hours |
| **HBS** | Harvard Business School |
| **HEPA** | high-efficiency particle absorption |
| **HPWT** | high-performance work teams |
| **HR** | human resources |
| **HS&E** | health safety and environmental |
| **ICE** | SMED formula, identify, convert, eliminate |
| **i.e.** | that is |
| **IL** | indirect labor |
| **IN** | inches |
| **INFO** | information |
| **INSP** | inspection |
| **ISO** | International Organization for Standardization |
| **IS** | information systems |
| **IT** | information technology (computing/networking) |
| **IT** | idle time |
| **ITCS** | intelligent tracking control system |

| | |
|---|---|
| **JB** | job breakdown |
| **JEI** | job easiness index |
| **JI** | job instruction |
| **JIC** | just in case |
| **JIT** | just in time |
| **JM** | job methodology |
| **JUSE** | Japanese Union of Scientists and Engineers |
| **KPI** | key process indicators |
| **KPO** | Kaizen Promotion Office |
| **KSA** | knowledge, skill, or ability |
| **LB** | pound or pounds |
| **LBDS** | lean business delivery system |
| **LCL** | lower control limit |
| **LEI** | Lean Enterprise Institute |
| **LIFO** | last in, first out |
| **LMAO** | laughed my butt off |
| **LMP** | lean maturity path |
| **LP** | lean practitioner |
| **LP1** | lean practitioner level 1 |
| **LP 2–5** | lean practitioner level 2 through level 5 |
| **LRB** | lean review board |
| **Max** | maximum |
| **MBD** | month by day |
| **MBTI** | Myers-Briggs Type Inventory—personality styles |
| **MH** | man hours |
| **Min** | minute or minutes |
| **Min** | minimum |
| **MM** | materials manager |
| **MPS** | master production schedule |
| **MRB** | material review board |
| **MSA** | measurement systems analysis |
| **MSD** | musculoskeletal disorder |
| **MSE** | manufacturing support equipment |
| **MSE** | measurement system evaluation |
| **MT** | meter |
| **MTD** | month to date |
| **MVA** | market value added |
| **NIH** | not invented here |
| **NOPAT** | net operating profit after taxes |
| **NOW** | not our way |
| **NRE** | Nonrecurring engineering |
| **NTED** | no touch exchange of dies |
| **NVA** | non-value added |
| **NVN** | non-value added but necessary |
| **OCED** | one cycle exchange of die |
| **OE** | order entry |
| **OEE** | overall equipment effectiveness |

| | |
|---|---|
| **OEE** | overall engineering effectiveness scale |
| **OPBSF** | one-piece balanced synchronized flow |
| **OPER** | operator |
| **OPF** | one-piece flow |
| **OPI** | office of process improvement |
| **OPS** | operations |
| **OR** | operating room |
| **ORG** | organization |
| **OSED** | one-shot exchange of dies |
| **OTD** | on-time delivery |
| **OTED** | one-touch exchange of dies |
| **OTP** | on-time performance |
| **PC** | production control |
| **PCDCA** | plan–control–do–check–act |
| **PDCA** | plan–do–check–act |
| **PDSA** | plan–do–study–act |
| **PEST** | political, economic, social, and technological |
| **PFA** | process flow analysis (following the product) |
| **PFEP** | plan for every part |
| **PI** | process improvement |
| **PI** | performance improvement |
| **PIT** | process improvement team |
| **P/N** | part number |
| **PM** | preventative maintenance |
| **PO** | purchase order |
| **POU** | point of use |
| **POUB** | point of use billing |
| **PPCS** | part production capacity sheet |
| **PPF** | product process flow, synonymous with PFA |
| **PPM** | parts per million |
| **PPV** | purchase price variance |
| **Prep** | preparation |
| **PSI** | pounds per square inch |
| **PWI** | perceived weirdness indicator scale (1–10) developed by Charlie Protzman |
| **QC** | quality control |
| **QCD** | quality, cost, and deliver |
| **+QDIP** | safety, quality, delivery, inventory, productivity |
| **QTY** | quantity |
| **RC** | running change |
| **RCCA** | root cause corrective action |
| **RCCM** | root cause counter measure |
| **Rchange** | resistance to change |
| **REQ** | requisition depending on the context |
| **Reqmt** | requirements |
| **RF** | radio frequency |
| **RFQ** | request for quote |
| **RFID** | radio-frequency identification |

| | |
|---|---|
| **RM** | raw materials |
| **ROA** | return on assets |
| **ROI** | return on investment |
| **RONA** | return on net assets |
| **RR** | railroad |
| **RTC** | resistance to change |
| **RW** | required work |
| **S** | second or seconds |
| **SASL** | signal acquisition source locator |
| **SIPOC** | suppliers–inputs–process–outputs–customer |
| **SJS** | standard job sheet |
| **SMART** | specific, measurable, attainable (achievable), realistic (relevant), timely |
| **SMED** | single-minute exchange of dies |
| **SMG** | strategic materials group |
| **SOP** | standard operating procedure |
| **SORS** | standard operation routine sheet, same as SWCS |
| **SPACER** | safety, purpose, agenda, code of conduct, expectations, roles |
| **SPC** | statistical process control |
| **SPEC** | specification |
| **SQC** | statistical quality control |
| **ST** | storage time |
| **STRAP** | strategic plan |
| **SWCS** | standard work combination sheet, same as SORS |
| **SWIP** | standard work in process |
| **SWOT** | strengths, weaknesses, opportunities, threats |
| **TBP** | Toyota Business Practice |
| **TCWQC** | total company-wide quality control |
| **TH** | throughput time |
| **TIPS** | transport, inspect, process, store |
| **TL** | team leader |
| **TLA** | three letter acronym |
| **TLT** | total labor time |
| **TM** | team member |
| **TOC** | theory of constraints |
| **TPM** | total productive maintenance |
| **TPS** | Toyota production system |
| **TQ** | total quality |
| **TQM** | total quality management |
| **TT** | takt time |
| **UAI** | use as is |
| **UCL** | upper control limit |
| **UHF** | ultrahigh frequency |
| **USW** | United Steelworkers |
| **VA** | value added |
| **VMI** | vendor-managed inventory |
| **VOC** | voice of the customer |
| **VOP** | Value of the Person |

| | |
|---|---|
| **VS** | value stream |
| **VSL** | value stream leader |
| **VSM** | value stream map |
| **W** | warm |
| **WACC** | weighted average cost of capital |
| **WADITW** | we've always done it that way |
| **WE** | Western Electric |
| **WFA** | Workflow analysis, following the operator |
| **WIIFM** | what's in it for me |
| **WIP** | work in process |
| **WMSD** | work-related musculoskeletal disorder |
| **WOW** | ways of working |
| **YTD** | year to date |

# Appendix C - Glossary

**5 whys:** Method of evaluating a problem or question by asking *why* five times. The purpose is to get to the root cause of the problem and not to address the symptoms. By asking why and answering each time, the root cause becomes more evident.

**5 Ws:** Asking why something happened—when, where, what, why, or who did the task.

**5W2H:** Same as the five Ws but adding how and how much.

**5Ss:** Method of creating a self-sustaining culture that perpetuates a neat, clean, and efficient workplace:

- **Shine:** Keep things clean. Floors swept, machines and furniture clean, all areas neat and tidy.
- **Sort:** Clearly distinguish between what is needed and kept and what is unneeded and thrown out.
- **Standardize:** Maintain and improve the first three *Ss* in addition to personal orderliness and neatness. Minimums and maximums can be added here.
- **Store:** Organize the way that necessary things are kept, making it easier for anyone to find, use, and return them to their proper location.
- **Sustain:** Achieve the discipline or habit of properly maintaining the correct procedures.

**Absorption costing:** Inventory valuation technique where variable costs and a portion of fixed costs are assigned to a unit of production (or sometimes labor or square footage). The fixed costs are usually allocated based on labor hours, machine hours, or material costs.

**Activity-based costing:** Developed in the late 1980s by Robert Kaplan and Robin Cooper of Harvard Business School. Activity-based costing is primarily concerned with the cost of indirect activities within a company and their relationships to the manufacture of specific products. The basic technique of activity-based costing is to analyze the indirect costs within an organization and to discover the activities that cause those costs.

**Affinity diagram:** One of the seven management tools to assist general planning. It organizes disparate language information by placing it on cards and grouping the cards which go together in a creative way. Header cards are used to summarize each group of cards. It organizes information and data.

**Allocation:** A material requirement planning (MRP) term where a work order has been released to the stockroom; however, the parts have not been picked for production. The system allocates (assigns) those parts to the work order; thus, they are no longer available for new work orders.

**Andon:** Andon means management by sight—visual management. Japanese translation means light. A flashing light or display in an area to communicate a given condition. An andon can be an electronic board or signal light. A visual indicator can be accompanied by a unique sound as well.

**Assembly:** A group of parts, raw material, subassemblies, or a combination of both, put together by labor to construct a finished product. An assembly could be an end item (finished good) or a higher level assembly determined by the levels in the bill of material.

**Backflush:** MRP term used to deduct all component parts from an assembly or subassembly by exploding the bill of material by the number of items produced. Backflushing can occur when the work order is generated or when the unit is shipped.

**Backlog:** All customer orders received but not yet shipped.

**Balance on hand (BOH):** The inventory levels between component parts.

**Balancing operations:** This is the equal distribution of labor time among the number of workers on the line. If there are four workers and 4 minutes of labor time in one unit then each worker should have 1 minute of work.

**Batch manufacturing:** A production strategy commonly employed in job shops and other instances where there is discrete manufacturing of a nonrepetitive nature. In batch manufacturing, order lots are maintained throughout the production process to minimize changeovers and achieve economies of scale. In batch manufacturing environments, resources are usually departmentalized by specialty and very seldom dedicated to any particular product family.

**Benchmarking:** Method of establishing internal expectations for excellence based upon direct comparison to the very best at what they do. Benchmarking is not necessarily a comparison with a direct competitor.

**Bill of material:** A list of all components and manufactured parts that comprise a finished product. The list may have different levels denoting various subassemblies required to build the final product.

**Bin:** A storage container used to hold parts. Bins range in various sizes from small to very large containers and can be made of plastic, wood, metal, cardboard, etc.

**Bin location file:** An electronic listing of storage locations for each bin. Generally, locations are designated to the work area, rack, and shelf, and location on the shelf, that is, 1—A—2 defines assembly area 1, rack A, and shelf 2 position on the shelf.

**Blanket order:** An order generally issued for a year or longer for a particular part number or group of specific part numbers. The blanket order defines the price, terms, and conditions for the supplier, thus allowing an authorized representative of the purchasing team to issue a release against the blanket order to the supplier.

**Blanket order release:** An authorization to ship from the customer to the supplier a specified quantity from the blanket order.

**Block diagram:** A diagram where the processes are represented in order of assembly by blocks denoting the process name, cycle time, utilities required, standard work in process (SWIP), etc.

**Bottleneck:** Generally referred to as the slowest person or machine. However, only machines can be true bottlenecks as we can always add labor. A true bottleneck runs 24 hours a day and still cannot keep up with customer demand.

**Breadman:** Centralized floor stock systems where the suppliers normally own and manage the material until it is used.

**Budget:** A plan that represents an estimate of future costs against the expected revenue or allocated funds to spend.

**Buffer:** Any material in storage waiting further processing.

**Buffer stock:** Inventory kept to cover yield losses due to poor quality.

**Capacity:** The total available possible output of a system within current constraints. The capability of a worker or machine within a specified time period.

**Carrying costs:** The cost to carry inventory, which is usually determined by the cost of capital and cost of maintaining the space (warehouse) and utilities, taxes, insurance, etc.

**Catch ball:** Communications back, forth, up, down, and horizontally across the organization, which must travel from person to person several times to be clearly understood and reach agreement (consensus). This process is referred to as *catch ball*.

**Cause and effect diagram:** A problem-solving statistical tool that indicates causes and effects and how they interrelate.

**CEDAC:** Anachronism for cause and effect diagram with the addition of cards. Problem-solving technique developed by Ryuji Fukuda. A method for defining the effect of a problem and a target effect statement. Through the development of a CEDAC diagram, facts and improvements will be identified that allow action.

**Cellular layout:** Generally denotes a family of product produced in a layout, which has the machines and workstations in order of assembly. Does not necessarily imply the parts that are produced in one-piece flow.

**Chaku-Chaku:** Japanese term for *load-load*. Refers to a production line that has been raised to a level of efficiency that requires simply the loading of parts by the operator without any effort required for unloading or transporting material.

**Checkpoint:** Control item with a means that requires immediate judgment and handling. It must be checked on a daily basis.

**CNC:** Acronym for computerized machining—stands for computer numerical control.

**Consigned inventory:** Normally finished goods stored at a customer site but still owned by the supplier.

**Constraint:** Anything that prevents a process from achieving a higher level of output or performance. Constraints can be physical like material or machines or transactional like policies or procedures.

**Continuous flow production:** Production in which products flow continuously without interruption.

**Continuous improvement (kaizen):** A philosophy by which individuals within an organization seek ways to always do things better, usually based on an understanding and control of variation. A pledge to, every day, do or make something better than it was before.

**Contribution margin:** Equal to sales revenue less variable costs leaving how much remains to be put toward fixed costs.

**Control chart:** A problem-solving statistical tool that indicates whether the system is in, or out, of control and whether the problem is a result of special causes or common system problems.

**Control item:** A control item is an item selected as a subject of control for maintenance of a desired condition. It is a yardstick that measures or judges the setting of a target level, the content of the work, the process, and the result of each stage of breakthrough and improvement in control during management activity.

**Control point:** Control item with a target. A control point is used to analyze data and take action accordingly.

**Cost cutting:** Eliminating costs in the traditional way, that is, reducing expenses, laying people off, requiring people to supply their own pens, making salary workers work much more overtime, etc.

**Cost of capital:** The cost of maintaining a dollar of capital invested for a certain period. Normally over a year.

**Cost reduction:** Reducing costs by eliminating the waste in processes.

**Correlation:** A statistical relationship between two sets of data such that when one brings about some change in the other it is explained and is statistically significant.

**Cp process capability:** Process capability is the measured, inherent reproducibility of the product turned out by a process. The most widely adopted formula for process capability (Cp) is

$$\text{Process capability} \left(Cp\right) = 6\sigma = \text{total tolerance} \div 6$$

where $\sigma$ is the standard deviation of the process under a state of statistical control. The most commonly used measure for process capability within ASA is a process capability index (Cpk), which is

$$Cpk = \text{lesser of } Cpu \text{ or } Cpl$$

where

$$Cpu = \left(\text{upper specification} - \text{process mean}\right) \div 3$$

and

$$Cpl = \left(\text{process mean} - \text{lower specification}\right) \div 3$$

Interpretation of the index is generally as follows:

Cpk > 1.33          More than adequate
Cpk ≤ 1.33 but > 1.00     Adequate, but must be monitored as it approaches 1.00
Cpk ≤ 1.00 but > 0.67     Not adequate for the job
Cpk ≤ 0.67          Totally inadequate

**CPIM:** APICS—acronym for certified purchasing and inventory manager. Rigorous course material required with five modules of testing to be certified.

**CPM:** Acronym stands for certified purchasing manager—this is a NAPM (national association of purchasing managers) certification for purchasing professionals. Requires passing rigorous testing and experience criteria.

**Cross-functional management:** Cross-functional management is the overseeing of horizontal interdivisional activities. It is used so that all aspects of the organization are well managed and have consistent, integrated quality efforts pertaining to scheduling, delivery, plans, etc.

**Cross-training:** Training an employee in many different jobs within or across cells.

**Customer relations:** A realization of the role the customer plays in the continuation of your business. A conscious decision to listen to and provide products and services for those who make your business an ongoing concern.

**Customer service:** Any specifications required to meet the customer demands, needs, or requests for information and service. Everyone in the company should be a customer service representative.

**Cycle:** Completion of one whole series of processes by a part or person.

**Cycle time:** Available time divided by the factory capacity demand, the time each unit is coming off the end of the assembly line or the time each operator must hit, or the total labor time divided by the number of operators.

**Cumulative:** The progressive total of all the pieces.

**Cumulative time:** Is equivalent to adding up the total times as you progress. For instance, if step 1 is 5 seconds and step 2 is 10 seconds, the cumulative time is 15 seconds.

**Daily control:** The systems by which workers identify simply and clearly understand what they must do to fulfill their job function in a way that will enable the organization to run smoothly. These items are usually concerned with the normal operation of a business. Also a system in which these required actions are monitored by the employees themselves.

**Data:** Any portrayal of alphabetic or numerical information to which some meaning can be ascribed. Data can be found in a series of numbers or in an answer to a question asked of a person.

**Data box:** Term apportioned to a box in a value stream map that underlies a process box and contains elements such as process cycle time, number of persons, change over time, lot size, etc.

**Demand flow:** Material only moves to a work center when that work center is out of work. Subject of the book *Quantum Leap* by the World Wide Flow College of Denver. Layouts are typically a conveyor down the middle of the line with subassembly lines feeding in both sides.

**Deming cycle:** A continuously rotating wheel of plan, do, check, act.

**Demonstrated capacity:** Term to depict capacity arrived at by nonscientific means. Generally, it is arrived at by feel or observing actual output without determining what the process could generate if all the waste was removed.

**Deviation:** The absolute difference between a number and the mean of a data set.

**Direct labor:** Labor attributable specifically to the product.

**Direct material:** Raw material or supplied materials that when combined become part of the final product.

**Distribution:** Term generally refers to a supply chain of intermediaries.

**Distributor:** A company that generally does not manufacture material but is a middle man. They normally hold some finished goods but not always. Sometimes they may make some modifications to the finished goods.

**Dock to stock:** Process where suppliers are certified by the company's supplier quality engineers or purchasing and quality professionals that result in the supplier's products bypassing inspection or sometimes receiving to go directly to the stock room or shop floor where it is used.

**Download:** Transfer of information from a central computer (cloud) to a tablet, PC, phone, or other type of device.

**Downstream operation:** Task that is subsequent to the operation currently being executed or planned.

**Downtime:** Time when a scheduled resource is not operating.

**Earned hours:** Standard hours credited for actual production during the period determined by some agreed upon rate.

**Economic order quantity:** Model used to determine the optimum batch size for product running through an operation or a line. It is equal to the square root of two times the annual demand times average cost of order preparation divided by the annual inventory carrying cost percentage times unit cost.

**Economy of scale:** Larger volumes of products realize lower cost of production due to allocating fixed costs against a larger output size.

**EDI:** Acronym stands for electronic data interchange which is the ability for computer systems between supplier and customer to talk to each other without human involvement. In some cases, this requires programing of an interface between computers so they can talk to each other.

**Effectiveness:** Is the ability to achieve stated goals or objectives, judged in terms of metrics that are based on both output and impact. It is (a) the degree to which an activity or initiative is successful in achieving a specified goal and (b) the degree to which activities of a unit achieve the unit's mission or goal.

**Efficiency:** Production without waste. Efficiency is based on the *energy* one spends to complete the product or service as well as timing. For example, we all know of the *learning curve*. The more one performs a new task, the better they become each time the task is practiced. As one becomes more efficient, they definitely reduce stress and gain accuracy, capability, and consistency of action. A person has achieved efficiency when they are getting more done with the same or better accuracy in a shorter period of time, with less energy and better results.

**Eight dimensions on quality:** Critical dimensions or categories of quality identified by David Garvin of the Harvard Business School that can serve as a framework for strategic analysis. They are performance, features, reliability, conformance, durability, serviceability, esthetics, and perceived quality.

**Elimination of waste:** A philosophy that states that all activities undertaken need to be evaluated to determine if they are necessary, enhancing the value of the goods and services being provided and what the customer wants. Determining if the systems that have been established are serving their users or are the users serving the system.

**Ending inventory:** Inventory present at the end of a period. Sometimes validated by taking a physical inventory.

**EPE:** Acronym stands for every part every—this denotes batch size of lots running through the process.

**Ergonomics:** The study of humans interacting with the environment or workplace.

**ERP:** Acronym for enterprise resource planning system. It is a business management software to integrate all business phases to include marketing/sales, planning, engineering, operations and customer support the third generation of MRP systems usually used to link company plants locally, nationally, or globally. SAP, ORACLE, and BPCS are examples of these types of systems.

**Excess inventory:** More inventory than required to do any task.

**Expedite:** To push, rush, or walk a product (or information, signatures, etc.) through the process or system.

**Expeditor:** One who expedites.

**External setup time:** Time utilized and steps that can be done preparing for changeovers while the machine is still running. Example—prepping for a racing car pit stop like getting tires in place, having fuel ready, etc. Focus of changeovers or setups moving internal elements to external elements.

**Fabrication:** The process of transforming metals into a final product or subassembly usually by machine. Generally, a term to distinguish activities done in a machine shop versus manually assembling components into a final product.

**Facility:** The physical plant or office (transactional areas).

**Failure analysis:** The process of determining the root cause of a failure usually generating a report of some type.

**Family:** A group of products (or information) that shares similar processes.

**FIFO:** First in, first out inventory management system.

**Flex fence:** Purchasing term used in contracts to mitigate demand risk by having the supply chain capable of flexing production plus or minus 10%, 20%, or 30%. This is accomplished by identifying long lead items and developing plans to stock some of those parts at the buyer's expense.

**Flexible workforce:** A workforce totally cross-trained, capable, and allowed to work in all positions.

**Floater:** Cross-trained workers moved around throughout the day to different positions depending on the takt time or cycle time and the staffing requirements for the day.

**Floor stock:** Generally less expensive C-type parts stored centrally on the floor and owned by the company.

**Flow:** Smooth, uninterrupted movement of material or information.

**Flow chart:** A problem-solving tool that illustrates a process. It shows the way things actually go through a process, the way they should go, and the difference.

**Flow production:** Describes how goods, services, or information are processed. It is, at its best, one piece at a time. This can be a part, a document, invoice, or customer order. It rejects the concept of batch, lot, or mass producing. It vertically integrates all operations or functions as operationally or sequentially performed. It also encompasses pull or demand processing. Goods are not pushed through the process but pulled or demanded by succeeding operations from preceding operations. Often referred to as *one-piece-flow*.

**FMEA:** Failure mode and effects analysis. A structured approach to assess the magnitude of potential failures and identify the sources of each potential failure. Each potential failure is studied to identify the most effective corrective action. FMEA is the process of mitigating risk by looking at a process to determine what is likely to go wrong, the probability of it going wrong, the severity if it does go wrong, and the countermeasures to be taken in the event it does go wrong.

**FOB:** Free on board—logistics term used to designate where title passes to the buyer.

**Focused factory:** A plant or department focused on a single or family of products. Where everything can be done within the four walls. Does not necessarily mean cellular or one-piece flow.

**Forecast:** An attempt to look into the future in order to predict demand. Companies use techniques that range from historical statistical techniques to systematic wild ass guesses (SWAGs). The longer the forecast horizon, the less accurate the forecast.

**FTE:** Acronym standing for full-time equivalent. The formula is to take the total number of hours being worked by one or multiple people and divide by 2,080 hours (per year) and come up with the equivalent of one person's worth of labor per year.

**Functional:** Organized by department.

**Functional layout:** Layouts where the same or similar equipment is grouped together. These layouts support batch production.

**GAAP:** Acronym for generally accepted accounting principles.

**Gain sharing:** Method of compensating employees based on the overall productivity of the company. The goal is to give the employee a stake in the company and share based on productivity. Measures and participatory schemes vary by company and philosophy. There are many different methods of gain sharing. Normally differentiated from profit sharing, which is based on formulas relating only to company profits.

**Grievance:** Term refers to complaint (contract violation) filed by an employee (normally union based) against someone who is union or nonunion in the company.

**Hanedashi:** Device or means for automatic removal of a workpiece from one operation or process, which provides proper state and orientation for the next operation or process. In manufacturing, a means for automatic unloading and orientation for the next operation or process. In manufacturing, a means for automatic unloading and orientation for the next operation, generally a very simple device. Crucial for a *Chaku-Chaku* line.

**Heijunka:** Japanese term for level loading production. Necessary to support Kanban-based systems.

**Histogram:** A chart that takes measurement data and displays its distribution, generally in a bar graph format. For example, a histogram can be used to reveal the amount of variation that any process has within it based upon the data available.

**Hoshin:** Type of corporate planning, strategy, and execution in a setting where everyone participates in coming up with goals through a process called catchball and everyone down to the shop floor knows what they are doing is directly supporting the top three to five company goals.

**Housekeeping:** Keeping an orderly and clean environment.

**Idle time:** When a person is standing around with nothing to do, visible by arms crossed. Also known as pure waste.

**Indirect costs:** Traditional accounting costs that are not directly related or accounted to the product. Also known as overhead costs.

**Indirect labor:** Traditional accounting of labor required to support production without directly working on the product.

**Indirect materials:** Traditional accounting of materials used to support production but not directly used on the product.

**Information:** Data presented to an individual or machine.

**Information systems:** Term used to designate manual or computer-based systems, which convey information throughout the department or organization as a whole. Term used in value stream mapping for boxes located at the top of the map with lines to the process (information) boxes with which they interact.

**Input:** Work or information fed to the beginning of a system or process.

**Inspection:** The act of multiple (two or more) checks on material or information to see if it is correct. Can also refer to a department of humans that checks incoming materials (receiving inspection), WIP (in-process inspection), or final inspection before the product leaves the plant.

**Internal setup time:** Term used to designate time when machine or process is down (not running). Example is time when the racing car is in the pit stop having tires replaced and fuel added, etc.

**Interrelationship diagram:** A tool that assists in general planning. This tool takes a central idea, issue, or problem and maps out the logical or sequential links among related items.

It is a creative process that shows every idea can be logically linked with more than one idea at a time. It allows for *multidirectional* rather than *linear* thinking to be used.

**Inventory:** Purchased materials used to assemble any level of the product or to support production. Inventory can be in various stages from raw materials to finished goods.

**Inventory turnover or turns:** The number of times inventory cycles or turns over during the year. Generally calculated by dividing average cost of sales divided by the average inventory (normally three months). This can be a historical or forward-looking methodology. Can also be calculated by dividing days of supply into the number of working or calendar days.

**Ishikawa diagram:** Referred to as a fishbone used to graphically display cause and effect and to get to the root cause.

**Item number:** Normally a part number or stock number for a part.

**Jidoka:** Automation with a human touch or mind, autonomation. Automatic machinery that will operate itself but always incorporates the following devices: a mechanism to detect abnormalities or defects and a mechanism to stop the machine or line when defects or abnormalities occur.

**Job costing:** Where costs are collected and allocated to a certain job or charge number. Can be based on actual or standard costs.

**Job description:** List of roles and responsibilities for a particular job.

**Job rotation:** Schedule of movement from machine to machine or process to process. Used to support and encourage cross-training.

**Job shop:** Term used for factories that have high mix and low volume typically nonrepeatable or customized products.

**Just-in-time manufacturing:** A strategy that exposes the waste in an operation, makes continuous improvement a reality, and provides the opportunity to promote total employee involvement. Concentrates on making what is needed, when it is needed, no sooner, no later.

**Kaizen (Kai = change; zen = good):** The process improvement that involves a series of continual improvements over time. These improvements may take the form of a process innovation (event) or small incremental improvements.

**Kanban:** Japanese for a sign board. Designates a pull production means of communicating need for product or service. Originally developed as a means to communicate between operations in different locations. It was intended to communicate a change in demand or supply. In application, it is generally used to trigger the movement of material to or through a process.

**Kit:** Collection of components used to support a sub- or final assembly of a product.

**Kitting:** Process of collecting the components used to support a sub- or final assembly of a product.

**Knowledge worker:** A worker, who acquires information from every task, analyzes and validates the information, and stores it for future use.

**Labor cost:** Cost of labor, can be direct or indirect. In Lean, we look at total labor cost versus indirect or direct associated with traditional cost accounting systems.

**Layout:** Physical arrangement of machines and materials or offices.

**LCL:** Lower control limit, used on control charts.

**Lead time:** The time to manufacture and deliver a product or service. This term is used in many (often contradictory) contexts. To avoid confusion, lead time is defined as the average total lapse time for execution of the product delivery process from order receipt to delivery to the customer under normal operating conditions. In industries that operate in a build-to-order environment, lead times flex based on the influences of seasonal demand loads. In environments where production is scheduled in repeating, fixed-time segments or cycles, the lead time is usually determined by the length of the production cycle (i.e., days, weeks, months, etc.).

**Lead time or throughput time:** Time it takes to get through the entire process or time quoted to customers to receive their orders (from order to cash).

**Lean production:** The activity of creating processes that are highly responsive and flexible to customer demand requirements. Successful Lean production is evident when processes are capable of consistently delivering the highest quality (defect-free) products and services, at the right location and at the right time, in response to customer demand and doing this in the most cost-effective manner possible.

**Learning curve:** A planning technique used to predict improvement based on experience. Uses log charts to trend the data.

**Level load:** Process of leveling or equally distributing demand or products across a cell or plant. Also known as heijunka.

**LIFO:** Last in, first out inventory management.

**Limit switch:** Various electronic devices used to trigger an action when a particular limit is reached. Used to control machines or count parts, used to turn on or off machines, used often for poka yoke, etc.

**Little's Law:** Throughput time divided by cycle time = amount of inventory in the system.

**Logistics:** The art and science of shipping materials, distribution, warehousing, and supply chain management.

**Lot:** Refers to a group of parts or information generally batched together through the process.

**Lot size:** Number of parts in a batch to be produced.

**LTA:** Acronym for long-term agreement. An agreement negotiated with a supplier for a longer term and more complex than a simple blanket (pricing) agreement, normally three to five years with other conditions centering on the supplier's improvement, quality and delivery certification, and price reduction goals.

**Machine hours:** Total hours a machine is running. Can be value-added or non-value-added time normally used for capacity planning. May or may not include setup time or unplanned downtime.

**Machine utilization:** The amount of time a machine is available versus the amount of time the machine is being used. Includes setup and run time compared to available time. It used to be the *be all and end all* for traditional cost accounting measures. With Lean, it is not as important unless it is a true bottleneck machine.

**Make or buy:** Study of costs of purchasing a part versus purchasing the raw materials and making it in house.

**Make to order:** A product that is not started until after the customer orders it. In some cases, a Kanban or inventory of parts produced to a certain level may then be modified to fit the customer requirements.

**Manufacturing resources planning (MRP II):** A second-generation MRP system that provides additional control linkages such as automatic purchase order generation, capacity planning, and accounts payable transactions.

**Master schedule:** Schedule with customer orders loaded by due date or promised date.

**Master scheduler:** Person who enters sales orders into the master schedule.

**Material requirements planning (MRP):** A computerized information system that calculates material requirements based on a master production schedule. This system may be used only for material procurement or to also execute the material plan through shop floor control.

**MBO:** Management by objectives—a system where goals are handed down from manager to employee where the employee participates in the process.

**Means (measure):** A way to accomplish a target.

**Min max:** Refers to a type of inventory system where once the minimum level is reached or a reorder point is reached, a quantity is reordered, which brings the quantity back up to the maximum level. Some computer MRP systems (Oracle) have this as an option to manage inventory.

**Milk run:** Term used to identify the path water spider uses to replenish materials for a line.

**Mistake proofing:** Also known as poka yoke or foolproofing. A system starting with successive checks by humans to inspection devices built into or added to machines to detect and or prevent defects.

**Mixed model production:** The ability to produce various models with different levels of customization one by one down the production line.

**Monthly audit:** The self-evaluation of performance against targets. An examination of things that helped or hindered performance in meeting the targets and the corrective actions that will be taken.

**MPS:** Master production schedule.

**MRO:** Term used to designate maintenance repair and operating supplies.

**MRP:** Material requirements planning; a computerized system developed by Olie Wright using lead time offsets, bill of material, and various planning parameters used to predict when to release requisitions or work orders in order to schedule the production floor.

**MRPII:** Material resource planning; a more advanced MRP system, which ties various systems together within a single company, that is, manufacturing and finance.

**MTM:** Methods time measurement; system that has studied and determined times for various operations or movements by operators. Generally used with motion study.

**Muda:** Japanese term for waste.

**Multiskilled or process workers:** Description for individuals at any level of the organization who are diverse in skill and training. Capable of performing a number of different tasks providing the organization with additional flexibility.

**Mura:** Japanese term for uneven.

**Muri:** Japanese term for overburden.

**Nemawashi:** Refers to the process of gaining consensus and support prior to implementing a strategy.

**Net sales:** Total sales less returns and allowances.

**Noise:** Randomness within a process.

**Nominal group technique:** Process of soliciting information from everyone in the group.

**Non-value added:** Designation for a step that does not meet one of the three value-added criteria.

**Non-value added but necessary (sometimes called business value added):** Any step that is necessary but the customer is not willing to pay for it but it is done right the first time.

**Normal distribution:** Statistical term where most data falls close to the mean ($\pm 1$ sigma), less fall away from the mean ($\pm 2$ sigma), and even less fall even further away ($\pm 3$ sigma), where the distribution when graphed looks like a bell-shaped curve.

**NTED:** No-touch exchange of dies.

**Objective:** What you are trying to achieve with a given plan. The desired end result. The reason for employing a strategy and developing targets.

**Obsolete:** Loss of product value due to engineering, product life decisions, or technological changes.

**Offset:** Time entered into MRP systems to designate how long it takes to get through a part of the system, that is, purchasing time entered as two days. MRP uses this information to develop a timeline to predict when to release the order or purchase requirement. When added up, it equals the total lead time of the product in the system.

**OJT:** Acronym for on-the-job training.

**One-year plan:** A statement of objective of an organizational event for a year.

**Operating system:** Refers to the type of system computer is using, that is, DOS, windows, etc.

**Operation:** A series of tasks grouped together such that the sum of the individual task times is equal to the takt time (cycle time to meet product demand requirements). It is important to distinguish between operations and activities. Operations are used to balance work content in a flow manufacturing process to achieve a particular daily output rate equal to customer demand. An operation defines the amount of work content performed by each operator to achieve a balanced flow and linear output rate.

**Opportunity cost:** Return on capital, which could have been achieved had it been used for something else more productive.

**Order policy:** Term used in MRP to decide lot sizing requirements.

**Organization structure:** The fashion in which resources are assigned to tasks. Includes cross-functional management and vertical work teams. Also includes the development of multiskilled workers through the assignment of technical and administrative personnel to nontraditional roles.

**Organizational development:** Process that looks at improving the interactions within and between departments across the overall organization. Generally led by a consultant or company change agent.

**Organizational tools:** These provide a team approach in which people get together to work on problems and also get better at what they are doing. Organizational tools include work groups and quality circles.

**OTED:** One-touch exchange of dies. Uses a human touch to changeover one or more machines at the same time.

**Overhead:** Costs not directly tied to the product. Normally refers to all personnel who support the production process whether it is physical or transactional.

**Overtime:** Work beyond the traditional 40 hours usually results in a premium paid per hour.

**Pareto chart:** A vertical bar graph showing the bars in order to size from left to right. Helps focus on the vital few problems rather than the trivial many. An extension of the Pareto principle that suggests the significant items in a given group normally constitute a relatively small portion of the items in the total group. Conversely, a majority of the items in the total will, even in aggregate, be relatively minor in significance (i.e., the 80/20 rule).

**Participative management:** Employees collaborate with managers to work on improvements to the process. Basis for QC circles.

**Pay for performance:** Pay is tied to overall output by a team.

**Perpetual inventory system:** System designed to always have the correct amount of inventory in the system.

**PFA:** Process flow analysis, looks at the flow of just the product through the process using TIPS.

**Phantom:** A bill of material (BOM) or non-production work order used to determine if there are any parts shortages. How to create the phantom varies depending on the type of MRP or

ERP system. In general, a work order is created and then backed out of the system prior to MRP running again.

**Physical layout:** A means of impacting workflow and productivity through the physical placement of machinery or furniture. Production machinery should be grouped in a cellular arrangement based upon product requirements, not process type. In addition to this, in most instances, there is an advantage in having the workflow in counterclockwise fashion. Similarly, in an office environment, furniture should be arranged such that there is an efficient flow of information or services rather than strictly defined departments.

**PDCA cycle:** Plan-Do-Check-Act. The PDCA system, sometimes referred to as the Deming cycle, is the most important item for control in policy deployment. In this cycle, you make a plan that is based on policy (plan); you take action accordingly (do); you check the result (check); and if the plan is not fulfilled, you analyze the cause and take further action by going back to the plan (action).

**Piece rate:** Form of worker compensation based on individual output targets that vary by employee and process.

**Pilot:** Trying something out for one or several pieces in a controlled environment to test a hypothesis.

**Plan:** The means to achieve a target.

**Planned downtime:** Downtime that is scheduled for a machine or line.

**Planner/buyer:** Combines planning and buyer jobs.

**Planner/buyer/scheduler:** Combines planning, buying, and scheduling jobs.

**Poka yoke:** Japanese expression meaning *common or simple, mistake proof.* A method of designing processes, either production or administrative, which will by their nature prevent errors. This may involve designing fixtures that will not accept a defective part or something as simple as having a credit memo be a different color than a debit memo. It requires that thought be put into the design of any system to anticipate *what* can go wrong and build in measures to prevent them.

**Policy:** The company objectives are to be achieved through the cooperation of all levels of managers and employees. A policy consists of targets, plans, and target values.

**Policy deployment:** Hoshin Kanri—policy deployment orchestrates continuous improvement in a way that fosters individual initiative and alignment. It is a process of implementing the policies of an organization directly through line managers and indirectly through cross-functional organization. It is a means of internalizing company policies throughout the organization, from highest to lowest level. Top managers will articulate its annual goals that are then deployed down through lower levels of management. The abstract goals of top management become more concrete and specific as they are deployed down through the organization. Policy deployment is process oriented. It is concerned with developing a process by which results become predictable. If the goal is not realized, it is necessary to review and see if the implementation was faulty. It is most important to determine what went wrong in the process that prevented the goal from being realized. The Japanese name for policy deployment is Hoshin Kanri. In Japanese, Hoshin means *shining metal, compass,* or *pointing in the direction.* Kanri means *control.* Hoshin Kanri is a method devised to capture and concretize strategic goals as well as flashes of insight about the future and to develop the means to bring these into reality. It is one of the major systems that make world-class quality management possible. It helps control the direction of the company by orchestrating change within a company. The system includes tools for continuous improvement, breakthroughs, and implementation. The key to Hoshin planning is it brings the total organization into the strategic planning process, both top down and bottom up. It ensures the direction, goals, and objectives of the company are rationally developed, well defined, clearly communicated, monitored, and adapted based on system feedback. It provides focus for the organization.

**POU:** Point of use, designates location where product or tooling or information is used.

**Preventative maintenance:** Term given to duties carried out on machines in order to prevent a breakdown or unplanned stoppage.

**Prioritization matrices:** This tool prioritizes tasks, issues, product/service characteristics, etc., based on known weighted criteria using a combination of tree and matrix diagram techniques. Above all, they are tools for decision-making.

**Problem-solving tools:** These tools find the root cause of problems. They are tools for thinking about problems, managing by fact, and documenting hunches. The tools include check sheet, line chart, Pareto chart, flow chart, histogram, control chart, and scatter diagram. In Japan, these are referred to as the seven QC tools.

**Process:** A series of activities that collectively accomplish a distinct objective. Processes are cross-functional and cut across departmental responsibility boundaries. Processes can be value added or non-value added.

**Process capability:** See CPK.

**Process control chart:** Chart that represents tracking the sequence of data points over a number of or 100% samplings. It serves as a basis to define common cause versus special cause variation and to predict when a part or machine is likely to fail.

**Process decision program chart:** The process decision program chart (PDPC) is a method that maps out conceivable events and contingencies that can occur in any implementation plan. It, in time, identifies possible countermeasures in response to these problems. This tool is used to plan each possible chain of events that need to occur when the problem or goal is an unfamiliar one.

**Process hierarchy:** A hierarchical decomposition from core business processes to the task level. The number of levels in a hierarchy is determined by the breadth and size of the organization. A large enterprise process hierarchy may include core business processes, processes, subprocesses, process segments, activities, and tasks.

**Process management:** This involves focusing on the process rather than the results. A variety of tools may be used for process management, including the seven QC tools.

**Process segment:** A series of activities that define a subset of a process.

**Product delivery process:** The stream of activities required to produce a product or service. This activity stream encompasses both planning and execution activities to include demand planning, order management, materials procurement, production, and distribution.

**Production control:** Employee that tracks status of daily production; normally used in batch environments but sometimes in Lean environments.

**Production schedule:** Orders lined up in order of priority based on due date, promised date, or some other planning parameters.

**Productivity:** Productivity is the *amount* of products produced in a certain amount of time with a certain amount of labor. The products could be physical products or transactional such as processing an invoice or Internet blogs. Productive means getting things done, outcomes reached, or goals achieved and are measured as output per unit of input (i.e., labor, equipment, and capital).

**Prototype:** First piece on which new process is tried.

**Pull production:** In a pull process, materials are staged at the point of consumption. As these materials are consumed, signals are sent back to previous steps in the production process to pull forward sufficient materials to replenish only those materials that have been consumed.

**Push production:** In a push process, production is initiated by the issuance of production orders that are offset in time from the actual demand to allow time for production and delivery. The idea is to maintain zero inventory and have materials complete each step of the production process just as they are needed at subsequent (downstream) activities.

**+QDIP:** Acronym stands for safety, quality, delivery, inventory, and production. Ideally, parameters are set by the employees on the shop floor or in the workshop.

**Quality:** Refers to the ability of the final product to meet both the customers required specification and unspecified specifications.

**Quality circles:** Quality circles are an organizational tool that provides a team approach in which people get together to work on problems and to improve productivity. Their primary objective is to foster teamwork and encourage employee by involvement employing the problem-solving approach.

**Quality function deployment:** A product development system that identifies the wants of a customer and gets that information to all the right people so the organization can effectively exceed competition in meeting the customer's most important wants. It translates customer wants into appropriate technical requirements for each stage of product development and production.

**Quality management:** The systems, organizations, and tools that make it possible to plan, manufacture, and deliver a quality product or service. This does not imply inspection or even traditional quality control. Rather, it involves the entire process involved in bringing goods and services to the customer.

**Queuing theory:** Applies to manufacturing orders, people, or information that is waiting in line for the next process. Based on Little's law.

**Queue time:** Amount of time an order, people, or information is waiting for the next process.

**Quick changeover:** Method of increasing the amount of productive time available for a piece of machinery by minimizing the time needed to change from one model to another. This greatly increases the flexibility of the operation and allows it to respond more quickly to changes in demand. It also has the benefit of allowing an organization to greatly reduce the amount of inventory that it must carry because of improved response time.

**Rate-based order management:** This order management system employs a finite capacity loading scheme to promise orders based upon the agreed demand bound limits. These minimum and maximum demand bounds reflect potential response capacity limits for production and materials procurement.

**Rate-based planning:** A procedure that establishes a controlled level of flexibility in the product delivery process in order to be robust to anticipated variations in demand. This flexibility is achieved by establishing minimum and maximum bounds around future demand forecasts. The idea is that both the production facility and the material supply channels will echelon sufficient capacity to accommodate demand swings that do not exceed the established demand bounds. As future demand forecasts move closer to the production window, updated demand bounds are periodically broadcasted to the material suppliers. At the point of order receipt and delivery promising (within sales or customer service), demand bounding limits are enforced to insure that the rate-based production plan remains feasible.

**Regression analysis:** Statistical technique that determines or estimates the amount of correlation explained between two or more variable sets of data.

**ROI:** Return on investment, generally compares investment versus the return to determine the payback that is often stated in years and expressed as a percentage of earnings.

**RONA:** Return on net assets.

**Root cause:** The ultimate reason for an event or condition.

**Run chart:** A statistical problem-solving tool that shows whether key indicators are going up or down and if the indicators are good or bad.

**Safety:** Ensuring that the work environment is free of hazards and obstacles of which could cause harm.

**Scanlon plan:** A system of group incentives that measures the plant-wide results of all efforts using the ratio of labor costs to sales value added by production. If there is an increase in production sales value with no change in pricing, mix, or labor costs, productivity has increased and unit costs have decreased.

**Scatter diagram:** One of the seven QC tools. The scatter diagram shows the relationship between two variables.

**Scheduled (planned) downtime:** Planned shutdown of equipment to perform maintenance or other tasks or lack of customer demand.

**Self-diagnosis:** As a basis for continuous improvement, each manager uses problem-solving activity to see why he or she is succeeding or failing to meet targets. This diagnosis should focus on identifying personal and organizational obstacles to the planned performance and on the development of alternate approaches based on this new information.

**Self-directed work team:** Normally, a small group of employees that can plan, organize, and manage their daily responsibilities with no direct supervision. They can normally hire, fire, or demote team members.

**Setup:** The changing over of a machine or also the loading and unloading of parts on a machine.

**Setup time:** The amount of time it takes to changeover a machine from the last good part to and including the first good part.

**Setup parts:** Preparation, mounting and removing, calibration, trial runs, and adjustments.

**Seven new tools:** Sometimes called the seven management tools. These are affinity and relationship diagrams for general planning; tree systems, matrix, and prioritization matrices for intermediate planning; and activity network diagrams and process decision program charts for detailed planning.

**Seven QC tools:** Problem-solving statistical tools needed for customer-driven master plan. They are cause and effect diagram, flow chart, Pareto chart, run chart, histogram, control chart, and scatter diagram.

**Seven wastes:** Seven types of waste have been identified for business. They are as follows:

1. Waste from overproduction of goods or services
2. Waste from waiting or idle time
3. Waste from transportation (unnecessary)
4. Waste from the process itself (inefficiency)
5. Waste of unnecessary stock on hand

6. Waste of motion and effort

7. Waste from producing defective goods

**The eighth waste:** Waste of talent and knowledge

**Shojinka:** Means labor flexibility. The term means employees staffing the line can flex up or down based on the incoming demand, which requires employees to be cross-trained and multi-process/machine capable. It also means continually optimizing the number of workers based on demand. This principle is central to baton zone line balancing (bumping).

**Shoninka:** Means *manpower savings*. This corresponds to the improvement of work procedures, machines, or equipment to free whole units of labor (i.e., one person) from a production line consisting of one or more workers.

**Shoryokuka[1]:** Shoryokuka means *labor savings* and indicates partial improvement of manual labor by adding small machines or devices to aid the job. This results in some small amount of labor savings but not an entire person as in shoninka. Again this becomes a goal of all follow-up point kaizen events.

**Simultaneous/concurrent engineering:** The practice of designing a product (or service), its production process, and its delivery mechanism all at the same time. The process requires considerable up-front planning as well as the dedication of resources early in the development cycle. The payoff is in the form of shorter development time from concept to market, lower overall development cost, and lower product or service cost based upon higher accuracy at introduction and less potential for redesign. Examples of this include the Toyota Lexus 200 and the Ford Taurus.

**SMED:** Single-minute exchange of dies, 9 minutes 59 seconds or less setup time.

**Smoothing/production smoothing:** The statistical method of converting weekly or monthly schedules to level-loaded daily schedules.

**SPC:** Acronym for statistical process control.

**Standard deviation:** Statistical measurement of process variation ($\sigma$) which measures the dispersion of sample observations around a process mean.

**Standard work:** Standard work is a tool that defines the interaction of man and his environment when processing something. In producing a part, it is the interaction of man and machine, whereas in processing an invoice, it is the interaction of man and the supplier and the accounting system. It details the motion of the operator and the sequence of action. It provides a routine for consistency of an operation and a basis for improvement. Furthermore, the concept of standard work is it is a verb, not a noun. It details the best process we currently know and understand. Tomorrow it should be better (continuous improvement), and the standard work should be revised to incorporate the improvement. There can be no improvement without a basis (standard work).

Standard work has three central elements:

1. Cycle time (not takt time)
2. Standard operations
3. SWIP

**Standard work (as a tool):** Establishes a routine/habit/pattern for repetitive tasks, makes managing such as scheduling and resource allocation easier, establishes the relationship between man and environment, provides a basis for improvement by defining the normal and highlighting the abnormal, and prohibits backsliding.

**Standard work in process:** The amount of material or a given product that must be in process at any time to insure maximum efficiency of the operation.

**Standardization:** The system of documenting and updating procedures to make sure everyone knows clearly and simply what is expected of them (measured by daily control). Essential for application of PDCA cycle.

**Statistical methods/tools:** Statistical methods allow employees to manage by facts and analyze problems through understanding variability and data. The seven QC tools are examples of statistical tools.

**Store, storage:** Any time a product (part, information, or person) is waiting in the process.

**Strategy:** The business process that involves goals setting, defining specific actions to achieve the business goals, and allocating the resources to execute the actions.

**Subprocess:** A series of interrelated process segments that forms a subset of a total process.

**Supplier partnerships:** An acknowledgment that suppliers are an integral part of any business. A partnership implies a long-term relationship that involves the supplier in both product development and process development. It also requires a commitment on the part of the supplier to pursue continuous improvement and world-class quality.

**System:** A system is the infrastructure that enables the processes to provide customer value. Business systems comprise market, customer, competition, organizational culture, environmental and technological influences, regulatory issues, physical resources, procedures, information flows, and knowledge sets. It is through physical processes that business systems transform inputs to outputs and, thereby, deliver products and services of value in the marketplace.

**Takt time:** The frequency with which the customer wants a product or how frequently a sold unit must be produced. The number is derived by taking the amount of time available in a day and dividing it by the number of sold units that need to be produced. Takt time is usually expressed in seconds.

**Target:** The desired goal that serves as a yardstick for evaluating the degree to which a *policy* is achieved. It is controlled by a *control point, control item,* or *target item.*

**Target costing:** Method for establishing cost objective for a product or service during the design phase. The target cost is determined by the following formula:

$$\text{Sales price} - \text{target profit} = \text{target cost}$$

**Target/means matrix:** Shows the relationship between targets and means and to identify control items and control methods.

**Target value:** Normally a numeric definition of successful target attainment. It is not always possible to have a numeric target, and you must never separate the target from the plan.

**Theory of constraints:** A management philosophy first put forth in the book *The Goal* by Eliyahu Goldratt to identify bottlenecks in the process. In the book, he follows a young boy scout named Herbie. We call bottlenecks *Herbies* today in some cases. His approach was to identify the constraint, exploit the constraint, subordinate all non-constraints, elevate the constraint, and if the constraint is broken in step 4, then go back to step 1.

**Throughput time:** A measure of the actual throughput time for a product to move through a flow process once the work begins. Many people incorrectly label this measure as manufacturing lead time but it is actually a small subset and often has little to do with the total time from order inception to fulfillment.

**TIPS:** Acronym for parts of process flow analysis—transport inspect process store.

**Total density:** One of the eight Lean wastes is the *waste of motion*. One of the first things we advise when trying to identify wasted motions is do not confuse motion with work. In offices, this concept is revised slightly to the following: *do not confuse effort with results*.[2] Total density = work divided by motion.[3] Not all motion is work. It is important to separate needed motions versus wasted motions.

**Total employee involvement (TEI):** A philosophy that advocates the harnessing of the collective knowledge of an organization through the involvement of its people. When supported by the management, it is a means of improving quality, delivery, profitability, and morale in an organization. It provides all employees with a greater sense of ownership in the success of the company and provides them with more control in addressing issues that face the organization. TEI does not allow top management to abdicate its obligation to properly plan and set objectives. It does, however, provide more resources and flexibility in meeting those objectives.

**Total labor time:** The sum of labor value-added and labor non-value-added times.

**Total productive maintenance:** TPM is productive maintenance conducted by all employees. It is equipment maintenance performed on a companywide basis. It has five goals:

1. Maximize equipment effectiveness (improve overall efficiency).
2. Develop a system of productive maintenance for the life of the equipment.
3. Involve all departments that plan, design, use, or maintain equipment in implementing TPM (engineering and design, production, and maintenance).
4. Actively involve all employees—from top management to shop-floor workers.
5. Promote TPM through motivational management (autonomous small group activities).

The word total in *total productive maintenance* has three meanings related to three important features of TPM: total effectiveness (pursuit of economic efficiency or profitability), total PM (maintenance prevention and activity to improve maintainability as well as preventative maintenance), and total participation (autonomous maintenance by operators and small group activities in every department and at every level).

**Transport:** Any travel a part or information does throughout the process.

**Tree diagram:** The tree diagram systematically breaks down plans into component parts and systematically maps out the full range of tasks/methods needed to achieve a goal. It can either be used as a cause-finding problem-solver or a task-generating planning tool.

**Value added:** Must meet three criteria from the AMA video *Time The Next Dimension of Quality*: customer cares, physically changes the thing going through the process, and done right the first time. Value added was expanded for hospitals to physically or emotionally change the patient for the better in addition to the other two criteria.

**Value-added work content ratio:** The steps that actually transform and increase the value of the product or test requirements legislated by industrial licensing agencies. The value-added work content ratio is formed by simply dividing the sum of all value-added work steps by the product lead time for the total process. This ratio can also be used to evaluate waste only in the manufacturing process segment by dividing the numerator by the manufacturing flow time.

**Vertical teams:** Vertical teams are groups of people who come together to meet and address problems or challenges. These teams are made up of the most appropriate people for the issue, regardless of their levels or jobs within the organization.

**Vision:** A long-term plan or direction that is based on a careful assessment of the most important directions for the organization.

**Visual management:** The use of visual media in the organization and general administration of a business. This would include the use of color, signs, and a clear span of sight in a work area. These visuals should clearly designate what things are and where they belong. They should provide immediate feedback as to the work being done and its pace. Visual management should provide access to information needed in the operation of a business. This would include charts and graphs that allow the business status to be determined through their review. This review should be capable of being performed at a glance. To facilitate this, it is necessary to be able to manage by fact and let the data speak for it.

**Water spider:** New role for material handler. Water spiders can be a low-skill or high-skill job. The water spider job is to replenish empty bins on the line daily, plays a vital role in mixed model parts sequencing, should stay 15 minutes or more ahead of the line, can be utilized as a floater, can be utilized to release parts orders from suppliers, and should have standard work and walk patterns/milk runs.

**Work groups:** Work groups are an organizational tool providing a team approach in which people work together on problems to improve productivity.

**World-class quality management:** The commitment by all employees. It is a philosophy/operating methodology totally committed to quality and customer satisfaction. It focuses on continuous process improvement in all processes. It advocates the use of analytical tools and scientific methods and data. It establishes priorities and manages by fact. World-class quality management has perfection (world class) as its goal. We should benchmark to be better than the competition by a large margin, the best. To obtain this status, all employees must be involved, everyone, everywhere, at all times. The result will be products and services that consistently meet or exceed the customers' expectations both internal and external. This group is always passionate with respect to improving the customer experience.

**Yo-i-don[4]:** It means ready set go. It is used to balance multiple processes and operators to a required cycle time using andon. This means each station or line is station balanced to one cycle time. When each operator completes their work, they press the andon button. Once the count-down or count-up clock reaches the prescribed cycle time, any station not completed, immediately turns the andon light to red. At this point, the supervisor and other team members will come to help that station.

**Yokoten[5]:** It is a process critical for creating a true learning organization. Sharing best practices (successes) is critical across the entire organization. In kanji, yoko means beside, side, or width and ten has several meanings but here it would mean to cultivate or comment. Yokoten is a means of *horizontal or sideways transfer of knowledge*, that is, peer-to-peer across the company. People are encouraged to Gemba, to see the kaizen improvement made for them, and see if they can apply the idea or an improved idea in their area. At Honeywell, this is referred to as horizontal linking mechanisms (HLMs).

# Notes

1. *Lean Lexicon*, John Shook, LEI, 2004.
2. Source unknown.
3. Kanban JIT at Toyota—Ohno, Japan Management Association.
4. Monden Yasuhiro, *Toyota Production System*, 3rd edition.
5. http://eudict.com/?lang=japeng&word=ten.

# Index

Note: Locators in *italics* represent figures and **bold** indicate tables in the text.

Printed in the United States
by Baker & Taylor Publisher Services